History of the Inca Realm

History of the Inca Realm, by María Rostworowski de Diez Canseco, is a classic work of ethnohistorical research that has been both influential and provocative in the field of Andean prehistory. Now the product of forty years of innovative archival research by one of Peru's most distinguished scholars, a wide-ranging critique of established interpretations of Inca history, is available to an English-reading audience.

The book begins with the mythical origins of the Incas and the formation of the great lineages, or *panaca.* It relates the creation and expansion of the Inca state, including the methods of conquest of the Inca rulers, especially the use of the ancient Andean tradition of reciprocity, along with the threat of military annihilation, to co-opt local rulers. It proposes that competition for rulership among the "most able," supported by royal lineages often mobilized by the mothers of the pretenders, became an inherently fragile political system. Inca social and political organization is shown to have been based on ancient Andean practices modified to meet the needs of the expanding state. Although rarely treated explicitly by the colonial chroniclers, who often used inaccurate analogies with European institutions, ancient political traditions such as dual rulership and the quadripartite division of space dominated Inca political organization. Economic organization is also treated in detail: the roles of elite administrators, commoners who provided labor for agriculture and public works, and specialists such as artisans, fishermen, women recruited to weave and to prepare beverages for public feasts, long-distance maritime traders, and camelid herders, among others. Finally, the book deals with the spectacular collapse of the Inca state as a result of civil war, Spanish military tactics and technology, the absence of a sense of national unity among the various ethnic groups, and unrest on the part of provincial lords, who saw their wealth and power reduced by the policies of the Inca rulers.

The author uses a great variety of published and unpublished documents and secondary works by Latin American, North American, and European scholars in fields including history, ethnology, archaeology, and ecology to examine topics such as the mythical origins of the Incas, the expansion of the Inca state, the organization of Inca society – including the political role of women – the vast trading networks of the coastal merchants, and the causes of the disintegration of the Inca state in the face of a small force of Spaniards. At each step, Dr. Rostworowski presents her own often original views clearly and forcefully, along with those of other scholars, providing her readers with varied evidence from which to draw their own conclusions.

María Rostworowski de Diez Canseco, Peruvian ethnohistorian, began her publications with *Pachacutec Inca Yupanqui.* Since then she has continued her indefatigable research in Peruvian and foreign archives in search of new sources for understanding the history of ancient Peru. She has published many books and articles in specialized journals. Dr. Rostworowski is a founding member of the Institute of Peruvian Studies and a member of Peru's National Academy of History.

History of the Inca Realm

MARÍA ROSTWOROWSKI DE DIEZ CANSECO

Translated by Harry B. Iceland

CAMBRIDGE
UNIVERSITY PRESS

PUBLISHED BY THE PRESS SYNDICATE OF THE UNIVERSITY OF CAMBRIDGE
The Pitt Building, Trumpington Street, Cambridge CB2 1RP, United Kingdom

CAMBRIDGE UNIVERSITY PRESS
The Edinburgh Building, Cambridge CB2 2RU, UK   http: //www.cup.cam.ac.uk
40 West 20th Street, New York, NY 10011-4211, USA   http: //www.cup.org
10 Stamford Road, Oakleigh, Melbourne 3166, Australia

Originally published in Spanish as *Historía del Tahuantinsuyu*
English translation first published 1999

Printed in the United States of America

Typeface Adobe Garamond 11/13 pt,   *System* Penta [BV]

A catalog record for this book is available from the British Library

Library of Congress Cataloging-in-Publication Data
Rostworowski de Diez Canseco, María.
[Historía del Tahuantinsuyu. English]
History of the Inca realm / María Rostworowski de Diez Canseco ;
translated by Harry B. Iceland.
p. cm.
Includes bibliographical references.
ISBN 0-521-44266-4. – ISBN 0-521-63759-7 (pbk.)
1. Incas.   2. Indians of South America – Andes Region – History.
I. Title.
F3429.R68513   1998
980'.00498323 – dc21   98-15504

ISBN 0 521 44266 4 hardback
ISBN 0 521 63759 7 paperback

Contents

Preface

Two serious difficulties are encountered in conducting research on the history of the Incas. One is related to the Andean mode of remembering and communicating events; the other, to the Spanish perspective in recording and interpreting the information left to us in what became known as the chronicles. This combination of difficulties is reflected in all the written information on Inca history that has come down to us from the sixteenth century. Although I have dealt with this subject in previous studies, the importance of these difficulties for ethnohistorical work on the Incas is such that I shall reexamine here some of the forms they have taken.

The study of the written sources is difficult, owing to their often contradictory and confusing contents. For example, evaluating the traditional native chronology of the Inca rulers has been an arduous task because of the uncertain data, with the same facts and events often attributed to more than one ruler. For this reason, it is necessary to carry out a critical analysis of such events as they appear in the traditional sources.

Several questions can be raised in connection with this problem. Was there some systematic means of transmitting memories of these events from one generation to another? We know that the pre-Hispanic cultures of Peru possessed no writing system, but this did not prevent them from remembering and evoking events, which they accomplished in various ways.

There is a consensus among the chroniclers that the natives possessed special songs in which each *ayllu* (a lineage group or kinship-based community) or *panaca* (a royal *ayllu*) narrated the principal events of its past during certain ceremonies held in the presence of the ruler. Those of the *hanan*, or upper, moiety would go first, followed by those of the *hurin*, or lower, moiety. Individuals were specially selected to praise the achievements and feats of the ancestors of their group. In this way, a kind of collective memory was retained.

Another way of recording the succession of local lords and the principal events of their reigns was by depicting them in paintings or on panels. Many of these were preserved, according to the chroniclers, in a place called Poquen Cancha (Acosta, 1940, book 6, chap. 8; Molina, 1943; RAHM A-92, folio 17v; Santillán, 1927:91). We know that Viceroy Toledo sent Philip II four tapestries illustrating Inca life. In a letter sent to the emperor from Cusco dated March 1, 1571, the viceroy wrote that these tapestries were painted by "the officials of that land," adding that although "the Indian painters did not have the curiosity of those over there [in Spain]," they were nevertheless worthy of being hung in one of the Spanish royal palaces (AGI, Lima 28b; Rostworowski, 1977:239; 1983:100).

A third way in which the Incas recorded events was by means of the *quipu*, small knotted cords of various colors, which could be used for accounting and for recording historic events (Cieza de León, *Señorío*, 1943: 81).

There were various means of preserving the native memories of pre-Conquest events: paintings, songs, and a mnemonic tool, the *quipu*; the absence of writing was not an insurmountable obstacle to the Inca people's keeping and commemorating their past. We cannot help but ask ourselves, Why, then, are there so many contradictions in the Inca narratives, if they possessed empirical methods for remembering the facts? To what can we attribute the many inconsistencies in the Andean record of the past?

The apparent confusion in the indigenous tradition concerning the Inca past cannot, however, be attributed to ignorance of the facts. Rather, answers must be sought in the interpretation of Andean sociopolitical structures by sixteenth-century Spaniards whose mentality prevented them from understanding a society with organizational and recording traditions radically different from their own. For this reason, I will examine briefly the Andean record and then the Spanish perspective in interpreting it.

THE ANDEAN RECORD

It is obvious that the natives did not share many of the concerns of the Europeans. The facts they wished to remember did not necessarily correspond to the demands of other latitudes. Assuredly, in the Andean context, there existed no historical sense of events as we traditionally understand it. Neither veracity, in the European sense, nor an exact chronology of events was required, or considered desirable.

The Inca custom of intentionally omitting an episode that might annoy the current ruler typifies the Andean approach to history. There are several instances of ignoring certain Inca rulers in order not to displease the sovereign in power. Oversights affected events as well as persons (Cieza de León, *Señorío*, 1943:77–79). In such cases, only members of the *ayllus* or the *panaca* adversely affected by such omissions kept alive, if hidden, their traditions. This intentional distortion of events and memories, combined with the absence of a native writing system and a lack of understanding of the native tradition on the part of the Spanish, explains the contradictory narratives of the chronicles.

Despite this obvious confusion, Inca history should not be classified as purely mythical, as claimed by many researchers. The documents, narratives, and many testimonies in which the natives claim to have known and seen the last Incas are irrefutable proof of the existence of the Inca state. Human beings, without the help of writing, can remember two and even three generations back.

THE SPANISH PERSPECTIVE

The Europeans who arrived on South American shores in the sixteenth century were concerned with conquering new lands, and few had sufficient preparation to understand the challenge represented by the Andean world. Their central intellectual concern was finding new justifications for their invasion. That they were less than eager to understand is explained by their desire to demonstrate that the Incas did not have the right to territory they had taken by violence. The mentality of the time and the interest in proving the rights of the king of Spain over the "provinces" of the Inca state made it difficult for the Spanish to comprehend the Andean reality.

One chronicler, Polo de Ondegardo (1917:47), assures us that "in the Inca record we frequently find all kinds of memories, with each province also having its records of the victories or wars and punishments affecting its lands. If for some reason it were important, we could easily specify the time in which each one became pacified under Inca rule, *but this is not important for the purpose at hand*, since it is enough to have found out the time at which they began their conquest here" (my italics).

The chroniclers, in the face of the inconsistencies of Inca history, tried to adjust and accommodate the various versions according to their own perspective, further distorting them in the process. In addition, they were too much imbued with the principles of primogeniture, legitimacy, and royal succession, according to European models, to understand Andean customs such as the right of the election of the "most able" to the offices of Inca and local lord. The Europeans could not conceive of the power of royal mummies who retained their servants, rights, and lands as they had possessed them in life. Equally incomprehensible were the moiety divisions, the Andean forms of kinship and reciprocity, and the complex system of symmetrical and asymmetrical obligations.

The Andean world was unique and too different to be understood by people come from overseas, preoccupied with enriching themselves, securing honors, and evangelizing the natives by force. An abyss must have formed between the Andean way of thinking and the Spanish perspective, an abyss that to the present day has continued to divide citizens of the same nation.

A PRELIMINARY CLARIFICATION

In this book, the reader will note the omission of the word "empire" with reference to the Inca. This is a deliberate omission based on the many Old World connotations of the term.

The originality of Inca culture is a result, in the first instance, of its isolation from other continents. The natives of the Andean region did not enjoy the advantages of the diffusion and cultural loans that permitted the development of the peoples of European classical antiquity. Their contacts with Mesoamerica were indirect and sporadic. The pre-Hispanic Andean world was forced to seek its own forms of development, to find solutions to its problems and its needs by going deep into its own roots. Andeans succeeded in dominating a harsh environment by joining forces and inventing methods to overcome unfavorable conditions. Their communal and organizational spirit enabled them to cope with disadvantages and adverse circumstances.

This spirit, this gathering into oneself, promoted and gave as fruit a creative and innovative force that enabled the Andean to find solutions to anguishing problems. Nothing was easy for the inhabitants of pre-Hispanic Peru. Their lands were situated in an environment tortured by inhospitable *punas*, craggy gorges, wide deserts, and tangled jungles.

This indigenous desire for unity is expressed in the term "Tahuantinsuyu," which means "the four united regions," referring to the regions of Chinchay, Antisuyu, Cuntisuyu, and Colla, roughly corresponding to the four cardinal directions. The term appears to reflect an impulse, possibly subconscious, toward an integration that was unfortunately never attained, cut short as it was by the appearance of Pizarro's forces. The Incas lacked sufficient time to consolidate their plans.

For these reasons, I am inclined to employ the term "Tahuantinsuyu" in place of "empire," since the cultural meaning of the latter term does not interpret or correspond to the Andean reality but is relevant to situations on other continents.

PART ONE

Rise and Apogee of the State

1

Primitive Cusco

What is called the Inca state was a late development among the high cultures of pre-Hispanic America; millennia separate it from the onset of Andean civilization. To understand better the timing of the appearance of Inca civilization within the Andean cultural sequence, we can view the chronological chart on page 4. Archaeologists begin the sequence of the rise of the Andean cultures with a Lithic Period of hunters and gatherers. They continue with the introduction of agriculture during the Archaic Period, after which, during the Formative Period, appear theocratic chiefdoms and societies that persist until after the Christian Era, giving way to an Early Regional Developmental Period, followed in turn by a final stage, that of the Militaristic States.

The first hegemonic state to appear during this final stage was that of the Wari, which lasted from the seventh to the tenth century A.D. Its collapse led to a resurgence of the Regional States, the Late Regional Developmental Period, from the tenth to the fifteenth century. The northern chiefdom of Chimor stands out during this transitional period between Wari and Inca hegemonies. The Inca state began to reach its apogee early in the fifteenth century, when its development was truncated by the appearance of the Spanish forces.

Previous to the chronology depicted in the chart on page 4, John Rowe had proposed an Andean chronological division by "horizons," characterized by territorial expansion by certain cultures, alternating with "intermediate periods" marked by local florescences. Thus, an Early Intermediate Period preceded an Early Horizon (Chavín), which was followed by a Middle Intermediate Period (Mochica, Nasca, among others) and a Middle Horizon (Tiahuanaco-Wari), which in turn gave rise to a Late Intermediate Period (Chancay, Chimu, Chincha, and others), finally followed by the expansion of the Inca, or the Late Horizon.

The ethnic groups that occupied the region of Cusco before the arrival of the groups of Manco Capac, the mythical earliest Incas, belong to the

Year	Periods		North Coast	Northern Highlands	Central Coast	South Coast	Central Highlands	Altiplano of Titicaca
1500	Inca State		Inca	Inca	Inca	Inca	Inca	Inca
	Regional States		Chimu	Local Kingdoms	Chancay	Ica-Chincha	Chancas	Aymara Kingdoms
1000	Wari State		Northern Wari	Wari	Pachacamac	Southern Wari	Wari	
500	Regional Developmental Period		Mochica and Gallinazo	Cajamarca and Recuay	Lima	Nasca	Huarpa	Tiwanaku and Pucara
A.D -0- B.C.	Formative Period		Salinar Cupisnique	Huaras Chavin	Ancon	Paracas	Rancha Chupas Wichqana	Kalasasaya Chiripa Wankarani
1000	Archaic Period		Huaca Prieta	?	Paraiso Encanto	Otuma Chilca	Cachi Piki	?
5000					Canario			
10000	Lithic Period		Paijan	Lauricocha Guitarrero	Arenal Chivateros Oquendo	?	Jaywa Ayacucho Pacaicasa	Viscachani
20000								

Militaristic States

Despotic urban societies

Theocratic kingdoms and chiefdoms

Village agriculturalists

Hunter-gatherers

Chronological framework for Andean society, with some examples of regional developments.

Tahuantinsuyu, the Inca realm.

Late Intermediate or Late Regional Developmental Period. The ceramic assemblages of this period contain considerable amounts of a style of poorly finished pottery known as *Kilke* that has been tentatively associated with Ayarmaca ethnic groups, whose chiefs had the generic names of Tocay Capac and Pinahua Capac.

Although relics of earlier archaeological periods have been found in Cusco, further research on earlier occupations is required to clarify several points. During the Middle Horizon, there was a city to the south of Cusco called Pikillaqta, which served as the Wari administrative center for the region. This Wari presence must have influenced many aspects of Inca development, including models of organization and of the exercise of power. In addition, it appears likely that myths and accounts from that period persisted until Inca times; a few centuries are not a barrier to the preservation of oral accounts.

These primitive stages of the history of Cusco belong to archaeology rather than to ethnohistory, which relies on sixteenth-century manuscripts and other documents. In this brief summary, I have tried only to place Inca culture within the broader chronological framework of the Andean cultures. At the close of the Middle Horizon, or period of Wari hegemony, a favorable moment for migratory movements appeared in the Andes. At that time, no central power controlled the various ethnic groups that roamed the land for unknown reasons. We do not know if these movements were a consequence of the decline of the centralizing power of the Wari, of invasions, fighting, wars, or prolonged natural disasters, such as droughts or heavy rains producing floods that destroyed villages and fields.

In the native myths, one can perceive movements of entire peoples throughout the mountains in search of fertile lands on which to establish themselves. Culture heroes, such as Manco Capac, Pariacaca, or Tutayquire (Avila, 1966; Salomon and Urioste, 1991), possessed divining and founding rods that, driven into the ground, indicated the places where the groups should establish themselves. Other groups, such as the Llacuaces, carried with them handfuls of earth and sought permanent places to settle whose soil matched that of their original homeland as closely as possible (AAL – *Idolatrías* leg. VI, exp. 18, folios 11r and 11v).

Legends tell of the presence of a number of minor chiefs, or *sinchi*, simple leaders of ethnic groups of diverse origins who inhabited the region of the future Cusco. In these myths, the first ancestors had been transformed into stones, and in their stony state watched over their descendants, a concept common to the entire Andean area.

The chroniclers have transmitted to us in a confused narrative the names of those primitive chiefs whose deeds were lost in the *purunpacha*, or deserted and depopulated time. Sarmiento de Gamboa (1943:45) mentions that in that first period three ethnic groups – the Sauaseray, the Antasayacs, and the Guallas – were established in the valley of the future Cusco. With time appeared newcomers who called themselves Alcavizas, Copalimaytas, and Culumchimas, and all together they coinhabited the region. Other ancient residents were the Lares and the Poques. It is difficult to pinpoint the zone inhabited by each group because the Incas later, when they acquired supremacy, proceeded to relocate them and redistribute their lands. Only a careful archaeological survey could perhaps shed more light on this early period.

The primitive village of Acamama was located on the future site of Cusco (Guaman Poma, 1936, fol. 84; Murúa, 1962:62), between the two rivers of that valley. The chroniclers tell of how in those early times the structures were of humble construction, and a marsh covered with rushes, originating in two free-flowing springs, was found at the foot of the place where later would be built the impressive structures of Sacsayhuaman (Betanzos, 1968).

Sarmiento de Gamboa (1943:59) heard directly from the lips of the high nobles of Cusco concerning the division of physical space in force during this early period. We are told that it consisted of districts with strong local affinities, quite different from the later divisions that developed during the apogee of the Incas. The village of Acamama comprised four sections: Quinti Cancha, or the District of the Humming Bird; Chumbi Cancha, or the District of the Weavers; Sairi Cancha, or the District of Tobacco; and the fourth district, Yarambuy Cancha, which is an Aymara rather than Quechua term, and which was probably a mestizo district inhabited by Aymara and Quechua speakers (from *yaruntatha*, to be mixed [Bertonio]).

Later on, other divisions, reflecting the increasing importance of the Manco group, replaced the four original districts. The division of space in four parts, however, was maintained as necessary to the organizational system.

Another Andean way of drawing boundaries was based on the principles of opposition and complementarity. In fact, the opposition of halves, whether of *hanan* and *hurin*, upper and lower, or *ichoc* and *allauca*, left and right, formed a dual division throughout the Andean world. *Ayllus*, towns, and valleys were all partitioned into dual opposites. The element of gender also enters into these divisions of physical space. Later, we will see how in Cusco the upper moiety relates to the masculine gender and the lower to the feminine.

In addition to these differences between the moieties, the concept of complementarity was fundamental to the sociopolitical-economic system. This concept had its roots in the complexity of Andean geography. The need for access to the different resources found at each ecological level led to the creation of various interaction mechanisms. It is interesting to note, however, that opposition as well as complementarity is present in other spheres of the natives' thought, as if their worldview revolved around these two concepts.

Both Acamama, which was a small primitive village, and Cusco, the later Inca capital, contained these dual and quadripartite divisions, which were fundamental to the entire Andean system. It is necessary to understand these underlying principles of division in order to understand the spatial divisions of that remote period, which were based on concepts that were retained after the settlement of the valley of Cusco by the first Incas. The subsequent rapid increase in the importance of the Incas required the later creation of new spatial divisions consistent with political developments, but the fundamental principles remained the same.

THE AYARMACAS

The region of Acamama was originally inhabited by, among others, a powerful chiefdom called Ayarmaca. Guaman Poma (1936, fol. 80), after referring to the four ages of the world, says that "some first Incas" called Tocay Capac and Pinahua Capac began to govern the region. Murúa refers to them as "kings," prior to the Incas, whose territory extended from Vilcanota to the Angaraes (1962), whereas Garcilaso assures us that they inhabited eighteen towns south of Cusco, stretching for three leagues from Salinas (1943, book 1, chap. XX). Tocay Capac and Pinahua Capac were the generic names of the rulers of Ayarmaca and Pinahua, according to the testimony of the chroniclers and the sixteenth-century documents. (See Rostworowski, 1969–70.)

It has been confirmed that the Ayarmacas played an important role in the founding of Cusco. They carried out prolonged campaigns against the Incas, and only with the expansion of the Inca state were the Ayarmacas definitively crushed and relegated to the category of simple local lords, chiefs of some few groups. They are not, then, another mythical group, as we have been able to trace them back to their beginnings, from the arrival of the people of Manco Capac at Cusco and then through the period of Inca rule, in the accounts of the chroniclers. The Ayarmacas continued to appear as such in the viceregal administrative testimonies and documents until finally they became, in the twentieth century, officially recognized peasant communities. Documents kept by these communities can be linked with colonial testimonies that confirm their descent from the Ayarmaca ethnic group. This long historical trajectory, confirmed by documentation, is rare in ethnohistory and deserves these few lines dedicated to it.

The name "Ayar" is shared by the mythical brothers who, with their respective sisters, left the cave of Pacaritambo and by an early ethnic group established in Acamama. The etymology of the name is significant. In the Quechua dictionary of González Holguín, *ayar* is the name of the wild quinoa plant. There was a *huaca*, or sacred place, called Capi ("quinoa root"), located on the hill of Quisco, which, according to one myth, represented the origin of the name "Cusco." According to Sauer (1950), the quinoa (*Chenopodium quinoa*) was an important food plant in the Andes that replaced corn in the high-altitude zones and was cultivated in parts of the Inca territory. It may also be that the name "Ayar" was applied retroactively, after the Incas had achieved domination over the Ayarmacas, in order to establish a continuity between the two groups and further justify Inca rule.

The four Ayar brothers also possessed second names, which distinguished among them. The etymology of "Ayar Cachi" does not present difficulties, since *cachi* is the Quechua word for salt, the preeminent condiment required by humans. *Uchu* can refer to the wild quinoa, but more importantly to chile or *ají*, the term used by the Spanish for the species *Capsicum*, whose varieties were the principal spices of the New World. The name of the third Ayar, called Mango or Manco by the chroniclers, may refer to an edible plant, *mango (Bromus mango)*, an ancient cereal now practically extinct but which in 1837 was still cultivated in Chiloé and used especially in the preparation of a beverage (Sauer, 1950). The name of Auca, the fourth brother, is related to a military term and not, like those of his brothers, to a plant or spice.

In this analysis of the derivation of the name "Ayarmaca," we must still examine the meaning of the word *maca*. This term refers to an edible root (*Lepidium meyenii*) whose habitat was the *puna* of the central region of Peru. This cultigen was formerly found throughout the high plateau, but today it is planted and used only in the towns near Jauja. According to popular belief, the *maca* has fertility properties, and for this reason a magical origin is attributed to it. The *maca* also represents an ancient agricultural tradition in the highlands, dating from long before the acclimatization of the potato to the *puna*. If this hypothesis is correct, the Ayarmacas, their name derived from two plants, represent an ethnic group adapted to the high mountain regions.

Two of the principal seats of the Ayarmacas were Tambo Cunga, or the Inn of the Gorge, and Amaro Cancha, or the Temple of the Serpent, situated near Pucyura. Another town frequently mentioned by the chroniclers is Aguayro Cancha, whose etymology may derive from the term *ahuani*, to weave. A document in the Archivo General de Indias in Seville, dated 1557, mentions that Aquillay, the principal *huaca* of the Ayarmacas, was in a ravine leading down from the lagoon of Guaypón toward the Yucay River. A fortress considered to belong to the Ayarmacas, now called Andinchayoc, is in the region of Chinchero (Rostworowski, 1969–70).

The importance of the Ayarmacas in times past is evidenced by the fact that at the height of Inca rule they retained a *ceque* of their own in the religious system of Cusco. The *ceques*, according to Polo de Ondegardo, and later Cobo, were imaginary lines that radiated from the plaza of the Temple of the Sun, surrounding the city and resembling a gigantic *quipu*. Although the Ayarmacas had lost all of their ancient power, the Incas could not take that privilege away from them. For this reason, the eighth *ceque* of Antisuyu, with eleven *huacas* along its length, instead of bearing the traditional names of Collana, Payan, and Cayao, was known as Ayarmaca. Also, the fifth *ceque* of Chinchaysuyu, on the road to Yucay, on the hill of Cinca, contained a rock that was an Ayarmaca shrine, which the Ayarmacas considered their *pacarina*, or place of origin.

The *ceques* were of profound religious significance. They were divided into four sections, and followed the *suyu* (divisions) of Tahuantinsuyu – that is, Chinchaysuyu, Antisuyu, Cuntisuyu, and Collasuyu – with a total of forty-two lines. Each *ceque* contained a number of *huacas*, or shrines, maintained by a specific *ayllu* or by a royal *panaca*. These *huacas* were served by many priests, women, and servants dedicated to the cult (Rowe, 1979).

Another prerogative preserved by the Ayarmacas was the celebration of the initiation rites of their youths during a different month from that of the Inca group. They celebrated the coming of age of their young men during the ceremonies of the *huarachicuy*, in the month of Oma Raimi, with the Omas, the Quivios, and the Tampus.

When they arrived in primitive Acamama, the Inca *ayllus* of Ayar Manco had to confront the existing inhabitants to make a place for themselves in the valley. They fought not only the neighboring minor chiefs but also their principal enemies, the Ayarmacas, at that time the most powerful and important group in the region. The chroniclers recount the wars initiated between the Ayarmacas and the Incas during several regimes; each new ruler had to maintain the struggle, with neither side achieving definitive conquest. In the narratives of Sarmiento de Gamboa, Guaman Poma, Santa Cruz Pachacuti, and others, we can glimpse the effort required for the Incas to survive in Cusco and retain their possessions.

The constant fighting between the two ethnic groups helped keep alive the oral tradition of the events. From generation to generation, they repeated their respective versions of long wars, defeats suffered, fleeting triumphs, and the destruction of their sacred places. The latent rancor between them prompted the abduction of the young prince Yahuar Huacac, son of the ruling Inca, whose unexpected tears of blood saved him from certain death. In attempts to diminish or put an end to the conflict, the two sides resorted to the exchange of women. This situation continued until the beginnings of the Inca state, when the final confrontation took place at Guaman Cancha, where the great Ayarmaca chief Tocay Capac was defeated. The Ayarmacas were broken, and are not mentioned again in the chronicles. Their towns were ruined and their proud chief taken as a prisoner to Cusco.

The Incas wisely divided the various Ayarmaca *ayllus* into three groups, separating them in order to prevent their rebelling and regaining their former strength. In viceregal times, after the reductions of Viceroy Toledo, the Ayarmacas inhabited Pucyura, Chinchero, and San Sebastián, where they appear in the colonial documents. At the present time, their ancient power long forgotten, they form peasant communities that were officially recognized by the Peruvian government in 1923.

The chronicles mention along with Tocay Capac another chief, called Pinahua Capac. The Pinahua *ayllus* were closely related to the Ayarmacas within the Andean dual system. During the colonial period there were two Pinahua *ayllus*, one in the district of Oropesa, Quispicanchis province, and the other in the Guaillabamba, near the valley of Yucay. The Pinahuas of Quispicanchis also continue to exist as a peasant community, which was officially recognized in 1965. Espinoza (1974) has published some documents from 1539–71 in which reference is made to various lands that belonged to the Pinahuas. Their territories extended south of San Jerónimo, from Angostura to the Vilcanota River and the Muyna Lagoon.

This account of events concerning Tocay and Pinahua Capac, which indicates the antiquity and importance of the Ayarmacas as a sovereign macroethnic group in the region, brings us to the arrival and settlement in Cusco of the group of Manco, the earliest Incas. It is necessary to clarify the sociopolitical situation in the Cusco region at the time of the appearance of the Incas, not only from an archaeological perspective but also from an ethnohistoric one.

This Andean version of the settlement of the site of primitive Cusco by groups that arrived and established themselves long before the arrival of the Incas is in agreement with the archaeological data. According to Rowe (1960, 1966), this replacement of one culture by another is reflected in the ceramics of the Late Intermediate Period at Cusco. Rowe emphasizes this phenomenon because it confirms that Inca culture has more important roots in the traditions of Ayacucho, Nasca, and Tiahuanaco than in the older cultures of the valley of Cusco.

2

The Beginnings of Inca Expansion

THE MYTH OF THE AYAR SIBLINGS

The arrival at Acamama of the groups led by Manco Capac marks the end of a long period of migration and search for lands suitable for agriculture. The myth of Manco Capac and of Mama Ocllo related by Garcilaso de la Vega is a classic. They left Lake Titicaca as a divine couple and headed north in hope of finding the "chosen" valley. On their arrival at the hill of Huanacauri, near what would one day be Cusco, Manco's magic staff sank into the earth. This was the much awaited signal, and there they founded the new state. This divine couple as civilizing heroes brought order, culture, and the arts, and it was the Sun himself who infused his children with heat and power.

Could this myth be the official version of the origin of the Children of the Sun? It seems likely that this version of the legend narrated by the Inca author is the work of Garcilaso himself, as a way of presenting the myth for European readers. For this reason, it is better to look for other, more Andean versions of the foundation story.

One of the principal myths concerning the origin of the Incas told of the Ayar Siblings emerging from a cave called Pacaritambo – Inn of Production, or Dawn, or House of Hiding. This cave was on the hill of Tambotoco, which had three "windows": Maras Toco, from which came forth "without parents," as a kind of spontaneous birth, the group of the Maras; Sutic, from which emerged the group of the Tampus; and Capac Toco, from which came four brothers, whose names were Ayar Uchu, Ayar Cachi, Ayar Mango, and Ayar Auca (Sarmiento de Gamboa, 1943, chap. 8). These latter were accompanied by their four sisters, Mama Ocllo, Mama Huaco, Mama Ipacura or Cura, and Mama Raua. Each chronicler recounts these episodes, as related by his informants, with minor variations.

The legendary Ayar brothers and their sisters began to wander slowly through the high plateau and mountain gorges, with the goal of finding an appropriate place to settle. It is interesting to note that in the Guaman Poma (1936, fol. 81) version, Mama Huaco is mentioned as the mother of Manco Capac, and there is a reference to an incestuous relationship between them.

Analyzing the myth from a psychoanalytical perspective, the two fundamental prohibitions, against incest and patricide, are absent, replaced by a network of fraternal relationships in which incest appears as a given. In this myth, the conjugal couple does not exist, only the binomial mother/son or brother/sister. There is no role for the father within this set of relationships. Rather, the kinship ties represented in the Ayar myth are limited to the relationship between son and mother (Hernández et al., 1987).

According to the narrative of the chronicles, the siblings quickly did away with Ayar Cachi for fear of his magical powers, since with just one shot from his sling he could knock down hills or create gorges. By trickery, they persuaded him to return to Pacaritambo to get the *napa*, or insignia of the nobles, and some gold cups they had forgotten, called *topapacusi*. When he entered the cave, they sealed it with blocks of stone, trapping him inside forever. After this episode, the Ayars continued on their journey through the mountains.

It is important to emphasize that the siblings, though without a permanent settlement, were still agriculturalists, since once established in a place they stayed there for years and then, after harvesting their crops, continued on their way. Sarmiento de Gamboa relates how during their wanderings the siblings reached a place called Guanacancha, four leagues from Cusco. There they remained for some time, sowing and harvesting their crops; but, becoming discontented, they renewed their march, eventually arriving in Tamboquiro, where they spent a number of years. When they reached Quirirmanta, at the foot of a hill, they convened a council among all the brothers and sisters in which they decided that Ayar Uchu must remain in that place, transformed into a principal *huaca* called Huanacauri. To adopt the form of a rock was, in the Andean world, a way of perpetuating the divinity or making sacred an individual, and so the lithic form assumed by Uchu did not prevent him from communicating with his siblings.

The same chronicler mentions that Mama Huaco was one of the fighters of the group, and that in the town of Matagua this "strong and able" woman took two shafts of gold and threw them toward the north. The first fell in Colcabamba but did not pierce the hard earth. The second was thrown to a place called Guayanaypata, where it penetrated easily. Other informants reported to Sarmiento de Gamboa that it was Manco Capac and not Mama Huaco who threw the magic staff that was to indicate the place of permanent settlement.

The wandering *ayllus* tried to reach the indicated place but, encountering resistance from the inhabitants, were forced to return to Matagua. Manco Capac then ordered Ayar Auca to go and populate the lands indicated by the shaft. Following his brother's orders, Auca rushed to the site, but no sooner did he step onto its soil than he was turned to stone. According to Andean beliefs, these *guanca*, or rocks, were landmarks indicating the taking possession of a space. Thus, Auca in his lithic form was the first to occupy the chosen site, so long desired, and he ordered Ayar Mango to be called, from that time forward, Manco Capac. According to Sarmiento de Gamboa, *cusco*, in the language spoken at that time, referred to occupying a space by means of magic. For Garcilaso, *cusco* was the "navel" of the world in the language of the Incas (1943, vol. 1, book 1, chap. 18). Cieza de León (1943) tells a similar story regarding the arrival of Manco and his people at Cusco and adds that the region was densely populated but that its inhabitants made a place for the new arrivals.

The myths narrated up to this point, referring to the manner in which ancient Cusco was occupied by the Incas, are totally different from the version given by Garcilaso. The legend of the Ayars, with the transformations of the characters into rocks or sacred *guanca*, along with the long pilgrimage of Manco's group, is a very Andean episode also present in the myths of other ethnic groups. The migrations of the Incas were those not of primitive bands of hunters and herders but of an essentially agricultural people concerned primarily with finding good lands to cultivate.

In these narratives, one of the two women of Manco Capac plays a special role. We have seen the episode in which, in spite of being a woman, Mama Huaco was the warrior who threw the founding shaft in the symbolic taking of possession of Cusco. According to the chroniclers, Mama Huaco took a *haybinto*, or *boleadora* (a lariat with balls on one end), and whirling it in the air wounded one of the Guallas, the ancient inhabitants of Acamama, after which she cut open his chest, took out his lungs, and blew strongly into them. This ferocity of Mama Huaco so terrorized the Guallas that they abandoned the town, ceding their place to the Incas.

In a previous study, I analyzed the feminine figure of Mama Huaco and what she might represent in the sociopolitical order of the Incas (Rostworowski, 1983). She was the prototype of the vigorous and warlike woman, in contrast to Mama Ocllo, the second partner of Manco Capac. Cabello de Valboa (1951) relates that Mama Huaco held the position of a brave captain who led armies. This masculine characteristic is represented in Aymara by the word *huaco*, which refers to a vigorous, free woman who is not frightened by cold or work.

According to Sarmiento de Gamboa (1943:59), the four leaders who commanded the *allyus* when they arrived in Cusco were Manco Capac, Mama Huaco, Sinchi Roca, and Mango Sapaca. Note that Mama Huaco is named among the four chiefs of the group. It is not so important whether these events are factual or mythical. More important is what the legend suggests about the social structure of these early Incas. In this personage of Mama Huaco we find a woman taking an active part in the conquest of Cusco, fighting alongside the men and leading an army. This appears to indicate that women could occupy high social positions and wield considerable power during this early period.

In the legends of Cusco, the example of Mama Huaco is not unique. In the war against the Chancas, a woman by the name of Chañan Curi Coca was the chief of the *ayllus* of Choco-Cachona. In the same legend, the chronicles tell of the help received by the Inca from the *pururauca*, magic stones that were transformed during battle into warriors and made possible the Inca triumph. The myth tells us that there were both masculine and feminine *pururauca*; that is, the practice of war was not a function of men only (Rowe, 1979).

These myths relating the Inca settlement of Cusco are basic because of what they reveal about the Incas' worldview and their sociopolitical structures. Manco Capac and his *ayllus* inhabited lower Cusco, and his residence was the Temple of Indicancha, while the followers of Auca occupied upper, or Hanan, Cusco. This division in halves, reflecting the opposition and complementarity of *hanan* and *hurin*, has also, in this context, a connotation of gender. Garcilaso de la Vega (1943, vol. 1:43) tends to confirm this view when he says that the older brothers populated upper Cusco and the younger brothers, who were followers of the "queen," settled Hurin Cusco.

According to Garcilaso, then, the men of *hanan* were masculine/masculine and those of *hurin* were masculine/feminine. With respect to the women, those of lower Cusco were classified as feminine/feminine and those of upper Cusco as feminine/masculine. The mythical prototypes of these women would be the feminine/feminine Mama Ocllo and the feminine/masculine Mama Huaco. (See Hernández et al., 1987; Rostworowski, 1983.)

THE *PANACA*

According to the chroniclers, a *panaca* was formed by the descendants of both sexes of a reigning Inca but excluded the ruler himself. According to the same sources, the *panaca* had the obligation to preserve the mummy of the deceased ruler and guard the memory of his life and achievements by means of songs, *quipu*, and paintings that were passed from generation to generation. For a people without writing, it was extremely important to organize the maintenance of these traditions.

The *panaca* of the last Incas were the most important, since their great estates expanded along with the Inca conquests. Apart from their extensive haciendas, worked by innumerable *yana*, or servants, they were also supported by priests, augurers, and women to care for them and help maintain their social status (Rostworowski, 1962, 1970a). The mummy of an Inca continued to enjoy the same possessions as he did in life. It constituted a kind of living ancestor the people could admire during the great festivals of Cusco, when he came out onto the great plaza of Aucaypata in all his finery, surrounded by his relatives and servants. This custom ensured that there was always a substantial clientele in the capital whose life and work revolved around the mummies of the deceased rulers, whose death did not prevent their active involvement in the politics of Cusco through their *panaca*.

Along with the guardian *ayllus*, the *panaca* constituted the elite and aristocracy of Cusco. Doubtless these groups formed factions and alliances that exercised great influence during the diverse episodes of Inca history. It should be remembered that each ruler had a great number of children by many wives. The court of the Inca encompassed all the members of the various *panaca*, including the ancestors of the living members, acting through their descendants as if they were still alive.

It is also useful to compare the significance of the term *panaca* with other terms referring to lineages and related social entities among the Aymara, the inhabitants of the coast, and other Andean peoples. In another work, I analyzed the term *parcialidad* in the context of the sixteenth and seventeenth centuries and considered certain aspects of the term *ayllu* (Rostworowski, 1981a). In the Andean world there were many such regional terms referring to these entities, and we cannot assume they all shared a single commonly accepted connotation. Bertonio notes the use of the term *hatha* in Aymara, which might be interpreted as "clan," "family," or *ayllu*, but also the seeds of plants, animals, and humans. There is no reference to the possession of common lands, although this might be inferred.

The dictionary of Fray Domingo de Santo Tomás (1951), which provides the coastal Quechua equivalents of highland terms, cites the word *villca* as the equivalent of *ayllu*. *Panaca*, according to this source, contains the idea of lineage and the extended family. Although the chroniclers consider the *panaca* to have been patrilineal, Zuidema (1964) believes the term refers, rather, to a man's siblings, and to matrilineal and exogamous, rather than patrilineal and endogamous, relations. In this way a man would belong to his sister's kin group and his children would belong to a different group. Zuidema (1964) suggests that the *panaca* existed since very early times and that it was from the *panaca* that the Inca was elected. I would further propose the hypothesis that the groups of Ayar Mango and Ayar Auca used the term *panaca* as a synonym for *ayllu* long before their arrival in Cusco.

It seems likely, then, that one of the differences between the *panaca* and other *ayllus* (as the *panaca* were also *ayllus*) was that the *ayllus* were patrilineal and the *panaca* matrilineal. The term *panaca* comes from *pana*, "sister in speech of a man, or first or second cousin, or from his place of origin or recognized lineage" (González Holguín). In other words, the mass of people that wandered in search of fertile lands to settle used the word *panaca* with reference to certain groups and lineages. In support of this assertion, the term *panaca* referred only to members of the Inca lineages, but the word *ayllu* was used in Cusco and Ayacucho long before the arrival of the Incas. Later, the Spanish spread the use of the term *ayllu* throughout Peru.

The chroniclers provide us with the names of five *panaca* residing in Hurin Cusco, and six in Hanan Cusco, as follows:

Hurin Cusco

Chima *panaca*	of Manco Capac
Raura *panaca*	of Sinchi Roca
Auayni *panaca*	of Lloque Yupanqui
Usca Mayta *panaca*	of Mayta Capac
Apo Mayta Capac *panaca*	of Capac Yupanqui

Hanan Cusco

Uicaquirao *panaca*	of Inca Roca
Aucaylli *panaca*	of Yahuar Huacac
Socso *panaca*	of Viracocha
Hatun Ayllu	de Pachacutec Inca Yupanqui
Capac Ayllu	of Tupac Yupanqui
Tumipampa *panaca*	of Huayna Capac

Regarding the *panaca* of Huayna Capac, it is important to point out that this lineage gave its name to the northern Inca administrative center of Tumipampa, in what is now Ecuador, and not vice versa, as has been erroneously proposed. In the execution of the will of Juan Sierra de Leguisamo, son of Mancio and of Beatriz Yupanqui, *ñusta*, or daughter of the Inca, some witnesses testified that Tumipampa was previously called Surampalli. (See Rostworowski, 1983.)

These royal *panaca*, together with the guardian *ayllus*, formed the elite of Cusco, and it is important to emphasize that these are not mythical groups, as there is abundant information about them in the archival documents, which tell us where they lived and what fields they possessed at the end of

the sixteenth century. A wealth of information is found in the books of the
Real Hacienda (Royal Treasury) of Cusco (Archivo General de la Nación,
Lima) and in the Libros Parroquiales (parrish records) of Cusco.

It is clear that during the period of Inca rule the *panaca*, in addition to
constituting the royal court, functioned as political factions. Their alliances
and enmities played a major role in Inca politics and the history of Cusco
society. Besides the traditional *panaca*, already mentioned, the chronicles
make sporadic mention of five additional *panaca* that appear to have had
important roles in earlier times but that were left behind in the competition
with more powerful rival groups. It is interesting to note that if we add
them to the traditional eleven, they form a total of eight *panaca* in each
half, that is, eight for Hanan Cusco and another eight for Hurin Cusco, a
common form of Andean *ayllu* organization, as multiples of the dual and
quadripartite divisions. On the other hand, the parrish records of Cusco
contain the names of a series of *ayllus* that existed during the sixteenth and
seventeenth centuries and are without doubt an important subject for future
research.

Two of these *panaca* were eliminated from the official list for Hanan
Cusco. The first was called Cusco Panaca, and was placed in Antisuyu
during the ceremonies of the Citua calendar festival. Perhaps it represented
the descendants of Ayar Auca, who gave his name to the place he conquered. The second was Iñaca Panaca, an interesting case that offers further
insight into the structure of the royal lineages. According to the accounts
concerning the *ceque* (Cobo, 1956; Rowe, 1979), the first *huaca* of the fifth
ceque of Chinchaysuyu, adjacent to the Temple of Coricancha, was called
Cusi Cancha or Recinto Venturoso (The Temple of Good Fortune). This
was the birthplace of Inca Yupanqui (who later would take the name Pachacutec), for which reason the members of Iñaca Panaca made their sacrifices
there (Rowe, 1979, chap. 5:1; Sarmiento de Gamboa, 1943, chap. 47).

The assertion that a reigning Inca did not belong to any of the "official"
panaca named in the chronicles suggests various possibilities that should be
considered further. First, this supports my hypothesis that there were larger
numbers of ancient *panaca*. Second, the name "Iñaca" has a markedly feminine connotation. González Holguín (1952, 368) offers the following
terms:

Yñaca: the mantilla for the head
Yñaca ñusta: the lady of the ayllo of Incas or nobles
Iñaca yñacally pachallicuni or pallapallalla: the elegantly dressed and heavily
    painted woman

In Bertonio (1956, 2nd part:175) we find:

Iñaca, vel Palla: an Inca woman of noble birth
Iñacachasita: to dress in the style of these women and make oneself very
    womanly

The presence of an *ayllu* called Iñaca Panaca supports the possibility that
this was a matrilineal lineage of noble women, unlike the patrilineal *ayllus*.
Further confirmation is found in the fact that Pachacutec abandoned his
ayllu of birth in order to join Hatun Ayllu. The difference between the
panaca and the *ayllus* lies in their social structures. If this conclusion is
correct, an Inca was born into one *panaca* and passed to another when he
received the *mascapaycha*, or royal tassel. Changing lineages did not mean
that a new group was created but that he passed from one group to another.
This unique practice of the Inca lineages gave enormous importance to the
ayllu or *panaca* of the mother of a ruler.

Sarmiento de Gamboa (1943, chap. 47) relates how Pachacutec tried to
merge Iñaca Panaca with Hatun Ayllu. We know that he was unsuccessful,
since they continued to survive as separate entities into colonial times. There
is documentary evidence that during the viceroyalty, Iñaca Panaca belonged
to the Parish of San Jerónimo, and a provision in a 1630 document from
Cusco concerning the determination of estate boundaries shows that the
lands of Iñaca Panaca bordered, on the one side, Sucsu and Aucaylli Panaca
and, on the other, the fields of the Chauincusco and the Arayraca (ACC,
book 22, 1713). Thus we have firm evidence that we are not dealing with
a mythical *ayllu*.

There were also three forgotten *panaca* among those of Hurin Cusco.
The first was Masca Panaca, mentioned by Molina, *el Cusqueño*, who situ-
ates it in Cuntisuyu during the Citua ceremonies (1943:3). It seems likely
that this group gave its name to the distinctive title used by the Sapa Inca.
The second *panaca* was called Sauaseray Panaca. Sarmiento de Gamboa
(1943, chap. 9) indicates its presence in Cusco long before the arrival of the
Manco lineages in the valley. Perhaps we are dealing with a first wave of
invaders who preceded the bulk of the Inca lineages. In Toledo's *Informaciones* (Levillier, 1940, vol. 2), we find testimony from natives who contend
that the Sauaseray came from Sutic Toco, unlike Mango, who belonged to
Capac Toco. The third *panaca* was the Yauri, which is also mentioned by
Molina during the Citua ceremonies in Cuntisuyu.

With the rise of the state, the *panaca* of the rulers who created the Inca
hegemony became the most powerful and wealthy, since they were the first
to possess great landed estates and large numbers of servants. Although in
the beginning they may have contributed importantly to the growth of
Tahuantinsuyu, with the passage of time their many members began to

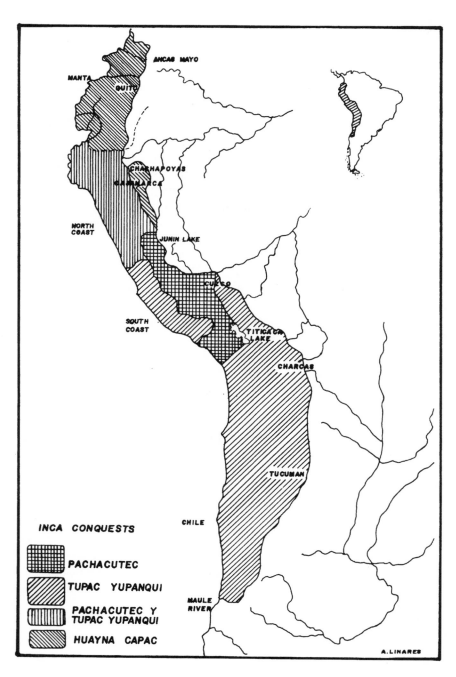

The expansion of the Inca state.

create problems for the reigning rulers. As we have seen, each mummy of a deceased Inca continued to participate in political life as if still alive, and by means of oracles rendered opinions and gave or denied approval concerning diverse issues.

These difficulties became more serious after the death of Huayna Capac, with the election of Huascar, and continued throughout the latter's rule until the *panaca* that supported Atahualpa finally triumphed.

3

Expansion and Development

THE LEGEND OF THE WAR AGAINST THE CHANCAS

While the myth of the Ayar siblings relates the settlement of the Incas in Cusco, that of the war against the Chancas deals with the beginnings of Inca greatness. These myths narrate two well-defined stages in the development of the Inca state. The first tells of its origins and efforts to make a place for itself in the valley of Cusco, and the second tells how it broke the circle of powerful neighbors and changed in its favor the long-existing equilibrium among the macroethnic groups of the region.

These narratives contain a fund of factual data enveloped in legend. Without doubt, the myth of Manco represents the movement of ethnic groups that arrived at Acamama, a small village occupied by other peoples. The legend of the war against the Chancas responds to the Incas' need to explain their existence, that is, to relate the events that unleashed the Inca expansion.

While we do not have a reliable account of events, owing to the absence of a native system of writing and the confusion of the chronicles, at least the legends offer an Andean version of what they might have been. It appears that circumstances favored the Inca rise to dominance, since we have the plain evidence of the Inca state from firsthand Spanish accounts. From that point their history is divided between myth and reality. It is also obvious that Inca might was not forged by itself, but resulted from a combination of favorable circumstances and the appearance of an elite group of capable people that knew how to take advantage of them.

When we are dealing with the Inca conquests, it should be clarified that, according to current archaeological evidence, this expansion dates to little more than a century before the arrival of the Europeans. Cieza de León (1943), as well as Castro-Ortega Morejón (1974), in their *relaciones*, affirm that the Incas were "modern" in the Andean panorama, that is, that their expansion did not belong to the ancient history of the region, a fact the Incas themselves recognized.

In the same way as the Incas tried to impose themselves and dominate their neighbors, the Chanca macroethnic group, located in the region of the Pampas and Pachachaca rivers, also aspired to territorial expansion some few generations before the arrival of the Spanish. Owing to the legendary character of the war against the Chancas, we cannot determine with certainty when it took place. It is possible that the confrontations between the two ethnic groups that led to the siege of Cusco and the total defeat of the Chancas began long before, some generations before the appearance of the Spanish.

The chronicle of Betanzos contains the most detailed information about the definitive wars between Incas and Chancas, whose victorious outcome he attributes to Prince Cusi Yupanqui, later to become the Inca Pachacutec. His narrative contains all the appearances of a piece of traditional indigenous song, and it appears that Betanzos had access to the oral tradition of the *panaca* of Pachacutec through his wife, Cusirimay Oello, who was related to Atahualpa. Both of them belonged to the lineage of Pachacutec in accordance with the Inca kinship system. This conclusion will be further explained later.

This *ñusta* had been Pizarro's concubine, with whom he had a son called Francisco, after his father. After the death of the Marqués, she married Juan de Betanzos, an expert Quechua speaker and official interpreter in Cusco. It is natural to suppose that he had long conversations with his wife's relatives, and that these were his principal informants when Viceroy Antonio de Mendoza ordered him to write an account, which he finished in 1551. His work remained unedited, and part of it was lost, until the recent discovery of the complete chronicle in the library of Bartolomé March, in Palma de Mallorca, thanks to the efforts of Mari Carmen Martín Rubio. The reader will understand why this is my chronicle of preference, since the data provided by Betanzos may be based directly on the Inca oral tradition.

The Chanca, according to their myths, considered the lagoon of Choclococha, near the town of Castrovirreyna, at an altitude of 4,950 meters, to be their *pacarina* (Cieza de León, *La Crónica*, 1941, chap. 15; Guaman Poma, 1936, fol. 85; Vázquez de Espinoza, 1942). The name Choclococha ("Lake of Maize Ears") originated, according to Murúa (1946, book 4, chap. 7), with a battle between the Huancas and the Huamanes, in which the former were defeated and, in their hasty flight, threw their loads of maize into the lagoon, whose ancient name was Acha. During the following summer excessive heat dried the lagoon, and the seeds germinated, producing tender ears of maize.

Another legend related to this lagoon is mentioned by Arriaga (1968). According to this author, during the procession of Corpus Christi the natives carried two "lambs of the earth" (llamas) in a litter, then sacrificed them to the lagoons of Choclococha and Urcococha, saying that the llamas had their origin there.

Like the Incas, the Chanca group comprised various *ayllus* divided into the moieties *hanan* and *hurin*. Those belonging to the upper moiety claimed Uscovilca as their mythical chief, while those of the lower moiety considered Ancovilca as their ancestor. Both were carried to their wars, like idols, in the form of *guanca*, or stones (Sarmiento de Gamboa, 1943, chap. 26).

Before discussing the various *ayllus* that made up this ethnic group, we should look at the meaning of the word *chanca*. The dictionary of Bertonio (1956) contains the word *cchancca*, wool thread. González Holguín (1952), in his Quechua dictionary, mentions *chanca zzapa*, to sway, walk shakily; *chanchani* or *zzanzzani*, go jumping; *chanca*, leg. According to Recaredo Pérez Palma (1938), *chanca* is the part of the body in which the extremities and the sex are united. Did the Chancas use this term for themselves? Or was it a term of ridicule applied to them by the Quechua-speaking Andahuaylas, or by the people of Cusco, referring to their manner of walking? The Chancas of Andahuaylas appear to have been close relatives of the other groups that inhabited the present-day province of Ayacucho. Garcilaso (1943, book 4, chap. 15) lists the Chanca *ayllus* as: the Hancohuallus, the Utunsullas, and the Urumarcas, inhabitants of the Valley of the Río Pampas; the Vilcas of the *meseta* who occupied the left bank of the same river; the Pocras, in the valleys that surrounded the present-day city of Ayacucho; the Iquichanos, of the mountains to the north of Huanta; the Morochucos, of Cangallo; and, finally, the Tacmanes and the Quiñuallas, who occupied the land between Abancay and the snowed-capped mountains.

Navarro del Aguila (1930), in his book *Tribus de Ankcu Wallokc*, gives the Chanca confederation control over a larger territory by allying them with the Huancas and by giving greater importance to the Pocra *ayllus*. It may be true that the Chancas formed part of a larger confederation of groups, but it does not appear that the other components of this proposed macroethnic group participated in the attack on Cusco. If this had been the case, the smaller forces of Cusco would not likely have been able to resist the assault. In addition, Betanzos refers to a dispersion of the Chanca forces toward other regions, which appears to indicate a limited cohesion of their armies. The Chancas seem, rather, to have been hordes dedicated to pillage. It can be hypothesized that, given their indomitable and bellicose spirit, they were responsible for the disintegration of the great Wari hegemony, or at least were the principal culprits in its demise.

During the regime of Viracocha, the Chancas left their lands to dedicate themselves to world conquest, departing from Paucaray, their principal town, situated three leagues from Parcos. Following Andean tradition, they divided their armies into three parts, one of which took the route toward Cuntisuyu with Malma and Irapa, or Rapa, as its leaders, representing the upper and lower moieties. The second army also moved toward Cuntisuyu, although Sarmiento de Gamboa contends that it went to Antisuyu. Its generals were Yana Vilca and Toquello Vilca, or Teclo Vilca. The third group, led by Tumay Huaraca and Astu Huaraca, took the most direct route to Cusco. This group was accompanied by Huaman Huaraca, who was to be responsible for negotiating the Inca surrender. (For an analysis of the names of the Chanca chiefs, see Rostworowski, 1953.)

Arriving at Vilcacunga, the Chancas sent their emissaries to Cusco to announce their intention of conquering the Incas. Viracocha, terrorized by the news, decided to abandon the city to its fate and sought refuge in the fort of Caquia Xaquixaguana. Viracocha's two sons, Urco and Socso, departed with him.

It will be useful to digress briefly on the subject of Urco. In a previous work I analyzed the selection of Urco as co-regent of the reigning Inca. I shall return to this subject when dealing with the successions of the Incas and practices by which the local lords sought to assure the nomination of a successor and avoid the normal practice of election of the "most able." The chroniclers who refer to Urco as ruler are the following: Cieza de León, Betanzos, Sarmiento de Gamboa. Santa Cruz Pachacuti, and Herrera. The chroniclers who only mention him are Murúa, Cabello de Valboa, Guaman Poma, Los Quipucamayoc, and Cobo. Father Acosta does not mention Urco by name, but says that the earliest victories of Pachacutec were owing to a "brother" who served as co-ruler with his father and was defeated in battle against the Chancas. Other chroniclers such as Las Casas (1923) and Román-Zamora refer to Pachacutec as the defender of Cusco. Calancha assures us that Pachacutec seized the government from his father and brother, "although Garcilaso says that the one who took the reign from his father was Viracocha." Herrera illustrates the cover of the fifteenth book of his chronicle with the Inca Urco with the insignias of command.

We return to the legend at the point when the conflict between the Incas and the Chancas acquires an epic character as the enemy troops approached Cusco. Only the young Cusi Yupanqui, supposed "son" of Viracocha, remained in the abandoned city, along with generals Vicaquirao, Apo Mayta, and Quiliscachi Urco Guaranga, and his four servants, Pata Yupanqui, Muru Uanca, Apo Yupanqui, and Uxula Urco Guaranga. Sarmiento de Gamboa indicates that seven men besides Cusi Yupanqui remained in

Cusco: Inca Roca, Quiliscachi Urco Guaranga, Chima Chaui, Pata Yuypanqui, Viracocha, Inca Paucar, and Mircoymana, the tutor of the Inca Yupanqui. The number eight, as we have seen, represents a multiple of the dual and quadripartite principles, and is of great significance in the Inca social structure.

The Betanzos narrative assumes here the tone of the long songs of the oral tradition, but still maintains a certain resemblance to the narratives of medieval epics. Cusi Yupanqui instructed the three nobles who remained with him to seek help among the neighboring *curacas*. The *curacas*, however, fearing the Chancas and seeing how few Inca defenders there were, refused their support. Later, the small size of the Inca force became a central feature of the mythology of their victory, increasing still further the magnitude of their accomplishment and the grandeur of their leader.

The legend tells of how alone and anguished the virtuous young Cusi Yupanqui slept, and of how in his dream there appeared to him the image of the god Viracocha, who prophesied his coming victory (this part of the myth has a markedly European flavor, since the Andean tradition would require offerings of numerous sacrifices to a *huaca* in order to obtain the oracle). On the day following this dream, the Chancas appeared on the hill of Carmenca and their squadrons came trampling down, shouting and screaming (see Hernández et al., 1987).

According to Cieza, the defenders of the city had dug great ditches covered with branches and earth into which the Chancas fell in their mad dash down the hill. Sarmiento de Gamboa (1943, chap. 27) mentions the female chief Chañan Cury Coca, of the *ayllus* of Choco and Cachona, who, at the head of her army, helped reject the enemy attack.

The myth tells of the miraculous intervention of the *pururaucas* in the critical moment of the fighting, of how these simple stones came to life transformed into fierce warriors at the height of the battle and were decisive in the Incas' victory (Cobo, 1956; Santa Cruz Pachacuti, 1927). The fame of the *pururaucas* was widely disseminated among the enemies of the Incas, and on occasion chiefs would surrender, fearful of confronting this veteran army.

Meanwhile, Cusi Yupanqui and his seven "brother" chiefs succeeded in stopping the advancing Chancas. Taking advantage of the favorable situation, the young prince threw himself at the enemy and seized the mummy of Uscovilca, as well as the Chanca banner. The Chancas, seeing themselves without their mummy and banner, took flight and did not stop until reaching Ichopampa. The neighboring lords who had waited on the heights above the city for the outcome of the battle, abandoned their positions to join forces with the victorious Incas and pursue their enemies.

According to Sarmiento de Gamboa (1943, chap. 28), the second confrontation with the Chancas took place at Ichopampa. This time the Incas were reinforced by the armies of the neighboring lords, who were anxious to join the victorious side. The two Chanca chiefs perished in the encounter and the disorderly dispersal of their forces permitted the Incas to collect a huge amount of booty, an event of great importance for their subsequent rise, as we will see shortly.

After Cusi Yupanqui's victory, according to the detailed narration of Betanzos, the young conqueror went to where the Inca Viracocha was waiting so that, following Andean practice, the ruler could trample the spoils of the defeated Chancas as a symbol of their conquest. The Inca was greatly confused when he saw the humiliated Chancas spread out on the ground. He refused to perform the triumphal act, however, preferring instead that Urco walk over the booty of the battlefield. Already suspicious of Viracocha's intentions, Yupanqui was alerted by one of his captains of preparations to ambush him. Viracocha's troops, he learned, had departed silently from their fortress for an unknown destination.

With this, Cusi Yupanqui ordered his troops divided into two groups, one remaining with him and the other following Viracocha's people to determine if they were planning an ambush or were marching on Cusco to initiate action against him from there. Meanwhile, Viracocha was waiting for Yupanqui with the humbled Chanca chiefs spread out on the ground. But Cusi, fearing an ambush, entered surrounded by his well-armed men. When Viracocha insisted that Urco receive credit for the triumph, Yupanqui decided to take the booty and return to Cusco. On the return road, however, he was attacked by Viracocha's troops in a narrow pass. Thanks to his prior warning, however, the ambush failed and the young leader made his triumphal return to Cusco.

Betanzos locates the second and final battle against the Chancas at Xaquixaguana. After his second victory over the Chancas, Yupanqui spared the lives of the Xaquixaguanas, saying that they were forced to fight against the Incas, and ordered them to cut their hair Inca style. The Chanca leaders, however, were severely punished as a warning. He ordered them to be hanged, their heads to be displayed on tall poles, and their bodies to be burned.

Following this victory, news reached Cusco that Inca Urco was in Yucay with an armed force. While there was no indication of an imminent attack, Yupanqui marched to Yucay accompanied by his "brother" Roca. In the confrontation, Urco was wounded in the throat by a stone while standing high above a river gorge. He fell into the water and briefly escaped by swimming downstream until he reached the crag of Chupellusca, one league below Tambo. There, however, he was caught and killed by Yupanqui's soldiers.

The Conqueror of the Chancas

In a work published in 1953, I devoted a chapter to analyzing the identity of the personage who achieved the victory over the Chancas. Although the identity of this individual is not relevant to an analysis of the myth, it is important for Inca history, especially because the final defeat of these adversaries of the Incas occurred just a few generations before the arrival of the Europeans. It is important to keep in mind that the events just narrated do not belong to the origin myths, but are accounts that explain the expansion of the Incas during the century before the Spanish Conquest.

Before examining the situation created by the defeat of the Chancas, it is worth asking if in fact an attack on Cusco by enemy tribes took place and when this might have occurred. This final confrontation must have been the culmination of many years of war between the Incas and Chancas, which could only end with the defeat of one of them. Obviously, the Incas were successful; were it otherwise, Andean history would have taken a very different course.

Early in the fifteenth century, the world of Cusco and its surroundings became too confining for the long-repressed ambition of the Incas. Their desire for conquest was frustrated by powerful neighbors, while at the same time they lacked an organizational structure to protect their possessions. Moreover, it appears likely that the repeated wars against the same enemies throughout the early Inca reigns were conducted in order to seize booty and not to acquire territorial possessions. Gaining control of large quantities of spoils was a major objective of these chiefs, since with booty they could be generous with their allies and secure their ties of reciprocity and kinship.

These circumstances changed as a result of the Inca victory over the Chancas. The Incas sought not only to take possession of valuable spoils but also to establish reciprocal relations with the chiefs of other ethnic groups, a subject I examine later.

Until the arrival of the Chancas in Carmenca, at the doors of Cusco, the Inca *señorío* was neither more extensive nor more powerful than their various neighboring ethnic groups. Each valley or village had a war chief for its defense, and interminable wars and conflicts kept all these small domains in a constant state of alert. Only the Chancas, after repeated victories over their neighbors, were able to widen their dominions. Chanca expansion was on an upward path, and it inevitably had to clash with the interests of the Incas, since both groups were determined to dominate their neighbors.

Given this situation, it is understandable that the victory of the Incas transformed the equilibrium existing up to that time. A breach was opened in the circle of hostile neighbors, and the Incas threw themselves through it and on to their wars of conquest.

Their victory gave the Incas an enormous advantage over the other war chiefs and local lords of the region. Many of these rushed to ally themselves with the Incas, and ties of reciprocity with the Incas were surely highly esteemed and much sought after. The road was open to a burst of expansion of the Inca domain. Strengthened by their newly won prestige, the Incas could destroy the Chancas in their own homeland, an unimaginable feat until that time. Following these triumphs, the Incas easily defeated the Ayarmacas as well, thus securing their territories in the immediate vicinity of the capital, a necessary step before they could think about distant conquests.

If we consider the war against the Chancas as the point of departure for the formation and subsequent expansion of the Inca state, we would expect that the chief who led them to victory would be the most distinguished figure in Inca history. This is, however, a very controversial subject, concerning which there are many serious historical discrepancies. For this reason, it will be useful to discuss further what the sources – that is, the chronicles – have to say on this point.

This confusion surrounding the individuals and episodes increases the mythical character of the events. What is the historical truth regarding these events? Are Viracocha and Pachacutec two distinguishable historical individuals, or did the native songs create two characters from a single historical figure? Did these events occur earlier, and was it the narrative of the chroniclers that shortened the elapsed time?

Undoubtedly, beginning with the assassination of Yahuar Huacac, the accounts of the chroniclers become vague and controversies begin to accumulate. Cieza de León (1943) mentions the election of Viracocha as ruler, following his nomination by a noblewoman of Hatun Cusco. He also lists the names of his military chiefs; if we compare this list with that of Yahuar Huacac's military chiefs, we see that they are identical, further evidence that Viracocha was not the son of Yahuar Huacac, although he belonged to the same generation (Sarmiento de Gamboa, 1943, chaps. 23 and 25).

Also, important aspects of events leading up to the Chanca attack on Cusco were Europeanized by the chroniclers. The episode relating the vision of the Creator god by Viracocha (or Cusi Yupanqui-Pachacutec) bears a striking resemblance to the European medieval romance ballads. The prayers of the future hero as related in these accounts were quite unlike what we know of native practices. An examination of the many colonial

Table 3.1.

Chroniclers who attribute the victory to Pachacutec	Chroniclers who attribute the victory to the Inca Viracocha	Chroniclers who do not mention the war but provide some indirect information
Cieza de León	Garcilaso de la Vega	Murúa mentions the
Las Casas	Cobo	existence of Urco
Polo de Ondegardo	Oliva	and the conquests
Sarmiento de Gamboa		of Pachacutec in
Acosta		Vilcas and Jauja
Gutierrez de Santa Clara		Molina, *el Cusqueño,*
Jesuita Anónimo		attributes the vision
Santa Cruz Pachacuti		of Pachacutec
Cobo		Cabello de Valboa
Calancha		speaks of the two
Román y Zamora		wars of Yupanqui
Herrera		against the Chancas
		Diego Fernańdez, *el*
		Palentino, mentions
		Pachacutec as the
		conqueror of
		Vilcas, an impor-
		tant Chanca center

proceedings against the idolatry of the natives shows that such an encounter would have been preceded by numerous sacrifices of llamas, guinea pigs, cocoa leaves, tallow, and even children. The Andean *huacas* and the *guanca* would have received offerings in return for their support and benevolence. Thus satisfied, they would have spoken, given their oracles, and maintained close ties with the faithful.

It is necessary, then, to compare the sources, the information provided by the various chronicles. One difficulty is that Garcilaso de la Vega, in opposition to most of the chroniclers, identifies the Inca Viracocha as the victor in the wars against the Chancas. In light of this claim we must examine the information provided by Garcilaso and compare it with the other sources. At the same time, we must look for motives that might have caused Garcilaso to change existing references regarding the events. For greater clarification, Table 3.1 shows the various chroniclers and their positions on this issue.

In the first column are listed the twelve chroniclers who attribute the victory over the Chancas to Pachacutec. Cieza de León's Inca Yupanqui must refer to Pachacutec, since various passages of his chronicle contain references to the identity of Yupanqui, such as "Inca Yupanqui, son of

Viracocha, increased his wealth" (referring to the Coricancha) and elsewhere, "in the time of the Inca Yupanqui, [his wealth] increased such that when he died and his son Tupac Yupanqui held the empire, it remained in this perfect state" (1943, chaps. 27 and 28).

There is no possible doubt concerning the identity of Inca Yupanqui as the successor of Viracocha and father of Tupac, the ninth ruler in the official version of Inca history. The chroniclers frequently refer to this Inca only as Yupanqui, explaining that he added Pachacutec to his name after the victory over the Chancas, and also that when an Inca assumed power he customarily changed his name (Santa Cruz Pachacuti, 1968).

Regarding the account of Oliva (1895, chap. 2), his informant was Catari de Cochabamba, according to whom Viracocha and Pachacutec were the same person, to whom he attributes the conquest of the Chancas without mentioning the attack on Cusco. Finally, Cobo (1956), faced with a difficult decision, decides to attribute the same events to both Incas, thus disqualifying himself as an informant.

In the third column appear those chroniclers who do not indicate either Pachacutec or Viracocha as conqueror of the Chancas, but whose information can contribute to our making this determination. The conquest of Vilcas involved the defeat of the Chancas, since this was an important center of that ethnic group. Also, the victor over the Chancas in Cusco would find it necessary to continue the war in enemy territory.

Guaman Poma does not mention the attack on Cusco, but refers to extensive conquests by Yahuar Huacac in territories belonging to the Chancas, which he attributes to the Inca Viracocha. I have shown that the conflict between Incas and Chancas lasted for many years and was likely renewed by each new ruler.

Guaman Poma's list of famous Inca captains reinforces my conclusions. He names Otorongo Achachi, son of Inca Roca, as the sixth captain; the son of Yahuar Huacac as the seventh, and the son of Pachacutec as the eighth. He omits from his list the captains of Viracocha (who would, of course, have included Yupanqui), possibly because these were the same as those of his predecessor, Yahuar Huacac. On the other hand, still according to Guaman Poma, the first Inca captain, son of Manco Capac and Mama Huaco, was also called Pachacutec. It appears likely that Cusi Yupanqui, or simply Yupanqui, was a descendant of Mama Huaco, since he was born to the lineage of Iñaca Panaca in Cusi Cancha, which was probably a matrilineal *ayllu*. This hypothesis would explain the preponderant place given by the Inca Yupanqui to the mythical couple Manco Capac and Mama Huaco at the time when he reorganized the *ayllus* and lineages of Cusco.

But let us return to Garcilaso's account and ask ourselves if his version, so different from those of most of the chroniclers, is the result of his ignorance of the facts, of the distance from his homeland or the passage of time between his departure from Peru and the writing down of his chronicle. Garcilaso, however, according to his own admission, knew and consulted the chronicles of Acosta and Cieza de León, both versions contrary to his own. An intentional error on Garcilaso's part, which can be proved, is one regarding the royal mummies found by Polo de Ondegardo in Cusco. In that case, Garcilaso's desire to hide the facts, to change or substitute the identities of the mummies and the names of the Incas, is undeniable.

We know that the mummy of the Inca Viracocha was found by Gonzalo Pizaro in Xaquixaguana, where he ordered it burned. The natives retrieved the ashes and kept them in a jar. Years later, Polo de Ondegardo discovered them (Acosta, 1940, book 6, chap. 20; Calancha, 1976, book 1, chap. 15; Sarmiento de Gamboa, 1943, chap. 25). The mummy of Tupac Yupanqui suffered a similar fate. It was burned by Challcochima, a general of Atahualpa. Again, it was Polo who found the ashes, in Calispuquio, together with those of Tupac Yupanqui's *huauque*, or double (Sarmiento de Gamboa, 1943, chap. 54).

The mummy of Pachacutec was found by Polo (1917) in Tococache, where it had been brought by the natives from its original place in Patallacta. It was in Tococache that the Inca had ordered the construction of a temple consecrated to the thunder deity, the idol he had selected as his *huauque*. Polo, referring to the mummy of Pachacutec, says the following:

> When I discovered the body of Pachacuti Inca Yupanqui Inca who was one of those that I sent to the Marqués in the city of Los Reyes, embalmed and also cured, as [were] all those we saw, and found with him *the principal idol of the province of Andavaylas, because he had conquered it* and placed it under the domination of the Incas when he defeated Barcuvilca, the principal ruler of the province, and had him killed. (My italics)

The Chanca idol found at the side of the body of Pachacutec is conclusive proof that it was this Inca who defeated the Chancas, since Cobo (1968, book 13, chap. 12) confirms that it was the custom for a conqueror to keep the idols of the places he had subjected. Upon the death of the Inca, these idols passed on to his lineage, or *panaca*.

Acosta (1940, book 6, chap. 21) also mentions Polo's discovery, and describes the mummy of Pachacutec in the following terms:

> He found it transferred from Patallacta to Tococache, where the parish of San Blas was founded. The body was whole and well-prepared with a kind of

pitch that made it seem alive. The eyes had been made from a thin sheet of gold, so well done that he did not miss the originals; and he had on his head a scar from a wound they had given him in a certain war. He had gray hair, as if he had died that same day, although he had been dead for 70 or 80 years.

The detail recalled by Acosta regarding the scar that appeared on the head of the mummified Pachacutec is confirmed by Cabello de Valboa and by Sarmiento de Gamboa (1943, chap. 39; Cabello de Valboa, 1951, chap. 4; Santa Cruz Pachacuti, 1927:187). These chroniclers reported that the Inca had received a wound during an encounter, a fact that assisted in the identification of the mummy. Another bit of evidence that helps identify the Inca is the mention of his gray hair, since all the data are in agreement concerning his advanced age when he died.

So, then, in spite of Garcilaso's having access to the books of Acosta and Cieza, the references to the mummies that appear in his chronicle are entirely different. Of the three male mummies he saw in the lodging of Polo de Ondegardo, he refers to one as belonging to Viracocha, the second to Tupac Yupanqui, and the third to Huayna Capac (Garcilaso, 1943, vol. 1, book 5, chap. 29). Garcilaso tells of how Polo showed him the mummies, giving him the name of each one. Polo could not, however, have provided the information as reported by Garcilaso because it was diametrically opposed to what he had learned and written.

It cannot be said in his defense that Garcilaso had simply forgotten details and confused the mummies because many years had elapsed since he had seen them. He himself says that Acosta's chronicle was available to him. It is surprising that Garcilaso makes no mention of the mummy of Pachacutec, and instead tells us about that of Viracocha. In doing so, his account arbitrarily exchanges the physical remains of Pachacutec for those of Viracocha, much as it exchanges their achievements in life. Nor, of course, does Garcilaso mention the Chanca idol that accompanied the body of the deceased Pachacutec.

What are the reasons behind Garcilaso's hiding and distorting the historical facts? Rather than search for European motives, we must look for an explanation in the purest indigenous perspective with which Garcilaso viewed these events, which for him involved all the political passions of the Cusco *panaca*.

Two major political factions confronted each other during the war between Huascar and Atahualpa. One consisted of the *panaca* of Tupac Yupanqui, called Capac Ayllu, and the other of the *panaca* of Pachacutec, called Hatun Ayllu. Garcilaso was descended through his mother from the *panaca* of Tupac Yupanqui, to which Huascar also belonged, through his mother, Raura Ocllo. On the other hand, research shows, Atahualpa belonged through his mother to Hatun Ayllu. The wars of succession to Huayna Capac quickly became disputes and rivalries between these two royal clans. But these issues will be more fully discussed later; they are anticipated here only to the extent that they can enlighten us concerning the motives of the Inca writer.

All this accumulation of rancor and hatred, increased by the burning of the mummy of Tupac Yupanqui and by the cruelty of Atahualpa's generals toward Huascar and his followers, affected Garcilaso profoundly and caused him to distort the historical facts. At the same time, as we have seen, ignoring and altering events was a frequent practice in Andean historiography. The same passions moved Betanzos in the opposite direction, when he omitted Huascar from his *capaccuna* or list of Inca rulers. If the development of the Incas has not been cut short by the arrival of the Spanish, all events involving Huascar would have disappeared from the native songs, *quipu*, and official paintings. His memory would have been preserved only among the members of his own diminished *panaca*.

Because of this Andean custom of distorting events, it becomes impossible to relate a true, coherent, reliable history of the Incas. Ideally, each event should be individually confirmed, an impossibility owing to the absence of adequate documentation. The case of Garcilaso's confusion of the royal mummies, with its flagrant intentional falsehood, is provable only because it occurred during the colonial period, for which it is possible to compare multiple written sources.

This again demonstrates that Inca history could be told in three or four different ways, on which the chroniclers would base their versions. For this reason, the war against the Chancas must be investigated with great caution to be able to distinguish myth from reality. In some cases, there are archaeological studies that corroborate the ethnographic evidence, or contradict it. González Carré et al., (1981), in their research on the history of Ayacucho, find that the weakening of Wari power around A.D. 1200–1470 coincided with the rise of ethnic groups they identify as the Chancas and groups related to them.

Archaeological studies have enabled us to locate more than 120 settlements in the Pampas River basin. These villages are at altitudes of 2,000 to 4,000 meters, which appears to indicate that the inhabitants felt the need to dominate such strategic points for defensive reasons. Their coarse ceramics have no relation to the sophisticated wares of the Wari period. They point, rather, to invasion by peoples of inferior culture. According to González Carré, the Chancas and their allies were hordes who dominated the region of Ayacucho, Huancavilca, and Andahuaylas, and were responsible for the destruction of the Wari capital.

These archaeological finds support our hypothesis and permit the discussion of one final question: why Cusi Yupanqui chose the ruling name of Pachacutec. I shall provide a conjectural answer to this question, a speculative one, since sometimes this is the only way to make advances in research: if it were in fact the Chancas and their related tribes that destroyed the Wari hegemony, the Inca victory would constitute a kind of remote revenge for a legendary defeat that took place centuries earlier. The inhabitants of Cusco at the time of the Inca victory must have preserved myths and memories of this distant past, even though many centuries had passed between the end of the Wari period and the beginnings of Inca expansion. An example of the perseverance of Andean oral traditions is found in the myth of Mama Raiguana, a goddess of the central and north-central sierra, which is preserved in the present-day village of Pampas, in the high valley of Chancay, as a folktale about a peasant mother (Arteaga León, 1976; Rostworowski, 1983). Based on this assumption, I venture that some Wari rulers used the name Pachacutec, and that Cusi Yupanqui chose a name that reminded him of the ancient greatness of that past culture. Possibly he felt himself heir of the legendary Wari lords and wished to emulate them (see the long list of rulers, who may be Wari lords, provided by Montesinos).

On the other hand, whenever a major disturbance occurred in the royal succession in Cusco, the Inca who obtained the royal tassel affirmed his victory by selecting a spectacular name, as in the cases of Viracocha after the assassination of Yahuar Huacac; of Cusi Yupanqui, after the war against the Chancas and the death of Urco; and finally, of Atahualpa, who planned to take the name of Tisci Capac when he triumphed over Huascar (Santa Cruz Pachacuti, 1927).

To claim, as does Imbelloni (1946), a thousand-year record and cyclical repetition of events it is necessary, above all, to have some kind of writing system and means of computing the passage of time. The *quipu* was not sufficient for this purpose. The natives did not keep counts of this kind because they did not measure time in solar years. When the Spanish wanted to know the number of years that had elapsed between the death of Huayna Capac and the arrival of Pizarro on his third voyage, the responses were confusing, and different in the case of each informant. If the Spanish could not determine with exactitude the chronology of events that occurred just a few years earlier, even less could the natives grasp the notion of a thousand-year record. And the Indians kept records of their individual ages not by years but, rather, by biological cycles. This is also noted in numerous ad-

A carved stone outcrop, possibly used as a ceremonial seat, at the Inca site of Puma Orco, south of Cusco. Photo by Edward Ranney.

ministrative and judicial documents in which native witnesses affirm they do not know their age because "they do not count by years" (Espinoza, 1971:204).

Likewise, the data regarding ages provided by Guaman Poma and narrations of the great flood are transpositions of Judeo-Christian beliefs, without Andean antecedents. When an Andean myth tells of great floods or torrential rains, it probably refers to appearances of El Niño, involving disturbances in the maritime currents.

The nine Pachacutis of Imbelloni and his cyclical counts are simply a transference of Old World thought to the Andes, a frequent occurrence in Andean historiography.

THE SYSTEM OF RECIPROCITY

Reciprocity was a system of socioeconomic organization that regulated the provision of services at various levels and served to interlock the production

The Coricancha, located in Lower Cusco on the present-day site of the Church of Santo Domingo, rebuilt and richly refurnished during the reign of Pachacutec Inca Yupanqui. Photo by Martin Chamb.

and distribution of goods. A means of ordering relations among the members of a society with an economy what did not use money, it was found throughout the Andean world and provided links among the diverse kinds of economic organization that existed within the vast territory of the Incas.

Many anthropologists have conducted studies of contemporary reciprocity in peasant communities throughout Peru to determine its means of social articulation and the reasons for its perseverance (Alberti and Mayer, 1974). Others have done comparative research on ancient cultures that did not use money (Polanyi et al., 1957; Sahlins, 1972).

According to studies by Murra (1972), we can distinguish between two levels of reciprocity. At the lower level were the principles of reciprocity that governed the relationships among the rural communities (*ayllus*) united by kinship ties. At the upper level occurred reciprocity as it was practiced by the Inca state, surrounded by its military and administrative apparatus, which benefited from the services provided by its subjects and redistributed the accumulated surpluses. Wachtel (1974:1353) finds that with the expansion of the Inca state, an earlier form of reciprocity, as it was practiced at the rural level, underwent structural changes. The principle of reciprocity remained the same, but its function changed. In its new context, it served the growth of the state apparatus, while the ancient expressions of reciprocity served only ideological functions that disguised and justified the new social relationships.

We can distinguish two stages or periods in the development of reciprocity. The first stage corresponds to the beginnings of Inca development, when it regulated the relations among the various lords of the Inca region. During this period, the power of the Inca ruler was extremely limited, and he was unable to order freely the construction of the principal infrastructure works required to further Inca domination. This underlay the great importance the Incas gave to the management of reciprocity to achieve their ends and take maximum advantage of the system. The second stage in the development of reciprocity was its functioning during the peak of Inca power, when the system underwent great transformations as it was adapted to the requirements of the state.

Reciprocity in Its Primitive Form

To understand the development of reciprocity and its functioning at the time of the beginnings of Cusco, we turn once again to the chronicle of Betanzos, since it is the only account from an Andean perspective of the first steps of the relatively weak Inca ethnic group toward becoming a powerful centralizing state.

After the Inca triumph over the Chancas, a new balance of power took hold in Cusco. Although Yupanqui had acquired great military prestige and could count on many allies, he was far from possessing absolute or direct domination over the other lords. He could not order works, or carry them out, without the approval and support of the local lords. It was impossible for him to command the workforce directly, without the agreement of his

The massive stone walls of Sascayhuaman, on a hilltop overlooking Cusco, which may have served as a monument to the great Inca victory over the Chancas, rather than as an actual fortress. Photo by Charles H. Coles, Neg. No. 288578, courtesy of Department of Library Services, American Museum of Natural History.

neighbors. When Inca expansion began, then, authority was exercised not directly but by means of reciprocity, of the *minka*, a term whose verb form, *minccacuni*, according to González Holguín (1952), means "to beg someone to help me, permitting him something" in return.

What events can be gleaned from the chronicle of Betanzos that illustrate these initial steps toward Inca domination? Above all, we can see the nature of the early relations between the Incas and the local lords. Any work that Yupanqui wished performed had to be requested and "begged" from the neighboring lords. He had first to invite them to convene in Cusco, to entertain them with presents, food and drink, and days filled with uninterrupted merriment. Only then could the Inca present his request (*ruego*) and ask the chiefs' cooperation in providing the necessary workforce to carry out the project at hand.

If the Inca wished to please and flatter his neighbors, he perforce had to show himself to be generous with them, by giving them women, clothes, luxury objects, and coca, among other things. In this situation, the Incas found it necessary to possess great quantities of gifts. In other words, it was essential to have large amounts of excess goods available for use as gifts, in exchange for which the Incas would receive an indispensable supply of labor. At that time, a simple rural chief must have been rather poor and rustic in terms of the objects of value at his disposal, and it was for this reason that the booty obtained by the Incas from the defeated Chancas acquired such importance. This large quantity of spoils was, in my opinion, the crucial factor that permitted the Inca to be "generous," thus oiling the gears of reciprocity. By this means he was able to attract into his orbit the assistance of the neighboring lords, which meant, in other words, access to their labor, without which it would have been impossible to undertake the construction work necessary to begin expansion.

The booty recovered in the final defeat of the Chancas must have been enormous, if we take into account that part of their army had successfully invaded the area of Cuntisuyu. It is likely that the Incas, when they occupied the principal Chanca centers, gathered up all the goods previously seized by the Chancas in their rapine.

According to Betanzos, all the important construction projects initiated and executed by Yupanqui were accomplished according to a comprehensive plan. We have already seen that it was essential to put in place the basic infrastructure that permitted the establishment of the Inca system of organization. For the purposes of history, it is not important to know who began these works, without which it would have been impossible to begin to extend the Inca domain. The interesting aspect of Betanzo's description is how these essential works, on which the state organization would rest, were being executed.

One of Yupanqui's first measures after being named ruler of Cusco was to effect a new distribution of the lands around the city. We will return to this measure later, but it is mentioned here because it represented a way of satisfying the *panaca* and *ayllus* allied with the Incas and of compensating those who had fought for the Inca triumph. The old romances of Hatun Ayllu burst forth in Betanzo's narrative when he tells of Yupanqui's stroll through the town and its surroundings, inspecting and reflecting on the projects that would be most useful and desirable to execute.

Yupanqui also ordered the construction of storage facilities around the city. This was a logical place to start his construction works because without adequate storage space for foodstuffs and craft products it would have been impossible for him to show his "generosity," that is, he would have been unable to continue meeting the requirements of reciprocity. For this purpose, he invited the neighboring chiefs to come to Cusco, receiving them with great presents and ritual meals, since no labor could be performed in the Andes without this fundamental and indispensable prerequisite, after which Yupanqui made his "petition." He informed the chiefs of his desire to build a great number of storehouses with the labor force at their command. "All of which the chiefs agreed to do because they understood that the Inca Yupanqui was a ruler who knew well how to reward whatever service was rendered to him" (Betanzos, 1968, chap. 12:35). And they asked "that he show them the places and locations where the storehouses should be built, what each of them should do" (ibid.). This request by Yupanqui demonstrates that the power of the Inca was still limited, and that he apparently still did not have sufficient manpower to carry out such a task alone.

When the construction was completed, "the Inca Yupanqui ordered the chiefs and lords to come together, and to those who . . . had rendered services to him, he granted numerous favors, giving them clothes and women from his lineage, and permitting them to rest on their lands for one year" (Ibid., p. 36).

When this period of rest was over, the Inca again convened the neighboring chiefs, and each brought with him products to fill the storehouses. On this occasion the celebrations lasted five days. On others the rejoicing might go on for a full lunar month. When the celebrations ended, the lord of Cusco made a new "request": the construction of the city "fortress."

Here we are primarily interested in illustrating the means employed at first to fill up the storehouses with goods. Other methods would be used when the power of the Inca became unlimited. At this point these undertakings did not involve firm and direct orders imparted by the ruler to the lords. Rather, he requested their help and cooperation, and they, in turn, accepted what he proposed. Yupanqui sent many such requests to his allied lords, always within the limits of the ritually established norms, while setting priorities among the works to be executed. In this way, reciprocity played a crucial role in the first Inca successes and in the birth of the Inca state.

We can assume that as the conquests widened, the number of *curacas* joined to the Inca by reciprocity and by kinship ties continued to increase, which resulted in the increasing availability of labor for Cusco. We can also assume that, according to Andean practice, if the "request" was not formulated in line with established custom, or if the petition did not satisfy the lords – whether because the Inca did not show himself to be sufficiently "generous" or for whatever motive – there existed the possibility of rejection on the part of the lords. To avoid such rejection, the Inca was considered obligated to be extremely "generous," and this may have sometimes resulted in proposals and counterproposals. It was possible for the lords to refuse the

Inca's "request" if they were displeased or offended by some omission on his part.

It appears likely that when the power of the Inca rulers had sufficiently increased, they began to find the reciprocity mechanism a nuisance and source of delay in their plans. Their desire to put aside the "request," at least occasionally, in favor of the direct demand for action must have strained the close ancestral ties that united the Sapan Inca with the subordinate high lord. We can catch glimpses of this tension during the Inca apogee, as we shall see.

Naturally, there were many levels of reciprocity: among members of the same *ayllu*, among the various factions belonging to the same ethnic group, in the relations of the commoners with their immediate lords, and so on. Reciprocity encompassed all levels of society, from the common people to the gods. It is important to emphasize that within the nobility itself there was a vast social hierarchy, and the ties that bound subordinate with superior were extremely diverse. The social composition of the Inca state is the subject of a more detailed analysis later on. It is not, of course, limited to a simple hierarchy from commoner to chief and, above him, the Inca. Andean society was much more complex, and within its vast territory there were, by the end of the early sixteenth century, a number of great lords at the head of macroethnic groups that exercised more power than that of a simple rustic village chief.

Reciprocity under the Inca State

With the territorial expansion of the Incas, it became impossible to continue the original pattern of reciprocity. It is natural that the foundations of the system would undergo substantial changes to adapt to the newly created circumstances. Above all, the power of the ruling Incas increased in proportion with their conquests, which made it impossible for them to continue meeting with each village chief to eat and drink.

According to Morris and Thompson (1985:165), the creation of the administrative centers at this time had as its main purposes to confirm political loyalties and secure the necessary economic cooperation. Owing to the enormous proportions of the Inca state, there was a need to create places where neighboring ethnic chiefs could be convened to renew their reciprocal alliances with the ruler.

Morris and Thompson's archaeological interpretations indicate that in the principal plaza of Huanuco Pampa the priority was not on its military function, as might be expected at a forward post, but, rather on the ceremonial aspect, for rituals and feasts in connection with the residence of the

Inca or his representatives. Maintaining the ties of reciprocity required an open space suitable for convening a large number of people, and this was the reason for the extraordinary dimensions of this plaza (500 by 350 m).

Another means of overcoming the impossibility of the Inca's meeting regularly with all the lords of his vast domains was the presence in the capital of one of the dual lords of each chiefdom. The information provided on this subject by the chroniclers is confirmed in two legal testimonies of one Don Gonzalo, ethnic lord of Lima (Rostworowski, 1981–82).

An alternative that permitted the Inca rulers to find rapid and direct solutions to their problems, act according to their needs, and free themselves from the rules established by tradition was the *yana*, or individuals taken from their *ayllus* of origin to fulfill special tasks and who took no part in the communal labor of their towns or lands. The *yana* might have diverse status, from simple peasants tied to labor in the fields to specialized craftsmen or chiefs, with their tasks established according to their social condition. They could be assigned variously to the Inca, to the queen, to a sacred place, or to a provincial lord. There existed a wide range of *yana*, according to their social conditions, origins, and tasks to which they were assigned, but their common denominator was to be outside the reciprocal system of "requests" and "requirements."

In the case of state reciprocity, however, it is worth mentioning two levels of *yana* that were very useful to the government. The first was the replacement of a local chief by a *yanayacu curaca*, who took the place of the natural lord. This could occur when the chief resisted, by force, submission to Cusco rule. After his defeat, he was replaced by a *yana* designated by the Inca, to whom he owed personal loyalty. The advantage of having a *yana* in power consisted of his remaining outside the system of reciprocity. The Inca could command him and demand obedience to his will without any prior formalities. This new way of dealing with rebellious lords forced the ethnic chiefs to become submissive to the demands of the state and to cooperate with the many requirements of the Cusco government.

Yana served on another level to secure labor outside the system of reciprocity to work the great private estates of the Incas and their queens. Each *panaca* possessed through inheritance many haciendas in the valleys near the capital, which were cultivated by large numbers of these laborers (who will be discussed further when we study the Inca system of land tenure).

Yana were also important in another kind of land tenure, on those lands in diverse locations that were owned by the state. Innumerable specialized artisans occupied this status, including silverworkers and goldworkers, the majority of them from the coast, who were sent wherever their skills were needed to create luxury articles. In Cusco they produced art objects for the

Machu Picchu, an example of Inca mastery of landscape architecture, high in the Andes northwest of Cusco. Photo by Billy Hare.

Inca and his court. Many of these articles were used as gifts for the great lords, and a monopoly was established in Cusco over the production of luxury goods so that the ruler could distribute them according to the interests of the state.

In this way, the ancient social structures underwent profound changes brought about by new Inca practices in reaction to changed circumstances, at the cost of a complete mutation of the past. While these changes occurred at the upper levels of the governmental and the social hierarchies, the members of the common and peasant *ayllus* continued to follow their ancient traditions. And despite these transformations, within the Inca elite itself reciprocity continued to be practiced. The royal *panaca* remained united by the strong ties of kinship and reciprocity.

An example of the persistence of this custom within the elite is the experience of Huayna Capac when waging war with the Cayambis of the north. The Inca, in need of reinforcements, ordered into battle an army recently arrived from the south, commanded by generals related to him by

A stretch of Inca road in the northern coastal valley of Saña. Photo by Billy Hare.

kinship. Given the urgency of the situation, he dispensed with the ritual of reciprocity and with the requests for gifts. Infuriated, the general-in-chief, Michicuacamayta, together with the Inca nobles who accompanied him, took the shrine of Huanacauri, which they carried with them, and set out on the return road to Cusco. The ruler, informed of the desertion of the nobles, dispatched emissaries loaded with gifts, clothes and food. The lords, satisfied with this offering of favors, returned and fought valiantly at the side of the Inca.

In the European world, this reaction of the Inca nobles would have been considered an act of treachery, and exemplary punishment would have awaited the deserters. In the Andean world, it was the Inca who was at fault and he who was responsible for correcting, to the extent possible, his error, flattering the offended lords with the gifts they expected and deserved. To omit reciprocity was considered a major insult, and the chiefs could not tolerate disrespect toward their persons. For this reason they did not hesitate to abandon the Inca at a critical moment.

Among the Inca elite there were frequent ceremonial meals in the public plaza in which all the important *panaca* and *ayllus* participated, divided into their moieties and seated according to hierarchical order. These were solemn acts, filled with tradition of great sociopolitical significance. One of Huascar's many errors was not participating in such reunions in which mutual obligations were confirmed. His absence and his disrespectful attitude toward the *panaca* incurred the emnity of his kin and the resentment of many high-level personages (Pedro Pizarro, 1978:53).

The Incas were not the only ones accustomed to convening to participate in festivals and ritual meals. The great ethnic lords followed similar customs with their own people, at their own socioeconomic levels. Everywhere in the Andean region lords congregated to eat and drink and renew bonds of friendship. On the coast, it was also customary for the ethnic chief, when he left his palace for whatever destination, to have at his disposal a retinue of carriers with vessels containing drink; wherever his litter was put down, there the people would come to drink at the expense of the lord. Such generosity on the part of the lords of the coast was a form of asymmetrical reciprocity between a lord and his subjects, and constituted part of the ritual of the coastal peoples. When the Spanish, without understanding the significance of reciprocity, classified these practices as drunken orgies (*borracheras*) and had them suppressed, their action provoked serious problems for the nobles, who saw their authority diminished as a result (Rostworowski, 1977: 242).

In summary, we can say that in the beginning the power of the Inca was based on a continual renovation of the ties of reciprocity, for which the state had to maintain in its storehouses large quantities of luxury objects and subsistence goods destined for the nobles and military chiefs with whom he had to practice reciprocity. As the state grew, so did the number of lords who had to be satisfied. This obligation must have placed constant pressure and an ever greater imposition on the government, which had to meet the demand for goods for reciprocity. Thus, the state found it had to increase its income constantly in order to ensure the required quantities of goods.

The state met this demand in various ways. The first consisted of increasing the lands considered to belong to the Inca. For this reason, with the advent of Tupac Yupanqui and later of Huayna Capac, these lands were successively increased in every chiefdom. Castro and Ortega Morejón (1974) showed this to be the case for Chincha, and the same kind of evidence is found for the chiefdom of Quivi, in the valley of the Río Chillón, in the increasing numbers of coca plantations belonging to each successive Inca ruler (AGI – Justicia 413). Productivity was also promoted by constructing paved roads in suitable places, and also by extending the existing hydraulic systems.

A third solution was to improve unoccupied or lightly populated lands with a new workforce that would take charge of the agricultural and grazing production of the zone. This occurred in the lands of Huayna Capac in Cochabamba, where more than 14,000 *mitmaq* (those sent by the state to work in a distant location) labored (Wachtel, 1980–81).

Undertaking new conquests and acquiring access to new state lands by arms was a fourth means of satisfying the increasing demand for products needed for the reciprocity system. Although the immediate demand might be met, conquest also increased the numbers of ethnic lords with whom ties of reciprocity were maintained.

Conrad and Demarest (1984:132) suggest that the ambition and pressure of the *panaca* was a factor in the expansion of the Incas. I would emphasize, rather, the Andean system of reciprocity itself, which created an ever-increasing demand for state production.

CONSTRUCTION AND STATE WORKS

Throughout the region once ruled by the Incas, one can find today traces of their urban settlements, sanctuaries, palaces, temples, *tambos* (inns), storehouses, and roads. This escalating expansion necessitated an entire infrastructure of roads with storehouses and *tambos* constructed along the principal routes to supply the armies, administrative, functionaries, and great contingents of *mitmaq* sent from one point to another in Andean space. The Incas were unquestionably outstanding in state planning, and one cannot help but ask, What has become of this Andean spirit of organization? Why has this great virtue been lost?

The last Inca rulers were great builders. They quickly implanted their building methods throughout their new domains, which tended to homogenize the territories under their rule. This eagerness to build resulted from the changed circumstances that followed the Inca victory over the Chancas. This victory was a turning point that led to the expansion not only of the Inca armies but also of the labor forces available for the vast construction projects indispensable for expanding Inca state power.

In their study of Inca architecture, Gasparini and Margolies (1977) indicate that almost all the structures that today are considered Inca probably belong to building activity carried out after 1440. And the great number of works carried out in so short a time span can only be explained by Inca use of an abundant state workforce based on the system of rotational labor. According to the same authors, the most difficult thing is the identification of the functions of the structures (p. 203), deciding how buildings were actually used, since the same type of construction is repeated throughout the Inca state (Bouchard, 1983).

Cusco

Betanzos (1968, chap. 16) and Sarmiento de Gamboa (1943, chap. 32) show that one of Yupanqui's principal concerns after defeating the Chancas was the reconstruction of Cusco. As a first measure, he ordered the city depopulated for a distance of two leagues around, and proceeded with the relocation of the *panaca* and *ayllus* according to his own purposes. The act of awarding lands was transcendental, given the significance and implications of land tenancy, a subject to which I return later. In light of this fact it becomes important to look at the data that may be found in surviving documents concerning the locations of the *ayllus* and macroethnic groups of the Cusco region, since these will reflect the results of the reforms carried out by Yupanqui rather than those dating back to an earlier period.

Having carried out this repartition of lands, the Inca turned to the transformation of his capital as appropriate to its recently acquired status. Until that time, Cusco had been no more than a rustic village, frequently flooded by the overflows of its two small rivers, the Huatanay and the Tulumayo.

Sarmiento de Gamboa (1943, chap. 39), Betanzos (1968, chap. 10), and Garcilaso (vol. 1, book 2, chap. 37) mention the practice of assembling clay models of the buildings and the valleys before beginning full-scale construction. Betanzos (1968, chap. 17) relates how one day the principal lords found Yupanqui "painting" the modifications to be made in the city. Such reports would be difficult to believe were it not for references contained in a document dating to 1558–67 dealing with a lawsuit between two chiefs involving lands in the valley of the Río Chillón on the central coast. Both litigating parties appeared before the Real Audiencia de Los Reyes with their clay models representing the location of the valley in question, and used their models to plead their cases before the judges (AGI – Justicia 413; Rostworowski 1988b).

When an army conquered a region, qualified individuals prepared models of the subjected zone and presented them to the Inca so that he might indicate the changes to be made. Then they were given to those responsible for executing the orders of the ruler. These examples illustrate the methods employed by the Incas to carry out the state works.

Betanzos (1968, chap. 16) relates how the reconstruction of Cusco was initiated by means of reciprocity. Yupanqui asked the ethnic chiefs to come to the capital bringing food, supplies, and the largest possible number of workers. In the meeting that followed the traditional festivities, thirty nobles were assigned to search the towns and "provinces" for supplies and to identify places that could provide the necessary materials, such as the stone quarries. The same chronicler tells of the preparations carried out before construction. The various tasks were divided up among the groups present, with some given responsibility for transporting the rough stones for the foundations, others for bringing the damp clay, to which was added wool or straw, for making adobe bricks.

Gasperini emphasizes the stoneworking skills of the highland Collas (which they inherited from the ancient Tiahuanacotas), many of whom were residents of Cusco. In the dictionary of González Holguín (1952), we find terms that indicate the various kinds of stone, including *callanca y callqui rumi* (worked stone slabs for paving).

Reconstruction began with the canalization of the streams, to avoid formation of swamps during the rainy season, and of the channels that brought water to the city. Betanzos relates that when the models were ready and the materials gathered together, the Incas proceeded to evacuate the sites where the new buildings were to be raised, relocating the inhabitants temporarily in neighboring villages. When the terrain was leveled, Yupanqui proceeded, with cord in hand, to measure and mark the outlines of the new city, indicating open areas and buildings. The construction took twenty years. Cieza (*Señorío*, chap. 51) indicates that 20,000 men worked continuously on the project. Nevertheless, it was not as difficult a task as might be supposed, since the laborers resided in Cusco for a limited time, after which they were replaced by others according to the *mita* system.

To the natives, according to Betanzos (chap. 17), Cusco represented the body of a puma: the space between the two rivers formed its trunk, with the head in Sacsayhuaman and the tail in Pumap Chupan, at the confluence of the rivers. According to Rowe (1963 and 1967), the puma could be represented as seated on its haunches, and the space between its front legs included the great plazas of Aucaypata and Cusipata, which delimited the sacred zone. Within its outlines were located the twelve barrios mentioned by Garcilaso: Colcampata, Cantut Pata, Munay Senga, Rimac Pampa, Cayaocachi, Chaquilchaca, Piqchu, Quillipata, Carmenca, Huaca Puncu, Puma Curcu, and Tococache.

The Inca plazas were extraordinarily broad and trapezoidal in form. When weather permitted, they were the scenes of intense religious and social activity. The rites of reciprocity took place in the principal plaza of Aucaypata, in which the Inca elite would meet to eat, drink, and participate in the ceremonial dances that marked the festivals of the Inca calendar. Also celebrated were the victories of the Inca armies, on which occasions part of the war booty would be laid out on the ground, along with the conquered trophies and even the captured lords and chiefs, so that the Inca might walk over them to symbolize his victory and the submission of his enemies. To adorn the plaza better, according to Sarmiento de Gamboa, it was covered with two and a half spans (about 20 inches) of sand brought from the coast (1943, chap. 30; Polo de Ondegardo 1917:109–10). The name of the plaza, Aucaypata, comes from the word *auca*, which means both "soldier" and "enemy" (González Holguín, 1952).

During the reconstruction of Cusco, it became evident that a new division of space was required, more in accord with the prevailing circumstances. We recall that when the group of Manco Capac arrived in primitive Acamama, the local boundaries were the four districts of Quinti Cancha, Chumbi Cancha, Sairi Cancha, and Yarambuy Cancha. Later, with the permanent settlement and consolidation of Manco Capac's situation vis-à-vis the principal lords of the region, came the second, more extensive division that gave rise to the four *señoríos* of Manco Capac, Tocay Capac, Pinahua Capac, and Colla Capac.

After the Inca victory over their ancestral rivals, the ancient boundaries had no reason for being, and a third delimitation of space was undertaken. The old nomenclature no longer reflected the changed circumstances of the period of Inca expansion. Their conquests gave the Incas dominion over distant lands, and the great *suyu* took shape reflecting the new, state, vision and with the dimensions of a larger, state, scope. Thus were formed the regions of Chinchaysuyu, Antisuyu, Collasuyu, and Cuntisuyu, which together constituted Tahuantinsuyu.

The reproduction of space, as conceived and represented by the natives in the establishment of Inca urban centers, was the quatripartition. Morris and Thompson (1985) choose to see the *ceque* system in the new "centers," but this seems unlikely because ethnic groups that were not Inca, but existed much earlier than the period of Inca expansion, participated in this system.

The Coricancha

According to the chroniclers, it was Pachacutec Inca Yupanqui who rebuilt the sanctuary and furnished it with objects and adornments of gold and silver in such profusion that its name was changed from Inti Cancha, "Temple of the Sun," to Coricancha, or "Temple of Gold." Much has been discussed and written about its wealth, so there is no need to dwell on the subject here.

Sarmiento de Gamboa (chap. 31) relates that after rebuilding the temple, the Inca had new idols placed in it, which appears to indicate that he carried out a religious reform as well. Pachacutec ordered that the Sun occupy the principal, central location, with the image of Viracocha to his right and that of Chuquiylla, the lightning deity – whom the Inca took as his double, or *huauque* – to his left. With this ruler, the Sun ceased to be the exclusive cult object of the Inca kin group and became part of the official religion of the entire state. It was considered to be the father of the royal lineages, and when a new ruler was elected, the candidate waited for solar confirmation of his selection.

These religious changes in Cusco did not affect the veneration of the numerous *huacas* and idols found throughout the Andean region. On the contrary, Pachacutec wished the principal *huacas* to remain in Cusco and awarded them servants, lands, and goods. Such was the way of preventing possible uprisings, since the natives would not rebel for fear reprisals might be taken against their idols.

The Coricancha is located in Lower Cusco, on the site of what is today the Church of Santo Domingo. Its construction is distinguished by walls that up to a certain height were of finely worked stones, above which adobe brick was used. Gasparini believes that the often mentioned band of gold that adorned the temple served to hide the joint between the two materials. According to Garcilaso (1943, book 3, chap. 20), the ceiling was very high, entirely of wood covered with well-placed straw. The roof was designed to extend over the wall and cover part of the street outside. The thickness of roofs in Inca construction was such that during the fighting between Pizarro and Almagro the roof of the palace of Cassana took several days to burn (Pedro Pizarro, 1978:161).

The rather poor appearance of the straw was remedied during the festivals and other events by covering the roofs with beautiful cloths woven with feathers of many colors (Santa Cruz Pachacuti, 1927:205). Despite its painstaking construction, the Coricancha did not differ greatly in its ground plan from other Inca structures, except for its more finely worked stone.

Gasparini and Margolies (1977:242) compare the research results of Rowe from 1940 with those of their own study, after the earthquake of 1950 that destroyed much of Cusco. It is unfortunate that the ruins were not cleared, without the reconstruction of the church (which could have been relocated), for the purpose of conducting archaeological excavations at the site. If this had been done, the greatest Inca sanctuary could have remained surrounded by gardens, like the ruins of the Roman Forum in the modern city.

After the collapse of the Church of Santo Domingo, some of the ancient Inca walls remained visible, providing additional information about the indigenous structures. Gasperini has made a hypothetical plan of the Temple of the Sun, with its structures around a great patio framed on the north by two apartments that follow the direction of the walls of the church, on the south by two similar apartments, while the lateral spaces framing the square were occupied by smaller rooms.

Pedro Pizarro (1978:92) relates that in front of the room where the Sun was said to sleep, there was a small garden in which they planted "seasonal maize for the sun." His reference to Chincha as the source of the earth for this garden is curious (Relaciones Geográficas de Indias, 1885, vol. 2, appendix 1:IX). There is no explanation of why this earth was selected to cultivate the maize of the Sun; the reason remains open to speculation.

Sanctuary Palaces and Administrative Centers

Together with the remodeling of the Temple of the Sun, the principal sanctuaries near Cusco, including Huanacauri, Anahuarqui, Yauira, Cinga, Pical, and Pachatopan, were also repaired. In and around the city various structures were built by the Inca Pachacutec, which by virtue of this connection with his life, were later considered sanctuaries. These included Cusicancha, "The Temple of Good Fortune," located "facing the Temple of Coricancha," the birthplace of the Inca, which remained in the care of Iñaca Panaca, his *ayllu* of origin (Rowe, 1970, CH–5:1); Condor Cancha, his palace of residence (Rowe, CH–3:4); Patallacta, a house located in Carmenca, where he died, in which sacrifices were made in his honor (Rowe, CH–1:2); and Pomamarca, a house located on a plain near Cusco where the mummy of Pachacutec's mother was kept, to which children were sacrificed (Rowe, AN–6:5).

In the sanctuary of Tococache they kept an idol of solid gold called Inti Illapa, or "thunder of the Sun," which the Inca Pachacutec considered a *huauque*, or "brother." They made sacrifices to this idol and begged of it that the ruler not lose his strength (Rowe, CH–2:3; Sarmiento de Gamboa, chap. 47). Another temple was that of Poquen Cancha, near Cusco, where paintings related to the lives of the Incas were preserved (Molina, 1943:7).

In the archival documents, we find not only that Pachacutec possessed lands for planting maize in the high valley of La Convención and coca plantations at lower altitudes but also that he ordered built a palace called

Guaman Marca for his recreation (Kendall, preliminary report, 1980; Ros-tworowski, 1963).

Whereas this Inca initiated and continued for more than twenty years the reconstruction of Cusco, the determination to endow the capital with new buildings lasted throughout the reigns of the subsequent Incas. The chronicles indicate the principal works attributed to each ruler, not only in Cusco itself but also in the "provinces." The building efforts of Tupac Yupanqui are easily confused with those of his father because of the period of co-rule. It is possible that the old ruler was responsible for construction in the capital, while Tupac made war and enlarged the state.

According to most chroniclers, Tupac began the construction of Sacsay-huaman, the imposing structure that dominates Cusco, which was contin-ued by subsequent rulers. There is a question as to whether Sacsayhuaman was in fact a fortress, since the rest of the city does not show evidence of major fortifications. It should also be noted that during the period of Inca expansion Cusco was in no danger of being attacked. Accounts of the Chanca advance on Cusco do not refer to the existence of a fortress that might have defended the city. On the contrary, we find that nothing hin-dered the Chanca advance during their mad dash along the slopes of Car-menca.

It appears more likely that Sacsayhuaman was a monument to the great victory achieved by the inhabitants of Cusco and that ritual battles were fought between its walls (Hartmann, 1977). This hypothesis is supported by Pedro Pizarro's (1978:48) statement that Huayna Capac ordered a for-tress built in the north in memory of one of his victories. We will recall the reference by Santa Cruz Pachacuti (1927:193) to the celebration of the triumphal return of Tupac Yupanqui after his prolonged stay in the north. At that time, as part of the festival, a simulated attack on the fortress, led by young Huayna Capac, was enacted for an audience of elites and com-moners.

The palace of Tupac Yupanqui was called Calispuquio Huasi, and nearby there was a much venerated fountain of the same name. The nobles used it to make their ablutions during the festivals of Raymi (Rowe, 1979 CH–3: 7; and CH–3:8). Tupac chose for his private estate the valley of Chinchero, near Cusco, and had large palaces built there. The places of Guaillabamba and Urcos were also his (Alcina Franch, 1976; Rostworowski, 1970).

Among the sites attributed to Tupac Yupanqui are the structures of Inca Huasi, in the valley of Lunahuaná on the left bank of the river, near the village of Paulo. Its uniqueness lies in the young Inca's having named it Cusco. He also gave the plazas, streets, and heights the same names as those of the capital (Cieza de León, *Señorío*, 1943, chap. 59).

All this was a result of the long war initiated by the Incas against Guarco (Cañete), a coastal chiefdom bordering on Lunahuaná, in the valley at the edge of the sea. The resistance of the Guarcos lasted four years, since the Inca troops would withdraw during the summer months for fear of the heat and not return before winter.

After the Inca triumph, according to Cieza, New Cusco was abandoned, probably occupied only by administrators and others sent by the Inca. The possibility that Inca Huasi was a replica of Cusco gives it special importance, and this hypothesis deserves further analysis. It should be emphasized that its construction reflects the quadripartite partition of the mythical space of the city, rather than the actual plan of Cusco before the apogee of the city. We find in its structures and layout not a model of the ancient capital but its symbolic representation. We should also consider the adaptation of the plan of New Cusco to the ravines of its broken, arid terrain, quite unlike the relatively flat terrain of the ancient capital. This, in turn, raises the question of the rationale for its traditional quadripartite division.

In a previous work I mention that according to a map of the valley's sites prepared by the architect Carlos Williams (Williams and Merino, 1974), the westernmost ruins (called El Arca by Williams and El Acllahuasi by Harth-Terré) appear to correspond to Lower Cusco. We are led to this conclusion for several reasons. First, this zone is separated from the other groups of structures by the spurs of several hills, and is also distinguished by the presence in its main plaza of an *ushnu,* or small stone throne of a type we know existed in Hurin Cusco (Rowe, 1979 AN-5). Also, according to Hyslop's (1985:15) map of the various groups of structures, four principal well-defined sectors can be distinguished in the ruins. The first, sector F, would correspond to Hurin Cusco, or Collasuyu; the second, sector E, to Aucay Pata of Hanan Cusco or Chinchaysuyu (with another *ushnu* in its main plaza); the third group, comprising sectors A and C, to Cuntisuyu; and sectors B and G, the fourth and most clearly defined group of structures, to Antisuyu. This, however, is all speculative.

Other Inca structures about which we have some documentary evidence include the so-called fortress of Guarco, at the edge of the sea (Matos Mendieta), and farther south, at the other end of the same valley, the palace of Herbay Bajo, described by Squier (1974/1877) and by Larrabure y Unanue (1941), which must have been luxurious. Thanks to the archival documents, we know that in 1562, Herbay, now totally destroyed, was known as Tambo de Locos (Rostworowski, 1978–80).

I conclude this discussion of the construction works undertaken by Tupac Yupanqui with an analysis of the state works, which can be classified as administrative centers, of which we can distinguish two types. The first consists of structures within the conquered settlements. New buildings were constructed, or older structures were converted, to use as housing for Inca administrative personnel. Examples of this type include the Temple of Hatun Cancha in Lurín Chincha and various building complexes in Collasuyu (Castro and Ortega-Morejón, 1974).

The Temple of Punchao Cancha or ("Temple of the Day") in Pachacamac was a religious variant of this type. This building is unusual in that it consists of several platforms in the form of truncated pyramids surmounted by structures, and it appears to represent an Inca adaptation to local coastal stylistic norms, probably because it was a famous sanctuary with a long tradition. It appears likely that Punchao Cancha also served two functions, as a temple dedicated to the Sun and as an Inca administrative center. From seventeenth- and eighteenth-century documents, we learn that the ancient sanctuary was also known as "El Castillo" (the castle) after losing its religious significance. Another group of structures at the site, called the Convent of Mamacona, is typically Inca.

The second type of administrative center undoubtedly represents the height of the Inca state. These imposing edifices are situated strategically in specially selected locations to serve their governmental functions best. Outstanding examples of this type are Huanuco Pampa and, on a much smaller scale, Tambo Colorado, on the coast of Humay, near Pisco.

Huanuco Pampa, a site studied archaeologically by Morris and Thompson (1985), covers an area of two square kilometers and contains some 3,500 visible structures, perhaps 4,000 in all. The Incas constructed this center on virgin land, beginning in the mid-fifteenth century, and construction was still under way at the time of the arrival of the Spanish. Its architecture is unlike that of the neighboring villages. It gives the impression of efficient imitative construction, lacking the virtuosity and loving craftsmanship evident in the structures of Cusco. The principal plaza, with an imposing *ushnu*, measures 550 meters by 350 meters, a truly enormous expanse. From this plaza radiates a series of streets that are still clearly visible. The most important are the Capac Nan, the trunk route that connected Cusco with Quito, and the street that divided the center into its upper and lower districts. Two other streets subdivided the city into four wards corresponding to the quadripartite division of space indispensable to the Inca organizational system.

The most novel suggestion of Morris and Thompson (1985) is that Huanuco Pampa, with its numerous storehouses, not only was an administrative center but served economic, religious, and possibly social functions as well. In societies such as the Andean these various functions are not easily separated, since they are all combined in a global vision of life. It seems likely that one of the principal functions of the center was to bring together nobles from a wide area for the renovation of the custom of reciprocity, since *el ruego*, the ruler's request, had to be repeated periodically. This would explain the enormous size of the plaza, which could hold all the participants in these socioreligious festivities with their ritual feasts. The participants in the ceremonies, whether ethnic chiefs or pilgrims, according to the circumstances, were not permanent residents of the center but temporary visitors from distant regions. Among the permanent inhabitants were the *mamacona* occupied with textile production and the preparation of beverages for rituals and enjoyment, and the *mitmaq* assigned to special state tasks. There were also the numerous participants in the seasonal *mita*, who came from more or less distant places.

Morris and Thompson (1985) find convincing evidence of social stratification in Huanuco Pampa and, to a lesser extent, of economically diverse groups. It is evident that state planning served to obtain the necessary labor force and the products to fill the storehouses, but it is also obvious that in Huanuco Pampa the state did not try to create a uniform, integrated society but, rather, preserved differences to facilitate political manipulation.

The authors doubt that Huanuco Pampa was a center of craft production, other than the textiles and beverages for ritual purposes. On this point I differ, since there must have been workshops for the production of utilitarian ceramics, as in Cajamarca, where potters were brought from Xultin on the coast to meet the needs of the state (Espinoza, 1970). Also, Morris and Thompson maintain that Huanuco Pampa represents a concept of the city very different from the European. This is also true of many other aspects of Andean culture and society.

These administrative centers were characterized by large numbers of storehouses where a variety of supplies were kept. These were not necessarily local or regional products, but might be brought over long distances, sometimes from as far as the coast and even the jungle region. Numerous documents from the central coast refer to the transport of products from that region to either Cusco or Huanuco Pampa.

The principal centers were located along the length of the Capac Nan, or dorsal spine of the road network of Tahuantinsuyu. Inca remains are numerous in the region of Collasuyu, which has maintained contact with Cusco since pre-Inca times. There, according to Gasparini and Margolies (1977:124), the Incas opted for a strategy of exploiting the already existing institutions of the region, modifying them only as necessary to suit their needs. In the south, there was a proliferation of centers strategically situated to control the surrounding valleys.

The Sanctuary of the Sun on the island of Collao in Lake Titicaca and the Sanctuaries of the Moon on the island of Coati are among the buildings attributed to Tupac Yupanqui (Ramos Gavilán, 1976). The Inca assigned 2,000 *mitmaq* for the support of these temples and that of Copacabana, while displacing the natives of Yungayo from their natural habitat. (Concerning the idol of Copacabana, see Rostworowski, 1983.)

Vilcas Huaman, in the present-day province of Cangallo in the Ayacucho region, was one of the important centers on the Chinchaysuyu route (see González Carré, Cosmópolis, and Lévano, 1981, 1987). Tumipampa, in Ecuador, originally built by Tupac Yupanqui, was only an administrative center in its beginnings but acquired great importance during the reign of Huayna Capac, who transformed and embellished his native city. Later, its agreeable and temperate climate so pleased the Spanish that they built the modern city of Cuenca on the site.

All this refers to the building accomplishments of Tupac Yupanqui. Although Pachacutec may rightly be considered the rebuilder of Cusco, Tupac was the initiator of many public works throughout the Inca realm.

Huayna Capac continued the work begun by his predecessors. In Cusco, he ordered the construction of the palace of Cassana. Sarmiento de Gamboa (chap. 58) and Cobo (1958, vol. 2, chap. 16) indicate that Sinchi Roca, brother of the Inca, was in charge of public works and the builder of the palaces of Yucay.

In the organization of the *ceque* of Cusco, the palace of Cassana is mentioned as belonging to Huayna Capac. It was said that there was a lake or spring called Ticcicocha within its walls. This much venerated water source was dedicated to Mama Ocllo, mother of the Inca and one of the most revered women in the Andean world (Rowe, 1979, CH–6:5 and CH-3:3). Pedro Pizarro (1978:87–88, 161) claims that the Marqués chose it as his residence because it had belonged to Huayna Capac, but, as is frequent in such cases, Garcilaso disagrees and contends that it belonged to Pachacutec (1943, vol. 2, book 7, chap. 10). He is undoubtedly mistaken, since we know that the latter Inca had another palace.

Two other palaces were on the plaza of Aucaypata, according to Pedro Pizarro and Estete, chroniclers who saw the city intact, before its destruction. Hatun Cancha was a large, enclosed building with just one entrance on the plaza, which belonged to the *mamacona*. Amarucancha, on the other side of the plaza, was the residence of "ancient Incas," according to Pedro Pizarro (1978:88). Possibly it was the residence of Amaru Yupanqui, son of Pachacutec, who was briefly co-regent with his father before being replaced by Tupac Yupanqui. Garcilaso, in his eagerness to hide the fact that Atahualpa belonged to the *panaca* of Pachacutec, deliberately altered the historical data and included a nonexistent Yupanqui on his list of rulers. Since he was for a long time the only chronicler consulted on such matters, the errors of his account have endured (Rostworowski, 1953). (I return to this topic later when dealing with the Inca successions.)

Following the example of his predecessors, Huayna Capac appropriated the valley of Yucay with its warm and generally agreeable climate. As he was originally from Tumipampa in the north, we can guess that he would dislike the harsh climate of Cusco. Another of his many estates, encompassing a large expanse of land, was in Quispeguanca (Cobo, vol. 2, chap. 16; Relaciones Geográficas de Indias, 1885, vol. 2, appendix 1:X; Rostworowski, 1970; Sarmiento de Gamboa, chap. 58). This Inca continued the construction of public works throughout Tahuantinsuyu, and above all in Tumipampa, where he erected the Temple of Mullu Cancha, whose walls were covered with coral-colored *mullu* (*Spondylus* sp., or spiny oyster) shells. To increase the splendor of the buildings, Huayna Capac ordered stones to be hauled from Cusco using thick ropes of hide (Cieza, *Señorío*, chap. 64). The sanctuary held images of the Sun and of the principal *huacas* of the Inca. Wishing to honor his mother, the Inca ordered a statue of Mama Ocllo placed in a special room of the temple, with responsibility for its care given the Cañar ethnic group (Cabello de Valboa, 1951:364; Cobo, vol. 2, chap. 16). It appears likely that most Inca construction in Ecuador, such as the Inga Pirca and the buildings of Quito, dates to the reign of Huayna Capac.

In general terms, Inca architecture was characterized by simplicity of form and somber decoration. Walls were distinguished by the extraordinary carving of the massive blocks of stone, and the rusticity of the straw roofs was offset by their coverings of bright cloth interwoven with the feathers of tropical birds. In the streets of Cusco, the silky brilliance of the roofs and the gold of the trimmings must have contrasted effectively with the cold symmetry of the stone walls.

The Incas differed in their esthetic concepts from other Andean cultures such as the Chavín, Tiahuanaco, and Wari, which employed statues, stelae, and sculptured heads to decorate their buildings. They differed also from the coastal cultures in their treatment of building exteriors, since the Andeans painted their buildings and also used friezes and stuccos in low relief (Bonavia, 1974–85; La Gasca, 1976; Muelle, 1939; Ravines, 1975; Schaedel, 1966).

The coastal peoples made profuse use of pictorial elements and decorated their walls with scenes of gods, birds, fish, animals, and plants, perhaps to counterbalance the desert aridness and gray skies. Alternatively, they painted their smooth walls a solid color, most frequently red ochre and lemon yellow.

The Temple of Puchao Cancha in Pachacamac and the Temple of Paramonga were spectacularly situated buildings, located for the simultaneous adoration of the sea and the setting sun. That of Paramonga is described by Estete in 1533 as comprising five superimposed terraces, with interiors and exteriors painted in many colors, and the images of two felines on either side of the principal entrance (Fernández de Oviedo, 1945, vol. 12:52).

The Incas were great masters of landscape architecture. They situated their temples and palaces so they would harmonize with the environment, and their structures followed closely the contours of the land. They made full use of nature for their esthetic purposes, a successful example of which is the architecture of Machu Picchu and, on a smaller scale, of Pisac, Guaman Marca, in the valley of La Convención.

The Road Network

The most important public works were without doubt the construction of the vast road network, including bridges, inns, and storehouses, that permitted the territorial expansion and organizational integration of the Inca state. Few nations in the fifteenth century possessed such a fantastic road complex as that of Tahuantinsuyu.

These roads did not originate with the Inca state; they must have existed since long before to unite the diverse ethnic groups and the principal sanctuaries or *huacas*, so that at the appropriate times they might carry out pilgrimages and trade involving religious centers such as Pachacamac and Pariacaca in the central highlands (Avila, 1966; Salomon and Urioste, 1991). Surely the Wari made use of the same roads to transfer their armies to places under their domination or influence and found them essential to maintain their political organization. Later the Chimu, whose territories included a broad zone along the coast, employed routes that are still archaeologically recognizable.

Nevertheless, it should not be assumed that these roads were open to all and at all times. The *Relación de Chincha* (Castro and Ortega Morejón, 1974/1558:93) mentions frequent wars among the chiefdoms, which prevented the inhabitants from leaving their valleys without the permission of their local lords. Movement along the roads was expedited during times of truce, which likely coincided with the religious festivals of the most important *huacas*. The absence of unity until the time of the Inca conquest meant that the roads were until then essentially local, and could vary considerably, depending on whether the macroethnic group responsible for a given portion of the road possessed a sufficient workforce to maintain it, or whether the road passed through regions divided into small, lightly populated chiefdoms

With the expansion of the Inca state, there was an extraordinary increase in the number of roads. According to the estimates of Hyslop (1984), the road system reached a total of 30,000 to 50,000 kilometers. The strength of the Incas lay in their deep spirit of organization and their ability to plan the use of the available workforce, which enabled them to build a road system that would become the basis of the state infrastructure.

These routes were indispensable to the Inca regime for the mobilization of its armies; the massive transfer of populations, often to distant places, under the *mitmaq* system; and the transport of products harvested on state lands to the storehouses in the administrative centers. Inca organization required roads and related facilities to transport its officials, administrators, inspectors judges, *quipocamayo*, and runners, carriers of news and messages, among others, an entire world revolving around the needs of the state. For these reasons, the road network served the exclusive ends of the central government and not those of the ethnic groups or of individuals. That is the basic point that distinguishes the Inca system from modern communications networks.

There were two principal trunk roads. One extended through the highlands, from south to north, while the second connected the coastal valleys. Numerous subsidiary roads connected these two trunk routes, linking the coast with the highlands and continuing on to the jungle region.

The first Spaniards to travel the Inca roads left descriptions of them. In the coastal valleys they were wide, clean, and closed off by high walls and trees that provided shade, at least according to the earliest information, provided for the northern region of San Miguel, in 1534, and Cristóbal de Mena y Estete, writing in 1533–34 (Fernández de Oviedo, 1945, vol. XII: 52–53; Porras, 1937). This is not the case for roads outside the valleys, and it is natural that walls were absent in the coastal deserts, where the way was marked only by piles of stones or by stakes. In the north, some roads have been found to have been lined by rows of stones, while on rocky surfaces the stones were removed to provide a roadway that was flat and free of pebbles (Hyslop, 1984). In the desert of Atacama, piles of stones were used to indicate the way (Santoro, 1983).

Documentary sources show that on the central coast, in the valley of the Chillón River, local roads extended from the coast toward the highlands along both banks of the river (Rostworowski, 1977:59–60). The valley of Pachacamac was crossed widthwise from north to south by five roads, each of which was reserved for a specific group of inhabitants according to their occupation; we know that the fifth road, bordering the sea, belonged to the *chasqui*, the Inca messengers and bearers of news, while the fourth was reserved for the movement of fish, that is, it belonged to the fishermen. The special functions of the other routes are unknown (Rostworowski, 1977: 218).

Early data concerning the mountain routes are also provided by Estete, who in 1533 accompanied Hernando Pizarro from Cajamarca to Pachacamac to undertake the ransom of Atahualpa, and then on his return through the central sierra in pursuit of General Challcochima. In his account he makes brief references to the roads they used near Huanuco Pampa. Most were paved "with much order and with channels to drain the water." In Piscobamba they found the road to be broad, bordered by boulders, and with "some steps made of stone." Continuing along the same route, they reached the town of Pombo or Pumpu, where two branches of the road came together, and whence they had previously departed for Pachacamac. There, the route passed through low fields, and the road was wide, ascending and descending by stone steps. In places with precipices, rails protected travelers and camelid herds from falling into the abyss.

In his investigation of Inca routes, Hyslop finds that there was no single pattern applied to all the roads in the network but, rather, that they were adapted to the geography of the region through which they passed. There has been some emphasis on the belief that the indigenous engineers tried to make the roads follow a straight line, but Hyslop (1984) maintains that it was impossible to fulfill this ideal except on the high plateaus or the coastal plains. According to him, road builders avoided curves or changes in direction to the extent possible, but they were forced to follow the dictates of the broken mountain terrain. One can discern in the construction of the roads the priority given to covering long distances over the immediate objective of uniting two nearby points. Supervision of the principal routes, such as the Capac Nan Guamanin, was the responsibility of a high-ranking official, generally an Inca noble (Guaman Poma, 1936, fols. 355–56).

The Bridges

Various types of bridges were used for crossing the rivers. In the mountains there were two principal kinds: those built of logs and those constructed of ropes. Logs were used when the distances to be spanned permitted. I return to Estete's account, because his information is based on observations made while the structures of the Inca state were still intact. After departing Huanuco Pampa, at a distance of about a half league, they passed a bridge "made of thick wood," unlike one they had seen in Andamarca, in the region of Cajamarca, which was of stone and wood with two large strong boulders projecting toward the river in order to shorten the span. At one end of this bridge there was an inn and a stone-paved patio that provided lodging and a place of recreation of the "lords of the earth" when they passed through.

The second type of bridge, which is also the best-known in the Andean region, was the rope bridge, which impressed not only the Spanish conquerors but also, later, foreign travelers who used them to cross the rivers of the region. Their construction utilized two large stone buttresses resting on solid foundations. Between the walls of each buttress crossed four or six thick beams to which the ropes of the bridge were fastened. The ropes were twined from twigs slender and flexible like wicker, plaiting three of these with a thicker one, and increasing the number of twigs until a diameter of some 50 centimeters, more or less, was reached (Cobo, 1965, vol. II, chap. 13). The material employed depended on what was available in the region. Gade (1972) indicates the use of twigs of the *lloque* (*Kaganeckia lanceolata*), *chachacomo* (*Escallonia resinosa*), *tasca* (*Escollonia patens*), and the sauce trees (*Salix humboldtiana*), as well as shrubs such as the *chilca* (*Baccharis sp.*). In the zones in which these plants were not found, they relied on the fibers of the maguey cactus (*Fourcroya andina*).

The best references regarding these bridges are the earliest, originating in the events in Cajamarca. In the *Relación Francesa de la Conquista* of 1534, we find: "There are very great and powerful rivers over which there are bridges made of thick ropes and between one and the other there are smaller, thin ropes; and of these bridges there are two, that used by the lords and that used by the common people" (Porras Barrenechea, 1937:74).

Farther on, the same *Relación* adds that on each side of the bridge there were permanent inhabitants whose occupation consisted of maintaining it and mending the ropes when they wore out. This is not the only account mentioning the existence of parallel bridges, one for the nobility and the other for the commoners (Estete, in Fernández de Oviedo, 1945, vol. 16: 60, 65, 66, and the Letter of Hernando Pizarro p. 85, dated in 1533). This information, suggesting a strongly hierarchical society, is found only in the earliest sources. Subsequently, during the civil wars among the Spaniards and the uprising of Manco II, many bridges were burned, and naturally they did not return to the practice of building two together.

Another bit of information in the earliest accounts concerns the collection of a toll. In a culture that did not use money, however, the "payment" could not justify the presence of the caretakers. Rather, it represented a form of control over the users of the bridge, which was recorded on the *quipu* and later passed on to the higher authorities. Guaman Poma mentions an Inca noble who was in charge of the bridges of Capac Nan. It is also likely that since the bridges were strategic places their vigilance was the responsibility of people of confidence, perhaps special *mitmaq* similar to those who guarded the borders of the Inca state. Similarly, Pedro Pizarro (1978:106) mentions that the four principal roads leaving Cusco were the responsibility of watchmen who observed all persons leaving and entering the city. Estete contends that in the town of Xauxa there were persons in charge of keeping a count of men who came for military service and of those who entered the town (Fernández de Oviedo, 1945, vol. 16:62).

Bridges can be classified according to their importance, as well as by material employed and method of construction. First would come those on the trunk roads, the Capac Nan, followed by the bridges on the routes joining the various ethnic groups and the local bridges that joined one village with another. Other bridges were used only during the rainy season, when the rivers rose (Mellafe, 1965; Thompson and Murra, 1966).

Rivers could also be crossed by means of the *oroya*. Cobo describes these as consisting of a rope made of *ichu*, a kind of strong reed that grows at high altitudes, thick as one's leg, which was tied to buttresses on either bank of the river. From this rope hung a basket with an arched handle through which the rope was passed. One or more persons could be seated in these baskets and drawn across by means of a cord attached to the basket and pulled from one end.

The construction of bridges and *oroyas* was the responsibility of the local ethnic groups, who distributed the work according to the *mita* system, with the population divided into *hanan* and *hurin* or *ichoc* and *allauca* (upper and lower, left and right). During viceregal times, the Andean method of distributing the labor obligations among the ethnic groups was preserved, which permitted the continued maintenance of these public works (Mellafe, 1965).

In the south, in the Desaguadero, near Lake Titicaca, there was a famous bridge that consisted of a row of reed boats arranged side by side and covered with a thick layer of reeds. Finally, on the coast, when the rivers could not be forded because of the strength of the current, in places where the valley narrowed, there were bridges of wood or rope crossing part or all of the river bed. Rafts made of logs were also used, and in the north there are references to rafts which utilized gourds contained within thick nets or mesh, which were driven and steered by expert swimmers who held onto them (for details concerning bridges, see Hyslop, 1984).

The Tambos, or Inns

The Spaniards made the Inca state famous by their accounts of the inns, also called *tampus*, placed at certain intervals along the principal roads. It is likely that, as with most of the Andean organizational system, the *tambos* existed in earlier times along the pilgrimage routes to the *huacas* and at the sanctuaries that housed the faithful who arrived from distant places. Perhaps a network of shelters was used by the Wari, and we cannot discard the possibility that the powerful Chimu chiefdom also used inns to facilitate the movement of its principals around their states. With reference to the tambos, I should note that there were various categories and dimensions according to their importance. In the great establishments of Vilcas or Huanuco Pampa, their many structures included palaces, temples, *tampu*, and storehouses, among others.

All along the principal routes there were inns to lodge the Inca and his retinue when he left Cusco, whether to visit his estates or to march to war. On the secondary routes there were lesser *tambos* for lodging the emissaries, inspectors, and all the officials necessary for the administration of the state who traveled for diverse reasons. Finally, the smallest shelters were used by the *chasqui*, or messengers, who, by relays, carried the governmental information usually contained on *quipu*.

We have, in addition to the well-known facts concerning the *tambos* in the chronicles, two lists of inns used in viceregal times on the routes between Cusco, Los Reyes, Lima, and Quito. These inns were maintained by means of the Andean system of the *mita* (Guaman Poma, 1936; Ordenanzas de las Tambos, prepared by Vaca de Castro, 1908/1543).

Guaman Poma establishes several categories of *tambos* according to their importance, which he illustrates with various drawings. This variety of *tambos* is further confirmed in the *Ordenanzas*, or statutes, decreed by the judge Gregorio González de Cuenca on his visit to Huamachuco. In this interesting 1567 document, the *mita* for the support of each *tambo* of the region was specified, and something can be learned of how each functioned. The significance of this manuscript lies in its having been written before the Toledo reforms, as well as before the forced resettlement of the natives, which means that the towns named were still in their original locations. Naturally, the *Ordenanzas* were Spanish and do not entirely reflect pre-Hispanic conditions, but the application of these reforms to the ancient system helps clarify how it must have functioned.

Nine *tambos* were in service in the area of Huamachuco, maintained by their six *guaranga* (each containing a thousand households). Two of them belonged to *mitmaq*, one of highland and the other of coastal people. Two of the *tambos*, those of Yagon and Huamachuco, are named as royal *tambos*, each served by thirty men, while the rest had only ten natives each at their disposal. These *tambos*, to be sure, were not situated along a single route but were dispersed throughout the area.

To improve one's understanding of the *tambo* system, one would have to undertake archaeological fieldwork to identify examples of these categories of structures, something that has not been accomplished. Various peoples of the six *guaranga* supplied labor for service in the *tambos*. Moreover, the native division of labor did not follow a European logic, by which each *guaranga* would send its people to the closest *tambo*; rather, in some cases, men would be sent to distant inns in spite of the availability of local labor. The testimony of the statutes specifies that "many of them would go to serve in very distant and remote *tambos*, although there were closer ones where they could serve" (Vaca de Castro, 1908). Undoubtedly, native reasoning obeyed factors other than the distances considered by Judge Cuenca. Understanding the indigenous way of thinking and the ease with which their actions can be judged erroneously are always sources of difficulty.

Scholars who have dealt with the subject of the pre-Hispanic *tambos* have questioned the actual distances between them. The earliest reference in the chronicles is a letter that Hernando Pizarro wrote to the king in 1533, in which he tells him that in his survey of the coast near Pachacamac, his people had found at certain intervals some structures built for the times when the Inca passed by the coast. (See Fernández de Oviedo, vol. 12:87.) Also, Mena in (Porras Barrenechea, 1937/1534) mentions that on the road from Cajamarca to the coast they found some shelters every two leagues. Each chronicler indicates the number of leagues covered between *tambos*, but the information differs from one to another because in sixteenth-century Europe, measurements had not been standardized. Information concerning distances used in the Andean region corresponds to the amount of energy expended rather than the actual distance covered. There were no standardized units of measurement in the Andean world, as each region kept its own system of measurements. The Inca regime, however, implanted a unit known as the *tupu* in Cusco. This term indicated the act of measuring, besides being a unit of measurement of area and distance. Analysis of the information that has been gathered concerning the native measurements indicates that the *tupu* was a relative measure that considered time expended before distance covered. One *tupu* of climbing was shorter than one of descending. It was, above all, a relative unit (Rostworowski, 1960).

According to Hyslop (1984), it is difficult to recognize *tambos* in the field because their architecture varied considerably. It appears likely that local building customs and the use of local labor influenced their construction (Morris and Thompson, 1985).

THE CONQUESTS

The Inca conquests must be discussed in depth both to examine the order in which they occurred and to explain the circumstances surrounding the most important ones. There are questions concerning the means employed by the Inca rulers to take control of such vast territories in a relatively short time. We need to explain the sudden rise of the Inca state and its almost explosive growth, as well as its rapid unraveling.

Archaeology has confirmed the limited duration of the Inca occupation, in contrast to a long stratigraphic sequence representing the development of the various earlier Andean cultures. The Incas took the achievements of these earlier cultures, above all in the area of sociopolitical organization, and applied them to their own system of government. It can be shown that the various practices of the system of reciprocity, such as the *minka* and the *ayni*, were not new and that, since ancient times, the macroethnic groups had built *tambos*, roads, and bridges. These earlier groups followed the practice of transferring populations from one place to another to serve their interests and used the institution of the *yana*, another long-established custom. All these customs were probably developed during the Middle Horizon, and perhaps earlier. The Inca rulers, however, were the first to employ them at the state level.

At present, it is difficult to attribute specific contributions to particular cultural groups. The cultural loans adopted by the Incas after the principal conquests must have been diverse, however, as were the factors that influenced them. Certainly the wealth and ostentation of the lords of Chimor must have had a great impact on the rude Inca warriors, and the example of the coastal chiefs must have encouraged the luxury and magnificence of the Inca rulers. This conjecture is supported by the presence in the Inca capital of groups of silversmiths from various coastal centers: Inca, Chincha, Pachacamac, Chimu, and Huancavilca, in present-day Ecuador. All these artisans worked for the lords of Cusco, and while they followed Inca stylistic models, they provided their own knowledge and technology.

Before considering the Inca conquests themselves, it will be useful to have an overview of the problems related to the disaster incurred at the hands of the Spanish invaders. One reason for the weakness of the Inca state when confronted by Pizarro's forces was the limited time of the Inca hegemony. The power enjoyed by the Incas was of short duration, and the arrival of the Spanish left no room for Inca supremacy to take root in the Andean world.

Perhaps the Incas desired to integrate the indigenous populations into their system. The mandatory use of the Inca dialect of Quechua as a *lengua general*, as the Spanish called it, may reflect such an objective. But it appears likely that these were subconscious desires at best, and that their principal objective was to facilitate the administration of the state. In any case, the integration of the Andean world never became a reality. The sentiments of local groups around their *huacas*, their pieces of land, and their immediate chiefs, continued to prevail.

The inhabitants of the vast Andean territory identified with their local nuclei and were not conscious of forming part of a whole. In this respect, Inca domination did not sink deep roots among the subjugated peoples. The brief time that had elapsed since annexation of the majority of the macroethnic groups by the Inca state had not erased the memory of their past liberty, and the majority of the great Andean lords were only waiting for the opportunity to shake off the Inca presence. For this reason, the Inca rulers were never able to form a nation, and it is not surprising that the ethnic chiefs saw the Spaniards as allies who would help them recover their past independence. They believed that collaboration with the Spanish would free them from their Inca masters, and for this reason attached themselves to the new arrivals. They could not know, or guess, that behind the soldiers of Pizarro stood the menacing presence of a country desirous of conquering the New World and possessing a more advanced technology that would overcome the Andean lords' desire for liberty.

It appears likely that Pizarro understood well the situation created by the Spanish presence, and took advantage of the opportunity to offer his self-interested support to the cause of the local lords of the country. Such was the case of the Huanca chief who, as just related, gave full support to Pizarro, in exchange for which he naturally expected that the Spanish Crown would award him with an *encomienda*, which never occurred. The natives could not foresee the power of the Spanish, nor the arrival en masse of fresh forces bent on dominating their land.

Another reason for the indigenous disaster at the hands of the Spaniards was the civil war between Huascar and Atahualpa. Undoubtedly the conflict for the succession to Huayna Capac weakened the central power as well as the country in general. Nevertheless, and even though the rivalry between the two brothers was the direct cause of the spectacular fall of the Inca state, the underlying cause was the desire of the Andean lords themselves to throw off the power of the Incas.

The Andean state was too recent and its authority not sufficiently established for it to survive the collision with a culture whose knowledge was superior to its own. Its collapse was caused, however, not by an internal decadence, as many have cited to explain its fall, but by an accumulation of adverse circumstances. Everything conspired against the natives of this land.

In a previous work (1953), I discussed in detail the Inca conquests and their sequence, but this was based entirely on the accounts of the chroniclers available at that time and an interpretation of their data. Now, thanks to advances in research and the appearance of new documentary sources, one can examine the data in terms of the conquests of specific places. It is now possible to broaden the horizon of the Inca conquests, and while I continue to maintain my original view regarding the period of expansion, for later times I am able to use concrete cases for which there is documentary evidence. In these testimonies we can see the diverse and changing conditions over the course of Inca rule, as well as the methods used by the Incas to maintain domination over the various ethnic groups.

The continuous wars against the Chancas until their final annihilation enabled the Incas to affirm their domination over the neighboring ethnic chiefs, whether by reciprocity or by arms. Sarmiento de Gamboa (chap. 35) tells of those battles against small chiefdoms located some few leagues from Cusco. Other, longer-distance, expeditions were directed against the Soras, in Cuntisuyu. The confrontation of greatest importance, however, was directed against the ethnic lords of the Altiplano, with whom the Incas had been in constant conflict for many years.

Cieza de León (*Señorío,* chap. 41) and Santa Cruz Pachacuti tell of the rivalries between the lords of Chucuito and Hatun Colla, and their hostility against the Canas and the Canchis. According to the chroniclers, during the reign of Viracocha, the Inca offered his support to the two Colla chiefs, but secretly made an agreement with Cari, the lord of Chucuito. Informed of the agreement, the chief of Hatun Colla decided to do battle against the Chucuito before the arrival of the Inca troops. After a violent battle in Paucarcolla, Cari claimed the victory, much to the Inca's displeasure. Based on this new situation, with conquest out of the question, the rulers of Cusco and Chucuito met peacefully and appear to have agreed to an alliance.*

With the regime of the Inca Pachacutec, the wars between the Collas and the Incas took a new turn. Sarmiento de Gamboa (chap. 37) relates in rich detail the fighting between the Incas and Chuchi Capac, also called Colla Capac, lord of Hatun Colla. In the midst of a battle in which neither side had the upper hand, Pachacutec, surrounded by his guard, carried out a direct attack on the Colla chief, who fell prisoner, demoralizing his men and giving the victory to the Incas. Betanzos mentions that this same tactic was used in the war against the Chancas, which gives the encounter something of a mythical quality. According to Sarmiento, Chuchi Capac was a great lord, as befit his title of Capac, and his domains stretched more than 160 leagues from north to south. His lands reached those of the Chichas, the region of Arequipa, the seacoast toward Atacama, and the jungle region of the Mojo. The Hatun Colla lands conquered by the Incas undoubtedly

---

* Many *keros* vessels portray a scene of peace between the Incas and the Collas, who can be recognized by their tall headdresses, an event that apparently had a great impact on the people of that time.

included their vertical enclaves on the coast and in the jungle region (Murra, 1964, 1972).

Cieza de León (chap. 52) in the *Señorío de los Incas* relates that the Inca Yupanqui marched from Cusco to Collao for the purpose of conquest. In Ayaviri, we are told, the inhabitants did not gather to offer him obedience; in reprisal for this, taking them unprepared, he destroyed their villages and carried out great slaughter in the towns. The region was left depopulated of its native inhabitants; to remedy this situation, the ruler ordered that numerous *mitmaq* be brought to repopulate it.

After the defeat of the Collas, the Inca returned to Cusco to celebrate his victory; at the close of the ceremonies, he ordered that the heads of the principal Colla leaders be cut off and preserved in a building called Llaxaguasi, in which trophies of this kind were kept (Sarmiento de Gamboa, chap. 37).

The remaining lords of the altiplano accepted Inca domination peacefully, surely preferring the booty expected through reciprocity with the Incas to embroiling themselves in new wars with a powerful enemy. The Lupaqas of Chucuito, the Paucarcollas, the Pacajes, and the Azángaros must have done the same. Sarmiento de Gamboa (chap. 87) contends that all the inhabitants of Cuntisuyu submitted out of fear (Santa Cruz Pachacuti, 1927:187).

The route to the sea lay open to the Incas, across the mountain lands and enclaves of the ethnic groups of Collao. It is likely that these "archipelagos" became the means of the first Inca contacts with the coast. Internal conflicts among the groups of Collao facilitated the Inca conquest of the zone, but later on they had to confront rebellions and other serious problems with these highland natives.

To better illustrate these events, let us examine briefly specific conquests that followed very different patterns of behavior. I have more information for the coastal conquests, based on my dedicating the last decades exclusively to researching the documentation concerning the coast.

Peaceful Conquest: The *Señorío* of Chincha*

The *Relación de Chincha* (Castro and Ortega Morejón, 1974/1558) is a report that discusses the peaceful conquest of this coastal valley by the Incas.

---

* That the term "Chincha" is the equivalent of "Chinchay" is supported by a document concerning the transfer of native silversmiths from there to Cusco. In Guaman Poma, we fine "Piscoy" substituted for "Pisco," "Lunaguanay" for "Lunahuaná," and likely "Ichmay" for "Pachacamac."

The first Inca army to appear in Chincha was commanded by General Capac Yupanqui. In this chronicle he is referred to as ruler, but the majority of chroniclers indicate he was only a military chief sent to the lowlands by his "brother" Pachacutec.

The Inca general arrived in Chincha with a large force, claiming to be the son of the Sun and to have come for the benefit of the inhabitants. He said that he desired nothing from them, neither gold, nor silver, nor women, because he had everything in abundance, and, on the contrary, brought many gifts by which he would be recognized as lord. In confirmation of these words, he offered the local lords great amounts of clothing produced in Cusco and other objects of value, which greatly pleased the lords of the valley, who in return recognized him as their master. This account is a good example of how reciprocity could be implanted without need for military confrontation, and how the local chiefs might voluntarily accept the Incas.

What advantages did such an arrangement offer the Inca, and what did he obtain in return for his gifts? The Inca general requested the construction of a house, a *hatuncancha*, which surely functioned as an Inca administrative center. He also asked for the assignment of *mamacona*, that is, women dedicated to producing textiles and preparing great quantities of beverages to cover the demands of reciprocity and the cult. Another benefit was the granting of a labor force of artisans and agriculturalists to work the Inca lands, whose products would go to fill the state storehouses.

These three requests by General Capac Yupanqui of the Chincha lords represent the bases of Andean wealth. The *mamacona* and *yana* were valuable sources of female and male labor, while the products of the cultivation of state lands filled the Inca storehouses. These were the three necessary requisites for undertaking the exploitation of the valley for the benefit of the Incas, who used the links of reciprocity to take control of its major resources. From the beginnings of its expansion, a principal goal of Inca organization was to secure the necessary labor force to undertake state infrastructure works.

After this brief appearance of General Capac Yupanqui, some time passed before the arrival in Chincha of young Tupac Yupanqui, then military chief, since his father, the Inca, was surely still alive. During this second stay of an Inca in the valley, the local lords spent considerable time in his company, after which Tupac ordered new social divisions of the population, dividing the commoners into groups of 10, 100, 1,000, and 10,000, with a chief for each unit, a system that had the advantage of facilitating a rapid inventory of the valley's inhabitants for administrative purposes. He ordered the construction of various roads joining the coastal valleys with each other, in addition to the principal coastal route, known as Capac Nan. He also had built a new palace for himself, *tambos*, and houses for the chosen women. Of great importance, he ordered the designation of new lands for the Inca, in addition to those previously set aside for Capac Yupanqui.

The donation of new lands to the Inca was of great significance for Inca policy, as well as a subject of displeasure for the lords of the valley, who lost their best fields. It constituted a major contribution to the highland conquerors that must have stirred considerable discontent among the coastal chiefs.

The third appearance of an Inca ruler in Chincha took place with the arrival of Huayna Capac, who ordered more lands assigned to the state and the transfer of women and of *yana*, both for himself and for the Sun. The arrival of a new Inca in the valley meant further impositions and donations for the inhabitants, in spite of their having received the Incas in peace and friendship. The central power was becoming steadily stronger and, as a result, more demanding and burdensome.

This *Relación* dealing with events in Chincha is extremely valuable because in a few lines it summarizes the successive arrivals in the valley of the highland lords and their increasing claims, the Inca policy of expansion and occupation in one valley, and the increasing oppression over time of the conquered peoples. This account makes clear the methods of Inca exploitation, however they might vary in each chiefdom according to its wealth and to whether the reception given the Incas had been peaceful or warlike. In the latter case, the Inca demands would be higher and onerous indeed for the conquered peoples.

Faced with the appearance of the Inca armies, a chief had two alternatives: to surrender to the offer of reciprocity and face the demands of the system or to take up arms to defend his independence. The prospect of defeat carried with it consequent loss of rulership and likely of life, which caused the ethnic chiefs to reflect and weakened the spirit of the lords. Thus, in most cases, the mere presence of the invading Inca troops was sufficient to accomplish the annexation of the macroethnic groups to the Inca state.

This reaction favored the rapid expansion of the Incas, even though the foundations and structures of the state lacked solidity. This fragility was clearly demonstrated with the arrival of the Spanish forces, whose appearance was sufficient to eliminate the tenuous ties of reciprocity between the chiefs of the great *señoríos* and the Inca rulers.

The peaceful domination of the *señorío* of Chincha surely resulted from its leaders' reluctance to harm their long-distance maritime trade with the peoples of present-day Ecuador or their trade with the highland region. Their desire to maintain their enterprises and their exchange system forced them to accept the demands of the Incas and reach an agreement with them.

While the Chincha needed to maintain good relations with the Incas, the latter, in turn, saw themselves fortunate to secure the precious red *Spondylus* shells they called *mullu* brought by raft from the warm northern seas for use in special rituals and ceremonies. One motive of the Incas for the conquest of Manta, Puerto Viejo, and La Puná was precisely to obtain direct access to the *mullu* shells.

Lightning Conquests: The Highland Chiefdoms of Chinchaysuyu

The next expedition of Capac Yupanqui was directed toward the region of Chinchaysuyu, and was the first Inca incursion into the northern mountains. We will follow the course of events in the consensus account of the chroniclers.

According to the account of Cieza de León, Capac Yupanqui, "brother" of Pachacutec, marched first to Andahuaylas, land already conquered from the Chancas, where he was joined by troops under a general of that ethnic group by the name of Anco Huallo. Continuing on the route, the Inca general met a minimum of resistance until confronting the Huancas, who were also defeated. Passing through Jauja, Yupanqui opened discussions with the inhabitants of Huarochirí and Yauyos, who from that time on proved to be firm allies of the Incas (Ciezas de León, *Señorío,* chap. 49; various documents confirm this interpretation).

The Inca armies next advanced toward Pumpu and Chinchaycocha, where the inhabitants hid among the rushes of the lake. In Tarma, the natives tried to oppose him, without success (Cieza de León, chap. 50). In the seat of Huanuco the Chanca contingent fled to a jungle region not controlled by the Incas (Cabello de Valboa, 1952, chap. 6; Sarmiento de Gamboa, chap. 37).

According to Sarmiento de Gamboa (chap. 38), Capac Yupanqui continued his advance by the northern route until reaching the *señorío* of Guzmango in Cajamarca. In the face of the Inca danger, Guzmango Capac, lord of six *guaranga* and chief of a macroethnic group, sought an alliance with the Chimu. In the ensuing confrontation with the Incas both lords were defeated, prompting the rapid retreat of Chimu Capac toward the coast.

The enormous amount of booty obtained in General Capac Yupanquyi's campaigns excited the distrust of the Incas who stayed in Cusco. Then the victorious chief took the return road to the capital. According to the chroniclers, the Inca, jealous of Capac Yupanqui's many triumphs and copious treasure, became suspicious of his brother and accused him of disobeying his orders and having permitted the escape of the Chancas. The repeated victories of Capac Yupanqui were a menace to the Inca rulers, whose criterion for accession to power was the right of most ablest.

On arriving in Limatambo, eight leagues from Cusco, Capac Yupanqui and his "brother" Huayna Yupanqui, the dual chiefs of the Inca armies, encountered a delegation sent by the ruler carrying an order condemning them to death for having disobeyed orders and holding them responsible for the Chancas' flight into the jungle. In fact, both chiefs were considered dangerous because of their successes and achievements, and because their having shown themselves capable threatened the right to power of the rulers who had remained in the capital (Cieza, *Señorío,* chap. 56; Sarmiento de Gamboa, chap. 38).

The rapid advance of the troops of Capac Yupanqui and Huayna Yupanqui through the northern sierra is an example of this kind of lightning conquest. It did not involve tenacious fighting with each chiefdom. The Inca forces were not delayed in their march, nor did they remain in those places that surrendered (at least, not during the initial period), where it was sufficient to establish a reciprocal agreement.

The first contact with the towns consisted of an offer to establish the ties demanded by the system; only later, with subsequent regimes, came increases in the obligations imposed on the ethnic lords. Once the customary requests had been granted, the Incas applied and restored the basic organizational structure. Let us look now at what happened when the local chiefs resisted Inca pressure.

Local Resistance: The Chiefdom of Guarco

Guarco, located in pre-hispanic times in the present-day valley of Cañete, was, in the middle of the fifteenth century, a traditionally warlike chiefdom that defended its liberty with ardor. It occupied a fertile valley, with abundant water throughout the year, with the further advantage that the river ran along the southern part of the valley, which facilitated its defense. The chroniclers are in agreement concerning the resistance offered by the inhabitants of Guarco to the Inca armies; their aggressiveness is evidenced by the network of fortifications that still exist in their ancient domain.

The chiefdom occupied the lower zone of the valley. Its frontiers from north to south were the deserts that bordered its cultivated fields. Its fertile lands extended eastward to the principal irrigation canals, and approaching the river bordered on the neighboring chiefdom of Lunahuaná. On the south, near the mouth of the river, was the Tambo de Locos, later called Herbay Bajo.

To the north of its borders rose the so-called Fuerte de Guarco (now Cerro Azul), situated on an escarpment facing the sea. Although the chroniclers mention this structure as having been built by the Incas, it probably dates from an earlier period. It may have served as a lookout to watch for the arrival of fleets of rafts and of foreign or local *caballitos de totora* (reed boats) putting into shore, not only to prevent possible enemy attacks by sea but also to maintain surveillance over arriving and departing vessels. It is likely that this observation contributed to the performance of rites and ceremonies involved in worship of the ocean, since the sea was the principal source of subsistence resources and considered to be a female deity. It is also likely that the Guarcos maintained a close watch over the coast for fear of maritime attack by their Chincha neighbors, who were attracted by their fertile lands and abundant water.

Cieza de León (1941, *Crónica,* chap. 73) gives a detailed description of the fort and concludes that it was built by the Incas. This version is repeated by other chroniclers, but it does not seem likely if it is assumed that the Guarcos continually sustained conflicts with all of their neighbors and only later against the Incas. This being so, it is reasonable to assume that its construction dates from pre-Inca times and that the Incas, after their triumph, proceeded to remodel it to house a garrison.

The second fortress of the chiefdom was that of Canchari, located on the edge of the valley, toward the east, on a natural rise of land. Its function was to control any attempt at invasion by highland peoples by way of the gorge of Pocoto, the natural approach route from the mountains to the coast for the inhabitants of Yauyos. The fort also protected the important irrigation canals of San Miguel, or Chiome, and María Angola, whose indigenous name was Chumbe (Rostworowski, 1978–80).

The third fortress, and the most important and impressive of all, was that of Ungara, near the intakes of the river. Its missions were to defend the starting point of the hydraulic system for the entire valley, to protect the southern part of the *señorío* from an enemy army able to cross the bed of the river, and to repel any attack coming from the neighboring valley of Chincha. According to Larrabure y Unanue (1941), these defenses of Ungara were complemented by a small fort on the left bank of the river, on the property of Palo. To the three fortifications of Guarco were added a wall of enormous proportions, built of adobe, that surrounded the fields and villages of the valley (Larrabure y Unanue, 1941).

All this information is necessary to demonstrate that the inhabitants of Guarco were accustomed to defending their lands from the designs of their enemies and that their security depended on their forts and walls. For this reason, they found it natural to resist the Incas tenaciously.

At the outset of the war between the Incas and the Guarcos, the small chiefdom of Lunahuaná fell to the Incas. This was a weakly defended coastal *señorío* whose lands bordered on those of Guarco and that extended on the east as far as Zúñiga and Pacarán in the upper valley. The riverbed, a natural penetration route to the coast, was selected by the Incas to descend to conquer the region. As mentioned earlier in this chapter, young Tupac Yupanqui ordered the construction of New Cusco in the valley of Lunahuaná.

It took the Incas three or four years to defeat this lowland people. Cieza de León (*Señorío,* 274–81) recounts that during the warm summer months the highlanders apparently abandoned the fight and returned to their villages to cultivate their fields. The *costeños* took advantage of these periods to repair their defenses and also to devote themselves to their agricultural tasks. This account provides significant information about how indigenous groups made war. When the agricultural cycle demanded, the highlanders abandoned their arms in favor of the *chaqui taclla,* or Andean plow, and the coastal peoples the *llampa,* or hoe, and both groups gave themselves over to the toils of the field. We find a similar occurrence during the siege of Cusco imposed by Manco II in 1534, further confirming that this was the custom in the Andes. Only during the relatively short duration of the Inca expansion, as a consequence of the great distances involved, were the armies restructured so warriors could remain in the field and absent from their homes for long periods of time. Recruitment was based on a system of wartime *mita* that took the recruits to distant places for longer periods. When Inca power disintegrated, the ancient tradition of short-term warfare reappeared.

Acosta (1940, book 3, chap. 15) and, later, Cobo tell of the resistance of the Guarcos, and how the end of the war resulted from a stratagem devised by the queen of Tupac Yupanqui. At that time, the chief of the valley of Guarco was a woman who was determined to oppose foreign seizure of her lands. The Incas' queen asked her husband to let her arrange for the submission of this rebellious chief by means of a ruse, to which the Inca agreed. She then sent an emissary to the chief, informing her of the desire of the Inca to leave her in her chiefdom and of his wish to celebrate a great and solemn ceremony in honor of the sea, in order to ensure peace. The chief, believing the words of the queen, ordered preparations for the festival. On the appointed day the entire Guarco population disembarked in rafts, accompanied by music and the beating of drums. When the Guarcos reached the open sea, far from the coast, the Inca armies quickly entered and seized control of the valley (Cobo, 1956, vol. 2, chap. 15).

In the accounts of the chroniclers, we can see the resistance of the Guarcos in the face of Inca might, and the subsequent cruel reprisals. According to Cabello de Valboa (1951:338–39), the name "Guarco" was given to the valley as a result of the exemplary punishments inflicted on its inhabitants, for the Inca apparently ordered that many rebels be hanged from the walls of the fort. (According to the Quechua *Lexicón* of Domingo de Santo Tomás, *guarcona* means hanging, and *guarcuni*, or *gui*, refers to the hanging victim.)

The severity of the Inca reprisals appears to be confirmed by the large number of *mitmaq* introduced into the valley after the conquest. The northern part of the chiefdom was given to the natives of the neighboring valley of Coayllo, and another stretch of land was given to Mochica peoples from the north. (Later, I will discuss the functions performed by these coastal people on the central and north-central coast.) Finally, the fields located on the left bank of the river were given to the Chinchas, who had received the Incas peacefully and became their allies.

Another Example of Local Resistance: The Collec

The Inca conquests can be best understood by looking at the largest possible number of individual cases or examples. Without these specific cases, we are left only with the accounts of the chronicles, which do not provide nearly as much detail and are therefore not as valuable as the administrative and judicial documents.

In the archives I have found documentary evidence of another coastal *señorío* that refused to accept the Incas peacefully and decided to defend itself by arms, that of Collique. Before my investigation, nothing was known of this *señorío*, whose existence, even, had been unknown. Such absence of information resulted, in great part, from the consequences of the Inca conquest and the extermination of the original population because of war and the subsequent punishments inflicted on the inhabitants. This demographic decline became more acute with the arrival of the Spanish, owing to their proximity to the city of Los Reyes, and this ethnic group had disappeared entirely by the end of the sixteenth century. We know of the existence of the *señorío* of Collique, or Collec, from various documents in the Archivo General de Indias in Seville (AGI – Justicia 413; Rostworowski 1988b).

The central coast comprises the valleys of Lurín, Rimac, and Chillón, divided in pre-Hispanic times into two principal *señoríos*: Ychsma, which includes the valleys of Lurín and Lima, and Collec, or Collique as the Spanish called it. The latter formed a prosperous ethnic group composed, in turn, of a series of small chiefdoms including Chuquitanta, Carabayllo, Zapan, Macas, Guaraui, Guancayo, and Quivi. Each contained various *guaranga, pachaca,* and *ayllus* ruled by their corresponding lords (Rostworowski, 1977).

The seat of the Colli Capac in Collique was a fortified structure surrounded by a great wall enclosing many fields watered by two bountiful springs, which permitted its inhabitants to survive prolonged sieges without hunger or thirst. These defenses were constructed by the inhabitants in response to the danger of attack by peoples from the valley uplands. The Canta, especially, coveted their land because of its suitability for planting a variety of coca adapted to the environment of the *chaupi yunga,* or middle coast. Various other upriver forts guarded access to the valley and to the cultivated fields.

The documents refer to repeated incursions by Canteños, who were unable, however, to defeat the Collecs, secure behind their strong walls. Thus, when the Inca armies appeared, the Colli Capac refused to submit, feeling secure within their defenses. We do not know the details of the conflict that ensued. We know only of the death of the lord of Collec in the ensuing combat, and the subsequent revenge of the Incas. To replace the deceased chief, the Incas appointed an individual belonging to the social status of *yanayacu,* as a warning to other chiefs that might wish to oppose them.

A short time later, the natives of Quivi were found guilty of performing witchcraft against the life of the Inca by means of a *huaca.* The Inca noble sent from Cusco to investigate the crime, and to impose an exemplary punishment, ordered the execution of the adult male population, freeing only the women and children (Rostworowski, 1977).

The Chiefdom of Chimu: An Example of Resistance

The third important confrontation between coastal people and highlanders involved the rich and opulent *señorío* of Chimor. I found no new information concerning its conquest, but as in the previous cases the Chimus refused the Inca offer of reciprocity. It was the Inca Tupac Yupanqui, at the head of his armies, who conquered the extensive domains of this northern coastal chiefdom.

The first encounter between the Chimus and the Incas took place during the hurried advance of General Capac Yupanqui toward Cajamarca. At that time, the ruler of Chimor, by the name of Minchaçaman, rushed to help Guzmango, lord of the six *guarangas* of Cajamarca. The latter was killed in battle and Minchaçaman quickly returned to the coast.

After Chincha, a second Inca personage to appear in the region was young Tupac Yupanqui, who devoted himself to war and to extending the borders of the Inca realm. This ruler is characterized as a great conqueror, and the chroniclers describe him as tireless in his long marches through the high valleys, ravines, and deserts. Even during the reign of Pachacutec Inca Yupanqui, Tupac Yupanqui was sent to Cajamarca as commanding general of the Inca armies, together with his "brother" Tupac Capac and with the experienced generals Anqui Yupanqui and Tilca Yupanqui (Sarmiento de Gamboa, chap. 44).

On his way northward through the mountains, the Inca overcame various forts where local lords offered resistance. After seizing control of Guzmango, he descended the Moche River, threatening to cut the coastal water supply. The Chimus were unable to resist the momentum of the Incas, and Minchaçaman, the Chimu chief, was defeated and taken as a prisoner to Cusco for the celebration of the victory festivals. In his place, Tupac Yupanqui named Chumun-caur as lord of Chimor, after which the Inca armies continued their advance toward Pacatnamú. At the same time, other Inca troops ventured toward the Chachapoyas, whose chief, Chuqui Sota, took refuge in the fort of Piajajalca. But he could not resist the Inca attack and fell prisoner to the invading forces (Sarmiento de Gamboa, chap. 44).

As a result of these conquests, the Incas obtained treasures of a quality and quantity never before seen in Cusco. On his return to the capital, the reception given Tupac Yupanqui became memorable for the sumptuousness of the festivities, the splendor of the booty, and the number of chiefs taken prisoner. In addition to the captured chiefs, the increased retinue of coastal people that the Inca brought with him included many artisans in the capacity of *mitmaq* or *yana*, among them experts in weaving fine textiles, others skilled in metallurgy, ceramicists, and specialists in the manufacture of other fine crafts, including featherwork. By tracking down unedited archival documents, I have been able to confirm the presence in the capital of silversmiths, brought there by order of the Inca, who were natives of Ica, Chincha, Pachacamac, and Chimu (Cieza de León, *Señorío*, chap. 58; Rostworowski, 1977). It would be useful to conduct an analysis of the pre-Hispanic metal artifacts from Cusco to determine the role of coastal craftspeople in this industry, as well as their influence on other aspects of Inca art and craft production.

According to our understanding, it was shortly after their conquest of the Chimu that the Incas acquired the magnificence so admired by the Spanish. It seems likely that the Inca elite adopted these customs of courtly luxury and sumptuousness from the defeated Chimu Capac and the Chimu nobility.

Before coming into contact with the northern macroethnic groups, the Incas were merely somewhat rustic warriors, as were the other chiefs of Cusco. Only as a result of this encounter did the rulers of Tahuantinsuyu begin to acquire the authority and wealth to match their conquests and cease to be simple local *curacas*.

Other Conquests of Tupac Yupanqui

After a period of rest, Tupac Yupanqui again left Cusco for the purpose of extending the borders of the Inca state. He took with him the same generals, Tilca and Anqui Yupanqui, and advanced by the principal mountain road of Capac Nan. Along the way, the ruler saw to it that Inca administration was in order and that the local lords were fulfilling their agreements, and he appointed and retired dignitaries according to the requirements of the incipient state. In this way they eventually reached the territory of the Cañaris, who had allied themselves with the Quito to confront the Incas.

After achieving victory over these ethnic groups, Tupac remained in Quito to rest and ordered that large numbers of *mitmaq* be brought for the purpose of building a city. Before departing, he left as governor an ancient noble by the name of Chalco Mayta, with permission to be carried in a litter and instructions to send Tupac monthly news by messenger about conditions in Quito (Cieza de León, *Señorío*, chaps. 56 and 57).

After leaving Quito, the Inca passed a place called Surampalli, where he ordered some structures built that were later named Tumipampa, after one of the royal *panaca* of Cusco (Rostworowski, 1983:141).

After several years away from the capital, Tupac embarked on a war against the Huancavilcas. He divided his army into three parts, taking command of one and entering the craggy mountains to attack his enemies from the east. The other two armies fought along the coast, by land as well as by sea, the latter with the assistance of Tumbesino raftsmen. There were actions all along the coast, from Tumbes to Guañapi, Guamo, Manta, Turuca, and Quisin (Sarmiento de Gamboa, chap. 46).

Tupac was occupied with conquering Manta and the island of La Puná when he was met by some merchants navigating rafts with sails. They indicated they had come from two islands called Auachumbi and Nina. Tupac was impressed by their account and decided to consult with the diviner who always accompanied him in his campaigns. He asked if what the "maritime merchants" said was true, since they "talked much" and he found it difficult to believe them. The diviner responded that he would go first, flying ahead to determine if the islands in question really existed.

Of interest in this somewhat unusual account by Sarmiento de Gamboa (chap. 46) is the mention of "navigating merchants" and the mysterious maritime voyage taken by the Inca. The expedition lasted nine months. On his return after so long an absence, Tupac decided to take the road back to

Cusco. He chose the coastal route and headed for Catacaos, Pacatnamú, and Chimor. The ruler advanced slowly through the coastal valleys, passing through Pachacamac, and from there continued by the mountain route, entering by way of Pariacaca and Jauja (Calancha, 1976, book 3; Cieza, *Señorío*, chap. 57). Another of his armies advanced on a parallel course by the opposite road, inspecting the various ethnic groups as it passed through (Sarmiento de Gamboa, chap. 46).

According to Sarmiento de Gamboa, it was after these northern conquests that Pachacutec died and Tupac Yupanqui, no longer co-regent, assumed absolute power together with his *yanapac*, or double, in the dual system. The chronologies of the Inca conquests are naturally somewhat vague, and it is likely that Tupac, after a long rest in Cusco, decided to lead his troops toward the jungle region of Anti, looking to broaden his access to the area's coca plantations. For this purpose he again divided his armies in three parts, personally leading one of them and entering the region by way of Aguatona. The second group was commanded by Otorongo Achachi, who entered through the town of Amaru; and the third by Chalco Yupanqui, who took the route through Pilcopata (Sarmiento de Gamboa, chap. 49).*

Once in the jungle, Tupac's armies suffered great hardships. The Inca himself became lost in the thick *monte* until he was found by Otorongo Achachi's troops, who were searching for him. On this occasion the Incas conquered the Opataris, the Manosuyu, the Mañaris, or Yanaximes, and the Chunchos, while an Inca captain by the name of Apo Curimache reached the Paititi. While the Inca was in the jungle region of Anti, a native of Collao by the name of Coaquiri fled the Inca ranks and reached the highlands, spreading news of the Inca's death. His talk excited the people and convinced them it was the opportune moment to rise up against the regime. Coaquiri himself took the name of Pachacutec Ynga, and under his command rebellion erupted throughout Collao (thus our supposition that the Inca's entry into the jungle took place earlier).

Once advised of events, Tupac hurriedly left the jungle, leaving Otorongo Achachi behind to conclude the conquest. The Inca passed directly through Paucartambo to face the rebels in Collao (Cobo, 1956, vol. 2, book 12, chap. 14). After pacifying the land, Tupac Yupanqui headed for Charcas, whose inhabitants were forced to submit. From there, he headed south

---

* This version is supported by Cabello de Valboa. Cobo (1956, vol. 2, chap. 15) mentions the same entry into Anti in connection with a voyage to Quito and a visit to Collasuyu. It seems to me that the march to Quito must have occurred earlier, since it is unlikely that the Inca could easily cover such great distances in a single voyage.

to Chile, where he seized two chiefs, Michimalongo and Tangalongo, and advanced as far as the southern borders at the Maule River.

After these conquests, subsequent departures from Cusco by the Inca were limited to visiting recently annexed zones in order to implant the new order. In some places, isolated cases of subversion were snuffed out, but the principal objective of these inspections was to ensure the implementation of the Inca organizational system, ordering the public works necessary for the good administration of the "provinces."

Owing to the imprecision of the chronicles, it is not possible to recount a precise factual history of the conquests of Tupac Yupanqui and Huayna Capac. One can only analyze the data and sketch an outline of the sequence of the territorial annexations. I have been more successful in providing detailed descriptions of specific conquests, as in the case of the Collec, which offers an example of the way in which the Inca conquests were accomplished.

Tupac Yupanqui was a great warrior. He led his armies personally and remained at the head of his troops in combat. To him are owed the majority of the conquests of the Inca state. Although Huayna Capac followed the path blazed by his predecessor, the same is not true of Huascar, nor of Atahualpa. The former did not leave Cusco except for some inspections, and only at the end of his reign, after continual defeats, did he himself assume command of the armies against his brother. Likewise, Atahualpa rarely took personal command, instead delegating the war against Huascar to his generals.

What might this attitude of leaving the task of preserving the enormous territory of Tahuantinsuyu in the hands of others indicate? Did it result from increased administrative responsibilities at home or perhaps from the loss of warlike spirit? Might it signal the beginnings of a division between military and administrative leadership?

On the other hand, if the Incas became soft and relied on their generals to preserve their domains, they ran the risk of sooner or later being deposed by more warlike leaders, since the law of the "most able" demanded a permanent state of alert.

The Conquests of Huayna Capac

Although the reign of Huayna Capac ended only shortly before the appearance of the Spanish on the coasts of ancient Peru, the chroniclers do not agree on the sequence in which his conquests occurred, nor on the events in general.

To this Inca fell the preservation of the acquired territories and the continued widening of his domains. It has been noted, however, that in the peripheral regions of the Inca realm, in Chile as well as in the jungle regions and in the northern reaches, the ancient Andean custom of reciprocity was not in force. Without its mediation, expansion could occur only through conquest and annexation of new peoples by means of bloody wars. What can we conclude from this fact?

The absence of the practice of reciprocity indicates that we are dealing with ethnic groups located in the regions farthest from the cultural nucleus, among which the customs of the most organized regions of the South American world did not exist. It is also likely that the natives of these remote regions did not see the advantages of joining the planned world of the Incas. Besides, they had little to lose, unlike the Chinchas, whose long-distance trading relations could have been ruined if they did not essentially submit to the Incas.

To analyze the differences among the chronicles concerning the conquests of Huayna Capac, I follow principally the word of Cieza de León, with a look at how it diverges from that of the others. The first years of Huayna Capac's rule were devoted to visiting his domains near Cusco. Cieza de León (*Señorío*, chap. 63) makes reference to an inspection of the Soras, Lucanas, and Andahuaylas. According to this chronicler, the Inca undertook no conquest or long-distance travel while his mother, Coya Mama Ocllo, was still alive. It appears that she begged her son not to absent himself for long periods from Cusco (Cobo, 1956, vol. 2, chap. 16; *Señorío*, chap. 61), while the extent of lands under his control was such that to visit all of them, a reigning Inca would have to spend several years away from the capital.

As recounted by Cieza and a consensus of the other chroniclers, Huayna Capac, after a prolonged stay in Cusco, during which he continued his building projects, left to visit the southern region of his domains. First, he traveled through Collao, observing how they filled the state storehouses with fine woolens, and selected the young girls for the *aclla huasi*, the Inca workshops. He passed through Chuquiapo and from there continued on to Charcas, reaching the region of the Chichas. During his stay in the south, the Inca observed the functioning of the state organization, the creation of *mitmaq*, the construction of *tampu*, roads, ritual baths, and so on. He continued his visits through Tucumán and La Plata, where he dispatched several captains to fight the Chiriguanas, although the harshness of the land forced them to return defeated.

According to the account of Sarmiento de Gamboa (chap. 59), while Huayna Capac was visiting the Collao, he sent his uncle Guaman Achachi by the route of Chinchaysuyu to inspect the country as far as Quito. Meanwhile, the Inca headed for Charcas, Cochabamba, and Pocona, continuing south by way of Coquimbo and Copiapó. During his stay in the south, news arrived concerning rebellions in Quito, Pasto, and Huancavilca that forced the ruler not only to return to Cusco but also to raise armies among the people of Collao for the new campaign in the north (Sarmiento de Gamboa, chap. 59). In this uprising against Cusco, the northerners killed the Inca governors. The same would happen when the Spaniards seized Atahualpa in Cajamarca, since no document we have found mentions the presence of Inca administrators living among the ethnic groups.

According to Cieza (chap. 62), the Inca remained in Chile for twelve lunar months, pacifying the country and building fortresses. Before abandoning the region, he left governors to continue the task of implanting the Inca system. It is worth mentioning that upon returning to Cusco, Atahualpa was born in the capital, to a princess by the name of Tuta Palla.

According to Cieza, it was after this stay in the south that Huayna Capac prepared his first voyage to the north in his capacity as ruler. Each departure of a reigning Inca involved elaborate preparations, which included many kinds of sacrifices, including *capaccocha*, the supreme human sacrifice. He also had to raise an army and convoke the chiefs so that they would provide men for the armies. The roads by which the Inca and his troops would travel were repaired or widened, and the storehouses had to be filled with the necessary supplies for the armies en route. The Inca could not depart Cusco without sumptuous festivals during which the ties of reciprocity and loyalty were reaffirmed between the ruler and the *panaca*, the chiefs of the macroethnic groups and the governors in charge of administering the state.

Once again Huayna Capac was on the march, with an entire entourage of military chiefs, lords, women, guards, and troops. It is probable that he advanced slowly, as the chroniclers of the conquest describe Atahualpa in the region of Cajamarca. Wherever the Inca passed, the local lords came to do him reverence and render him obedience. When he arrived in Vilcas, he was lodged in the quarters that had been ordered built by Tupac Yupanqui. Then he passed through the valley of Jauja, where he intervened in a controversy among the local lords over borders and boundaries. From there the Inca sent two envoys, one to the Yauyos and the other to the people of the coast, and continued advancing to Pumpu, where he remained briefly, anxious to arrive at Guzmango.

During his stay in Cajamarca, the Inca set out for Chachapoyas, where the local lords had rebelled and taken refuge in a fortress. Twice the ruler was repelled by the natives, until with the help of new reinforcements he ended the rebellion. Many Chachapoyas were sent to Cusco, while *mitmaq* composed of loyal and reliable people arrived to protect the borders of the Inca realm.

Differing from Cieza, Cobo (1956, vol. 2, chap. 16) says that after pacifying the Chachapoyas, the Inca returned to Cusco and went to rest in the
valley of Yucay, where he devoted himself to overseeing the construction of
palaces and temples. After a time, according to this chronicler, Huayna
Capac returned to the south, to Tiahuanaco, Cochabamba, Pocona, Lupaca,
and elsewhere; while in Collasuyu, he made his call for people to form
armies for the purpose of marching on Tumipampa.

According to Cieza de León, after achieving peace in Chachapoyas,
Huayna Capac continued north and entered the jungle against the Braca-
moros (chap. 64), but, as it was an inhospitable place with barbarous people,
he decided to withdraw. He then reached Surampalli, his birthplace, in
Cañar country, where he "relaxed to extreme." It is likely that during his
stay there he ordered it renamed Tumipampa, after his *panaca* (Rostworowski, 1983). While there, he received news of a revolt in Cusco and sent
orders to behead the principal rebels.

During this period, the Inca waged against ethnic groups in the north
wars that were won at great cost in human life. Whereas the soldiers of the
Inca fought without conviction, wishing only to return to their villages as
quickly as possible, the northerners were fighting in defense of their freedom
and their peoples. All were hard battles. According to Cieza, a defensive
league was organized among the Caranquis, Otavalos, Cayambis, Cochas-
quis, and Pifos, something the Inca did not expect. Before entering into
combat, he offered the establishment of ties of reciprocity, which they, of
course, refused (Cieza, *Señorío*, chap. 66).

Cobo recounts in detail the wars against the northern tribes. Huayna
Capac convened his military chiefs in Tumipampa to determine how they
would proceed in the conquest and pacification of the region. It was decided
to open the fighting in Pasto, in the extreme north. For this purpose, three
armies were organized: one with people from Collao, under the command
of captains Mollo-Cavana of the Lupaca nation of Hilavi, and Mollo Pucara
of Hatun Colla; the second army from Cuntisuyu, commanded by two
chiefs, Apu Cavac-Cavana and Apu Cunti Mullu; and the third army, composed of people of diverse provenance as well as two thousand Inca noblemen under the command of Auqui Toma and Coya Tupa. I mention this
information concerning the composition of the troops who marched north
because it shows the typical formation of the armies in the Andean world:
divided into three parts, with each army commanded by two chiefs (Cobo,
1956, vol. 2, book 12, chap. 16). This formation is identical with that of
the Chanca troops when they left their homeland to conquer the world of
that time, and it is clear evidence of the nature of the system itself.

The march on Pasto was a success. In their victory celebrations, however, the Inca armies neglected to remain on their guard, permitting the natives to fall on them and wreak great carnage. Huayna Capac reacted by rallying the dispersed troops and, with new reinforcements, personally marched at the front of his men to crush the rebellion.

The Inca, desiring to dominate the entire region, subsequently directed his forces against the Caranquis and Cayambis, with Apu Cari, lord of Chucuito, as one of his generals. The natives took refuge in a fortress, and in one of the battles that followed unexpectedly left their stronghold to attack the Cusco nobles who were the backbone of the armies. The surprise assault forced the Inca nobles backward, and in their confusion they dropped the Inca from his litter, leaving him to fall into enemy hands had it not been for captains Cusi Tupa Yupanqui and Huayna Achachi, both of the high Inca nobility. Still, according to Cobo's account (chap. 17), Huayna Capac returned to Tumipampa in front of his army and made his entrance into the city on foot, and not in his litter, as had been his custom.

Not content with these victories, the Inca sent new troops against the Cayambis and Caranquis under the command of his brother Auqui Toma. In a hard-fought battle, the noblemen had seized control of four walls of the fortress when Auqui Toma fell mortally wounded. The natives' accounts of their wars invariably emphasize the reaction of flight and disorder among the troops when the chief falls prisoner or dies on the battlefield, as was the case on this occasion.

In Cobo's account, it was after these events that reinforcements arrived from Cusco, led by Apo Mihi and the other generals. According to some chroniclers, these chiefs arrived at Tumipampa because of Huayna Capac's tumble from his litter. In any case, we have seen the attitude of the Inca nobles toward the requirements of reciprocity, as illustrated by this episode.

In his haste to fight and desire for revenge from the rebels, Huayna Capac overlooked the tradition of reciprocity and ordered the recently arrived troops to march to the front. Profoundly angered by this discourtesy, the Inca nobles grabbed the statue of Manco Capac, according to one version, and that of Huanacauri, according to another, and began to return to Cusco. Once advised of this, the Inca hastily dispatched rich gifts and favors for the nobles, who, satisfied by his attitude, returned to Tumipampa and prepared to attack the rebels. Cobo mentions the formation of the three armies: one under Apo Mihi and the second composed of people of Chinchaysuyu, although he does not name the commanders of the third army. The chroniclers are in agreement that the courage and valor of the Incas permitted them to win the battle, and that the Inca reprisals were so great that the lake near the fortress turned red from the quantity of blood spilled, for which it became known as Yahuarcocha.

According to Sarmiento de Gamboa (chap. 60), Huayna Capac spent many years in Tumipampa, his preferred residence. It appears likely that, as his birthplace, he considered it more enjoyable than Cusco.

Huayna Capac also spent long years fighting against the northern ethnic groups, and after arduous battles was able to incorporate them into the Inca state. News arrived in Quito of strange bearded people, sailing in great wooden houses, who had made contact with the coastal peoples. In the year 1526, Francisco Pizzaro and his men had made their appearance on the coasts of the Inca realm. Messengers reached the Inca with this disquieting news, leaving the ruler impressed by their accounts of the recently disembarked bizarre personages (Cieza de León, *Señorío*, chap. 62).

According to Sarmiento de Gamboa (chap. 62), before the third voyage of Pizarro a tremendous epidemic of smallpox and measles broke out in the northern provinces. These evils were unknown there until that time, and they produced great havoc in the Andean world, since the population lacked immunity against them. Among the victims of the plague was the Inca Huayna Capac, who died in Quito.

As has been noted, there are serious discrepancies in the chronology of the conquests of Huayna Capac, even though the end of his reign coincided with the appearance of the Spaniards. Nevertheless, the most striking feature of these campaigns is that in the extreme north, as well as in Chile, in the south, the traditions of reciprocity were unknown. The immediate consequence of the absence of this custom in these two regions was the resort to force.

Rebellions of the Local *Señoríos* and of Members of the Nobility

The history of the Incas would be neither complete nor accurate without reference to the frequent rebellions of the ethnic lords against the Cusco regime. Generally, in the narratives and accounts concerning the history of the Incas, one detects a certain tendency to idealize it, and to portray an idyllic Inca state in the Andes. The constant uprisings that shook the "provinces" of Tahuantinsuyu prove the existence of discontent among the ethnic chiefs in the face of Inca oppression and domination. The brief duration of the Inca expansion permitted neither consolidation of their territorial possessions nor development of a consciousness, on the part of these lords, of belonging to a state.

Predominant among the inhabitants of the Inca state was loyalty to the homeland, the *ayllu*, the village, and the local or regional lord. Loyalty to the state was totally missing. Therefore, it was impossible to awaken in the masses and among the local leaders a feeling of union or a defensive cohesiveness when the dangerous foreigners appeared. The Inca state had still not been able to create among its inhabitants a sense of belonging to a nation. If the Andean world had continued to evolve on its own, without European interference, perhaps it might have achieved with time the effective union of the ethnic groups around the Incas. We can only record that such a process was cut short and cannot guess what might have occurred.

These constant rebellions reveal the lack of unity within the Inca state. The so-called Inca peace was more apparent than real, interrupted, as it was, by frequent uprisings, at times bloody and prolonged. The numerous disturbances also help explain the rapid fall of the Inca state following the appearance of the Spanish conquerors. With the Spanish presence, the local lords felt themselves liberated from Inca rule, and the weak ties of reciprocity and kinship that linked the regional lords with the masters of the Inca realm were quickly broken.

Moreover, in addition to uprisings by the chiefs of the macroethnic groups, there were frequent revolts among the highest elite of the Inca nobility itself. The customs that governed the inheritance of power encouraged the pretensions of many candidates to the office of Supreme Inca, increasing the weakness of the central power during changes of government and encouraging confrontations among the members of the nobility. (I return to these internal difficulties in Cusco when dealing with the question of succession.) These unsettling revolts appear from the outset of the territorial expansion of the Inca state. Before this period they were internal conflicts that took place, above all, at the end of each Inca's rule.

During the early period of the subjugation of the Collao, at the time of the reigns of Pachacutec and Tupac Yupanqui, there were frequent revolts by the Aymaras. Only beginning with the rule of Huayna Capac do the highland ethnic groups appear to have become integrated into the Inca state, as evidenced by their full participation in the wars in the far north. At that time, a great contingent of troops from Collasuyu and Cuntisuyu fought in the campaigns against the Ecuadorian ethnic groups.

The first Aymara insurrection took place when Inca Yupanqui entered the Andean jungle region. The Huamallas, Hatuncollas, Chucuitos, and Azángaros, taking advantage of his absence in an inhospitable region with difficult communications, joined forces and took up arms. Their first action was to kill the governors appointed by the Incas (Cieza de León, *Señorío*, chap. 53). The rebels then took refuge in their fortress and declared war on the Incas. The latter were in time victorious, and the leaders of the movement were sent as prisoners to Cusco. The Inca ordered that from then on there were to be only a limited number of Aymara in the capital, so that when new contingents of soldiers from Collao arrived in Cusco, an equal number had to leave the city.

Sarmiento de Gamboa (chaps. 40 and 41) recounts that Pachacutec had to conquer the highlands three times, and that it was the Aymaras who most frequently rose up against him. A new insurrection broke out during the reign of Tupac Yupanqui (chap. 50). Although Sarmiento's account of it appears to be the same as Cieza's, he places it during the reign of another ruler.

One of the most dangerous attempts at rebellion occurred during the reign of Tupac Yupanqui. The source was not a subject lord, however, but the Inca's own brother, Tupa Capac. He was an important individual who occupied the position of inspector of the recently conquered territories and enjoyed the confidence of the ruler. His property, lands, and servants were numerous. Not content, however, with these possessions, he began to conspire against the ruler himself. In spite of the secrecy surrounding the conspiracy, word of it reached the Inca, who ordered an investigation and a cruel punishment for the guilty (Sarmiento de Gamboa, chap. 51). Cieza (*Señorío*, chap. 56) narrates the occurrence of another disturbance in Cusco, while Tupac Yupanqui was in Tumipampa, which was quickly put down by those responsible for the care and government of the capital.

One means of suffocating rebellions, by employing the magical powers of the idols, is described by Avila's informants (1966:131; Salomon and Urioste 1991). They tell of a curious intervention of the *huacas* in an insurrection by the inhabitants of the central coast. This occurred when the Alancunas, Calancus, and Chaquis rose up and managed to maintain a state of rebellion for twelve years. In response, the ruler convened his principal *huacas* so they could help him end this embarrassing situation. Convening the gods in the plaza of Aucaypata in Cusco, the Inca told them that he had always granted offerings and sacrifices to all the *huacas*, and that in this moment of need he expected to be able to count on their support.

A prolonged silence followed the words of Tupac Yupanqui. This silence was interrupted by Pachacamac, who said he could do nothing because, if he moved to vanquish the rebels, he would annihilate the Inca and the entire world as well. He was referring to his principal attribute, as the god of earthquakes, he who controls and sends earth tremors. Then Macahuisa, son of Pariacaca, replied to the Inca. As he spoke, "his mouth blew the words as if they had weight, and from his mouth came smoke instead of breath." This *huaca* promised to support Tupac Yupanqui and left in the Inca's litter for the rebellious region. When he reached a mountain above the rebel villages, it began to rain, first a little, then in torrents, flooding the ravines, villages, and fields. The enemies of the Inca were annihilated, as lightning bolts killed the lords and principal nobles of the region. So it was told in Huarochirí of the opportune intervention of the *huaca* Macahuisa. This mythical recounting of a rebellion in the Cisandean highlands may have some basis in truth, that is, that a rebellion ended as the result of a climatic disaster, with the precipitation of an avalanche of stones, mud, and water over the rebellious villages.

Perhaps Huayna Capac was the ruler who put down the greatest number of rebellions. The great extent of his state and his proximity to written history permitted better recording of the events of his reign.

According to Zarate (1944:46), one of the most serious uprisings was led by Chimu Capac, whose domains stretched along 100 leagues of coastline. The chronicler does not offer details concerning the events, only that the Inca emerged victorious and that the rebel leader was executed. After that time, the people of the coast were prohibited from carrying arms and were not called to join the armies of the Inca, indicating that the lord of Chanchan must have betrayed the Inca ruler while belonging to the forces of Tahuantinsuyu, after his submission to the Inca state.

That the peoples of the coast were not permitted to join the armies of the Inca is confirmed by other documents relating to the lowlands. In the 1549 inspection ordered by Licenciado La Gasca in the valley of Huaura, the ethnic lord at the *encomienda* of Nicolás de Riber the Younger was asked if formerly he sent men to serve in the wars of the Incas. He replied that as natives of the coast, they did not take part in those conflicts (Fernández de Oviedo, 1945, vol. 12:114). A statement to the same effect is found in the inspection of Atico and Caravelí in 1549. When a local chief by the name of Chincha Pula was questioned whether in pre-Hispanic times he contributed with men to the armies of the Inca, he responded negatively. This evidence tends to confirm the lack of confidence shown by the Incas in the inhabitants of the coast.

The suspicions produced by the insurrection of Chimor brought another consequence: the dispersion of its people, who were sent as *mitmaq* to numerous places throughout the Inca realm. Because of the important functions performed by many of these colonists in the towns where they were forced to live, I return later to this subject.

According to Cobo (1956, vol. 2, chap. 16), while Huayna Capac was in Jauja, news arrived of a rebellion by the lords of Chachapoyas. The Inca departed for that province, which he was able to pacify without much effort before continuing on to Quito.

According to Sarmiento de Gamboa (chap. 58), after spending a short time in Chachapoyas, the Inca returned to Cusco and then marched south to Cochabamba and Chile. During his stay in Tiahuanaco, he received the news of uprisings in Quito, which forced him to call for support and gather new troops. This time, his stay in the far north was longer, and he gradually came to dominate the entire region. Among the most rebellious chiefs was Tomalá of the island of La Puná, who took every opportunity to betray the Inca ruler.

It is likely that the lord of Pabur, of the region of Piura, became involved in one of these uprisings. In 1532, Francisco Pizarro, passing through the region en route to Cajamarca, was quartered in the great plaza of the chiefdom of the same name. He learned that it had been an important *señorío*, rich and heavily populated, but that it was destroyed and its towns burned for refusing to receive Huayna Capac peacefully (Fernández de Oviedo, 1945, vol. III:277).

In Tumipampa, Huayna Capac was informed by the *chasqui* of an attack on the Charcas by the Chiriguanas, a jungle people, who had killed the unwary fortress guards. The Inca sent a captain by the name of Yasca to put down the invaders. This captain took with him for support a number of idols, among them Catequil of Cajamarca and Huamachuco, Curichaculla of Chachapoyas, and Tomayrica of Chinchaysuyu (Sarmiento de Gamboa, chap. 61).

All these rebellions demonstrated the need to prevent uprisings, not only by the various ethnic chiefs but also in the core of the Cusco elite. One motive for insubordination that presented itself unfailingly, and at both levels, was the death of a reigning Inca. For this reason, the demise of a ruler was hidden until his successor was chosen, with every precaution taken to guard the secret of his death. Only the closest and most loyal members of the elite knew of the event, and only when the succession was decided was his death communicated to the inhabitants of the realm.

For this reason, the leading figures of the Inca court in Quito hid the death of Huayna Capac from the people and had his body embalmed and taken to Cusco, as if he were still alive (Guaman Poma, 1936, fol. 114). Later on, we shall see the disturbances in the capital, provoked by the nobility, in relation to the election of the new ruler.

The great distances of Tahuantinsuyu made it more and more difficult, in spite of the speed of the *chasqui*, to communicate the news of an uprising. To overcome to some extent the obstacles of distance, they devised the stratagem of having prepared firewood, well dried, on the peaks of the *cerros*, which could be ignited to announce the onset of a rebellion. Those waiting on the next elevation, on seeing the flames, would light another fire, with successive fires indicating both the existence and the direction of the rebellion. While waiting for the messengers with their *quipu* and news, the troops would be readied to march immediately.

The Inca Armies

There is no doubt as to the importance of the Inca armies and the preponderant role they played in the territorial expansion of the Inca state. I first examine the information provided by the chroniclers concerning the organization of the army, after which I analyze its development over time.

In the wars of conquest and in the organization of the troops the ethnic divisions were preserved, and the *señoríos* designated to contribute to the military *mita* provided soldiers led by their own chiefs. In the wars in the far north, during the rule of Huayna Capac, it was the Collas and inhabitants of Cuntisuyu who made the heaviest contributions of men. We can guess that the Inca had more confidence in them because they had been incorporated into Tahuantinsuyu long before, or simply because it was a large, heavily populated region that could afford the absence of so many men. In some cases, the violence of the fighting and high mortality rate of the northern wars was such that few warriors returned to their *señoríos* of origin.

According to Cobo (1956, vol. 2, book 14, chap. 9) the Incas, as conquerors, greatly esteemed their armies and military chiefs. The troops were organized along political divisions, that is, in units of ten and one hundred, commanded by their own chiefs. Nevertheless, the Inca lineages held the highest positions in a hierarchy above that of the local commanders. There were also armies composed of royal *ayllus*, who probably constituted the elite troops.

The armies marched to war by ethnic groups, with those groups that had belonged longest to Tahuantinsuyu situated closest to the person of the Inca. The armies were divided into squadrons, each of which carried just one kind of weapon. There were archers, slingers, bearers of flint-edged *macanas* and other varieties of clubs, among others. Nor were they lacking musical instruments, such as drums, trumpets made of great marine shells, and flutes.

Fernández de Oviedo (1945, vol. 12:30) relates the order followed when the battle was begun: first came men with slings and stones the size of eggs, carrying shields and wearing suits of quilted cotton to protect themselves against projectiles. Behind them marched soldiers armed with clubs and axes. The former carried the Andean *macana*, a club with a sharp star-shaped stone fixed to the end, or clubs with hafted stones the thickness of a fist or sharp stone points. As for the axes, Fernández de Oviedo describes them as being similar to the European *alabardes* or battle-axes with heads of copper, gold, or silver according to the bearer's rank (Salas, 1950). Then advanced the bearers of small lances, which were thrown like darts, and, in the rear guard, lancers, with long weapons supported on the left shoulder, which was covered by a thick cloth suited for that purpose.

Cristóbal de Mena (in Fernández de Oviedo 1945:83) describes the magnificence of Atahualpa in Cajamarca shortly before he fell prisoner, when Hernando de Soto and Hernando Pizarro went to see him: "The chief's entire camp [i.e., Atahualpa's camp], from one end to the other, was closed off by squadrons of lancers, *alabarderos* and archers; another squadron of Indians with slings and *tiraderas* [straps used to propel arrows]; and others with clubs and *macanas*."

The chroniclers tell of how all the soldiers went to combat well adorned with jewels and costumes according to the customs of their places of origin. They wore headdresses and feathers over the shoulder and chest, and large plates of copper, silver, or gold according to their military rank. In some regions, their faces were painted to frighten the enemy. They attacked singing and shouting to create fear among the enemy troops. The shouting was such that, according to the chroniclers, the birds of the field fell to the ground terrified.

Diego de Molina, in his account inserted in the work of Fernández de Oviedo (1945, vol. 12:97), refers to the strength of the Inca armies and to their intimidation of the civilian inhabitants who did not bear arms. He also mentions that the soldiers fought with bows, arrows, clubs, poles, slings, and *macanas*, which they wielded with both hands. Later on, Molina adds (p. 97) that the warriors marched in squadrons, each with its particular weapon. The body of the army advanced first, and in the middle of the troops, protected by a rear guard, marched the porters. According to Cieza (1943), the men carried their cargo only to a predetermined point, where others would relieve them. This *mita* system made the work less arduous and unpleasant. On the other hand, during the conquests of Pizarro and the civil wars, the natives delivered by their chiefs to serve the Spaniards carried cargo and arms for an indefinite period, and few returned to their *ayllus* of origin, whether stranded along the way or dying en route (Espinoza, 1971).

In another work (1983), speaking of the dual command of the armies, I indicate that in the documents and chronicles there is mention of two chiefs for each army, with one representing the upper moiety and the other, the lower moiety. This division reflected the concept of duality in the Andean world, which was repeated in the rule of the chiefdoms, among the Incas themselves, and in the command of the state. In addition to this dual command of the troops, the chroniclers mention a tripartite organization of the armies as they entered battle, which similarly reflected the structure of Andean symbolic thought. This tripartite distribution of their troops did not originate with the Incas. Before the Inca expansion, the Chanca troops followed the same practice, which I believe corresponded to a religious and social ideology.

According to my hypothesis, this tripartite military formation corresponded to the pan-Andean divisions of Collana, Payan, and Callao. Collana was the elder brother, the *curaq*, the most important. Payan represented femininity; it is a term that comes from *paya*, the noblewoman. In the myth of the Ayar Siblings, Mama Huaco was the warrior and played an active role in the arrival and settlement of Manco Capac in Cusco. Similarly, in the Chanca siege of Cusco, a female chief at the head of her troops repulsed the attackers, a triumph that marked the beginning of the Inca expansion. In both Inca myths, the women fought as chiefs. The term *callao* referred to the younger brother, or *sullca*, in the dual division, and also to the common people.

Another myth related to the Inca armies deals with the legendary *pururauca* that transformed themselves into valiant warriors during the Chanca attack on Cusco, thus contributing to the Inca triumph. Santa Cruz Pachacuti (1927:170) recounts that an old priest of the Temple of the Sun called Topauanchire put some stones near the sanctuary, to which he added weapons and helmets to simulate posted soldiers. In the heat of battle a miracle occurred and the stones were turned into fierce soldiers and contributed to the Inca victory.

In Andean ideology, the gods and mythical personages were transformed into stones, while maintaining the ability to communicate with human beings. It was a form of indefinite perpetuation and sanctification. In the myth of the *pururauca* the reverse occurred, that is, the stones took living human form. The supernatural power that emanated from them produced terror among the natives, and because of this fear many enemy chiefs surrendered to the Incas without a fight (Cobo, 1956). Among the *pururauca* stones, in Cusco they especially worshiped one named Tanancuricota, who was venerated as a woman who appeared among the legendary soldiers. Through her, the feminine aspect was included in the epic of war (Rowe, 1979, CU–8:1).

In wars of importance, led by the Inca elite or by the ruler himself, the armies carried with them either the idol Huanacauri or an image of Manco Capac. The Chancas did the same, bearing carved representations of their two progenitors, Uscovilca and Ancovilca. What can we learn from the above accounts of the armies and conquests of the Incas? We find that the conquests of the Incas can be divided into three categories. The first type was common during the Late Intermediate Period and at the beginning of the Late Horizon, when the future capital was just one more chiefdom in the Andean world. These were usually wars of plunder, whose objective was to seize the spoils of the adversary. The chronicles mention repeated attacks against the same neighboring towns during various Inca regimes, with little or no territorial annexation.

The second type of conquest had a very different face. It was carried out by means of reciprocity and kinship ties established through the exchange of women and gifts. The advantage of such conquests consisted of avoiding actual fighting. They involved an agreement to accept Inca rule, receiving in return, according to reciprocity, sumptuous gifts and the communal consumption of food and drink in the public plaza. As the power of the Incas increased, the ruler had greater quantities of goods at his disposal to establish reciprocity with the macroethnic chiefs. The prestige of battle-hardened soldiers and the well-known "generosity" of the Inca were the preferred means employed for the aggrandizement of the state. It also happened that overwhelming fear of the Incas on the part of the ethnic lords prompted them to accept Inca overlordship peacefully.

The third category of conquest took place when Inca expansion reached its peak in the south, as well as in the north. These are the conquests of Huayna Capac on the borders of the Inca realm. It appears that in these border regions there developed a greater belligerence and aggressiveness, possibly owing to the absence of a tradition of reciprocity among the inhabitants of these regions. There was no place for the customs of the formal request or the granting of favors and gifts. When a local lord rejected the ties of reciprocity and decided to offer resistance to the Inca armies, war was initiated, from which the troops of the Inca ruler generally emerged victorious. The Inca generals carried out severe reprisals against the defeated lords, creating a climate of terror to discourage future confrontations or uprisings.

A defeated local chief was generally taken to Cusco for the victory ceremonies and then put to death. In his place the Inca designated someone loyal to him. In some cases he would name as chief someone of *yana* status, who was not subject to the rules of reciprocity. If the war of conquest had been of long duration, as in the case of Guarco, or constituted a direct offense or plot against the person of the Inca ruler, as in the case of Quivi, the punishment inflicted on the defeated *señorío* was even greater, and the sanctions fell on the entire male population.

These customs encouraged the submission of the ethnic chiefs to the requirements of peace and obedience to the Inca. They also explain the rapidity of Inca expansion, which was based not on long wars but on rapid acceptance of the superiority of the Inca forces.

For the wars of plunder and those undertaken within the tradition of reciprocity, the armies were convened for a definite and limited period of time. In addition, the border posts were manned by special *mitmaq*, whose function was to watch out for any attempt by foreigners to encroach on the territory of the state. Such was the case of the Incas sent to help the Chupaychos guard the border with the aggressive Panataguas (AMRREE).

Expeditions were carried out when there was no need for the workforce in the fields; that is, troops were convened for a short time only. It can be said that when distances were not great, the armies did not have a permanent character and were dissolved when the time came for agricultural work. In the *Relación* of Chincha, we find that there was a time for war and during that period it was dangerous to be absent from one's valley or leave one's town or village without risk of death (Castro and Ortega Morejón, 1974).

More information related to a specific time for carrying out military activities, at least for attacks on the coast, is provided by Cieza de León, who reports that fighting did not occur during the summer months because of the effects of the excessive heat on the highland forces (*Señorío*, chap. 59). Another factor that hindered the conquest of the coast during the summer months was the swift flow of the rivers and resulting difficulty in crossing the valleys. The natural routes for travel to the lowlands followed the courses of the rivers. During seasons appropriate for military operations, the soldiers, led by their own chiefs, marched accompanied in the rearguard by their women, each woman taking care of her man and, if he was wounded, nursing and feeding him.

With the expansion of the Inca state and resulting long distances involved in the military campaigns, it became impossible for the troops to return to their villages to participate in the agricultural work. The Incas resorted in these circumstances to the war *mita*. This permitted Inca armies to remain at the borders of the state for several consecutive years and meant that other men were made responsible for the crops and that their women remained in their *ayllus*, perhaps working in the fields in place of their men.

A direct consequence of this situation was the need for great storage facilities for food and military supplies of all kinds. There was also increased demand for storehouses along the trunk routes on which the troops marched, especially along the principal Cusco-Quito axis. The Incas had to construct thousands of kilometers of roads, bridges, shelters, administrative centers, and storehouses with adequate supplies. The routes marked by *tambos* and the storehouses in administrative centers such as Vilcas Huaman and Huanuco Pampa are evidence of this organizational development.

It appears likely that the expansionist policy of the Incas resulted in a demographic decline in the indigenous population, which would accelerate with the arrival of the Spanish. In fact, first the wars in the far north during the reign of Huayna Capac and later the confrontations between Huascar and Atahualpa demanded enormous contributions by the male population of the Inca realm.

In the last phase of Inca rule, one can see a change in the leadership tradition of the armies, in the command of the troops. The rulers who forged the great expansion went personally at the head of their armies. These include Tupac Yupanqui and Huayna Capac, who on only a handful of occasions left the command to their subordinates. Huascar and Atahualpa, on the other hand, stayed away from the battlefront, in their respective cities or in the rearguard, and it was their generals who were responsible for conducting the war. Huascar left Cusco only for the final battle, in which he fell, defeated by his brother's generals.

To what should this unwarlike spirit of the last Incas be attributed? Had the Inca state become overextended? Were Huascar and Atahualpa not confident with leaving the management of state politics to others? Had power changed the aggressiveness of the rulers? Did they fear internal and local revolts owing to serious discontent among both the *panaca* and the ethnic lords?

This last point, an indication of a transformation in the Inca state, would explain the lack of cohesion between the diverse ethnic groups and the central power, one of the reasons for the ease of its collapse. In fact, the interminable Inca wars of conquest must have produced increasing discontent among the ethnic lords, since on them fell the responsibility for providing a constantly increasing supply of soldiers. This contribution represented a decrease in the labor available for the functioning of their own chiefdoms. Innumerable labor services were needed to fulfill the other obligations demanded by the Inca administration: working the fields of the state, of the Sun, and of the principal *huacas* found in each *señorío*; the contributions of women as *mamacona*, of craftsmen to satisfy the demands of the court, of stoneworkers and builders for the state construction projects, and of the labor required to maintain roads and *tambos*.

The coastal lords were not required to provide men for the armies, but they were no better off for that. Each new ruler increased the amount of lands required by the state, which also required porters to transport the harvest from the fields to the state storehouses. Naturally, these were the best lands in the valley and were subtracted from the hacienda of the local chief. In addition, the coastal lords contributed large numbers of craftsmen of all kinds.

This situation permitted the fermentation of discontent among the ethnic lords and weakened and undermined the domination of the Inca, which was maintained principally through fear. While authority remained in the hands of a ruler such as Huayna Capac, who was feared and respected, the Inca realm remained at peace. Nevertheless, given the way in which Inca hegemony was forged, there must have been an increasing restlessness among the Andean population subject to the Inca rulers. Only some fortuitous circumstance was required for that power, more apparent than real, to collapse, as in fact occurred with the appearance of Pizarro's forces.

The ethnic lords saw in this moment the opportunity for liberation, and yielded to the foreigners in the hope of recovering their ancient freedom. After a time, following the Spanish Conquest, the natives began to realize their mistake and were seized by a tremendous sense of frustration in their desire for independence. They realized that the situation had worsened: Not only had the weight of the yoke increased, but their beliefs and their religion were affected. It was then that a nostalgia for the past began to develop. The consequences would be the numerous peasant rebellions throughout the Colonial Period and the rise of Taqui Oncoy, the belief in a return to the primordial time of the rule of the *huacas* (Bornoz, 1967).

THE SUCCESSIONS AND CO-RULE

The civil war between Huascar and Atahualpa that broke out after the death of Huayna Capac was not a unique or even unusual phenomenon in Andean history. On the contrary, these circumstances were repeated at the end of each regime. The anarchic situation was a result of the traditions of succession and the struggle for power that broke out with greater or lesser intensity at the death of an Inca. The principal reason for conflict was the absence of laws governing the inheritance of power, aggravated because various members of a group of the deceased Inca's followers could aspire to rule and enjoyed equal rights and prerogatives.

The chroniclers accepted as given that in pre-Hispanic Peru the oldest legitimate son of a ruler inherited the throne. Nevertheless, by studying of the chronicles to verify the events that followed the death of each Inca, we discover that the traditions of succession were quite different.

If the indigenous laws had been similar to the European model, we would expect to find, in the archival documents and the chronicles, detailed references concerning the rights of primogeniture and genealogical trees, with mention of greater and lesser branches, among others, to indicate who was in the line of succession. On the contrary, we find no such thing among either the Incas or the other ethnic lords. The chroniclers themselves contradict their own affirmations regarding rules of succession when they refer to specific cases.

First, let us look at the evidence regarding the inheritance of power among the ethnic chiefs, after which I will examine in detail succession among the Incas. Observing the traditions in the Andean world enables us to appreciate the established customs, and we can assume that the Incas, at least in their beginnings, did not differ in their traditions from the other lords of the vast region.

In early times, the war chief was elected on the basis of his bravery and ability by the adult members of the ethnic group. Garcilaso (1941, book 4, chap. 10:325) mentions a variety of customs governing inheritance among the ethnic chiefs before Inca domination. Although he indicates the prevalence of the custom of primogeniture, he also mentions that in some "provinces" succession fell on "the son most beloved by his subjects," apparently more an election than an inheritance. Garcilaso goes on to say that in other places succession passed from one brother to another before returning to the son of the oldest brother. Castro and Ortega Morejón (1974) affirm that in the valley of Chincha, before and after Inca domination, they selected as lord the chief who was most appropriate for the office, and did not consider if he was son, uncle, brother, or cousin of the deceased ruler.

In the *Informaciones de Toledo* (Levillier, 1935, vol. 2:46, 50–51, 57) there are many references to the election of the most able son of a chief. Cobo (1956, vol. 2, book 12, chap. 25) affirms that on the death of a local lord, the Inca left authority in the hands of the eldest son only if he was capable, and that if he was not, another was selected. Santillán (1927, chap. 17) indicates that at the death of a lord of a *pachaca* (an administrative unit of 100 families), a "virtuous and competent" man was elected from among the group of lords, without taking into account if he was a relative of the deceased (Cabello de Valboa, 1951, book 2, chap. 17:330; Jiménez de la Espada, 1885, vol. 1:72; vol. II:111).

Las Casas (1923, chap. 14) says that the inheritance of rulership among the chiefs consisted of the election of the most capable person to govern, and that preference was given to the deceased ruler's sons. The elected individual "was given the responsibilities of rulership on a trial basis . . . while the lord was still alive, and could correct or amend his errors." Las Casas adds that this was a custom found throughout the Indies.

The government of the Viceroy Toledo produced a compendium of obligations of the local bosses during the Colonial Period (Las Obligaciones), for which questions were asked concerning the successions of the ethnic lords. In the *Recopilación de Leyes de Indias* it was recommended that regarding the inheritance of the office of local chief no changes be made, "leaving the succession to ancient right and custom." Nevertheless, Spanish custom quickly began to prevail, which caused an increasing number of lawsuits concerning the inheritance of leadership positions.

In the first years after the Conquest, and above all during the civil wars, the successions of the chiefdoms continued as during the time of the Incas, except that the approval of the selection belonged to the Spanish *encomendero* in place of the Inca. With the pacification of the country and establishment of the viceroyalty, judgments concerning the inheritance of the *señoríos* were sent to the Real Audiencia, and followed the ordinary course of decisions with all their terms and trials that could last months or years. The natives loved such lawsuits and prolonged them even more, with all the inconveniences and costs involved. For these reasons we find a good number of these proceedings in the archives.

Some years ago I worked with manuscripts from the north coast dealing with suits pursued by the ethnic chiefs for the inheritance of chiefdoms (Rostworowski, 1961). One of those dealt with the succession of the *señorío* of Reque, Callanca, and Monsefú. The evidence of these proceedings was that election to the office of chief could fall on a son, brother, or any other person who could be shown capable of filling the position. Not only do the facts as narrated in the proceedings support this conclusion, but the native customs operative in Reque and other towns on the coast are further confirmed in the *Probanza de Oficio* (AGN–Derecho Indígena, book 29, 1595). It should be emphasized that before the Spanish Conquest, each of the old chief's brothers governed the ethnic group in turn.

A similar situation is described in proceedings from the *señorío* of Nariguala of Piura in 1575. In the suit it is mentioned that it was the Inca who designated a chief's successor and that it was not considered whether a candidate was eldest son of the deceased or some other relative, but that he had "good understanding" and showed himself to be capable and adequate (Rostworowski, 1961).

In La Punta de la Aguja, Nonura, and Pisura in Piura, the absence of primogeniture is evident in that all the sons and daughters of a lord could aspire to power. According to native law, the principal condition for ascent to power was the ability and capacity to carry out the duties of the office, and for this same reason children under legal age were automatically excluded.

The *señorío* of Lambayeque emphasized generational successions, that is, from brother to brother before passing on to sons. An example confirming this practice is the succession of Chullumpisan and of his brothers Cipromasa and Fallempisan (Cabello de Valboa, 1951; Rostworowski, 1961). In the manuscript cited by Vargas Ugarte (1942), Fallempisan was followed in office by his four brothers, each in turn (although all of them had sons), before the next generation succeeded to power. The same pattern is found in the 1573 *Visita* to Guancayo, in the valley of Chillón, near Lima, where brothers, rather than sons, succeeded to office (Rostworowski, 1977).

On the other hand, everything appears to indicate that among the Incas inheritance passed to the son of the sister, as happened to the son of Inca Roca and Mama Micay. She belonged to the *señorío* of the Guallacanes, whose chief, her brother, sent messengers asking Inca Roca to send him their son to make him heir to his title and chiefdom.

More information can be found in the wills of the ethnic lords. These colonial-period proceedings are extremely valuable for the information they provide about indigenous customs of inheritance and the practices and priorities of the relatives of the deceased. While to some extent they follow Spanish inheritance models, these wills also preserve important remnants of indigenous traditions.

In the will of Don Hernando Anicama, lord of Lurín, in Ica, in 1561, we see that this individual, although he had several sons, bequeathed his *señorío* to his brother Alonso Guaman Aquije, who held the office of "second person." In addition to the title, the new lord inherited most of his brother's possessions, including his lands. Also favored in the will was the deceased chief's sister, who also received lands. The old lord also indicated his wish that his sons succeed in turn upon the death of his brother (Rostworowski, 1977b, 1982).

Another example is that of Don Diego Collín, who in 1598 was lord of Machangara or Machocco in the valley of Panzaleo, Ecuador (Caillavet, 1982). Don Diego had inherited the office from his father and decided at that time, for unknown reasons, to divide his *señorío* in two parts. Half remained under his authority, while the other half was given his "principal nephew," Don Andrés Espín. (We do not know why this individual was considered a principal.) In his will Don Diego Collín left his half to the son of the daughter of his sister, adding in his testament that his two heirs were "very capable."

A case that illustrates the native tradition, despite its late date, 1622, is that of Don Luis de Colán, who in his testament indicated that he did not have children and that he was leaving the chiefdom to his brother, Don Domingo, instead of to Phelipe Temoche, his grandson. In the north it was common to find women performing the functions of lords. They governed with the title of *capullana*, and the inheritance could be passed down through the female lines.

The examples just given emphasize the importance of the candidates' ability as the principal criterion for inheritance of power. Naturally, as I said, underage children were not considered for succession. Second, in cases where more than one individual was qualified for the office, elections were held that might vary according to local norms and customs. Third, it can be seen that among some ethnic groups the rights of brothers predominated, in the sense of exhausting first the members of one generation before passing on to the next. Among others, we can see the authority of the lord to name his successor or to bequeath his power to: (1) his own son, whether the eldest or a younger son; (2) a brother; (3) a son of his sister's. Under Inca rule, the elected chief had to receive the approval of the Inca and could be deposed in favor of someone considered more loyal to the Inca.

If such were the Andean traditions of succession among the ethnic lords, the Incas could not, in their beginnings, be distinguished from the general rule. What happened, then, in Cusco, according to the information in the chronicles?

Betanzos (1968, chap. 16), referring to the selection of the eldest son of the *coya* or queen, indicates that if she had had only daughters, the selection would have been made among the sons of the secondary wives, for the one who "showed himself to be able to rule and govern his kingdom and republic."

Santillán (1927) says that sons succeeded their fathers, but that the succession fell not

> necessarily on the eldest, but to the one who the father loved best and whom he wished to leave as king and in life gave him the tassel which was the insignia of kings, and with it he was selected to rule upon the death of his father . . . and *the Inca always chose the best man among his sons, or one who he had had with a sister or woman of his lineage.* (My italics)

If the Inca and his heir died, "the Inca *orejones* or principal persons chose another of his brothers and gave him the tassel" (as happened on the death of Ninancuyuchi, son of Huayna Capac).

Guaman Poma (1936, folio 18) relates that the heir had to be a son of the *coya*, "and they did not consider if he was older or younger, but someone who was elected by the Sun." Here, in place of mentioning dignitaries with the right to elect, it is the Sun who is the giver of power. Murúa (1946) considers the sons of the *coya* to be the natural heirs. Among these, we are told, succeeded "the one among all who was the most astute and capable man for war and for government . . . and if the first prince in line was not apt for rule and did not have brothers, then, in the same order, he among the bastard sons who was "the best man and possessed the required qualities" would inherit. The principals convened to elect the successor, who was frequently the son of the sister of the deceased ruler.

This information is extremely important because it shows that the right to succession was based on the prerogative of the son of the sister, a situation similar to the case just cited of the the *señorío* of the Guallacanes, which requested the son of Mama Micay, wife of Inca Roca, as ruler of its lands. Owing to the preponderant role of the maternal uncle, the later custom of matrimony between the Inca and his sister can be explained as an effort to assure the inheritance of power, not via the paternal side, but through the maternal line.

Thus, an analysis of the information provided by the chroniclers themselves indicates that their often-cited affirmations concerning succession from father to son reflected their own European cultural assumptions rather than accounts or observations of actual Andean traditions.

According to traditional historiography, the first Incas belonged to the dynasty of Lower Cusco, with power subsequently passing to that of Upper Cusco. The tradition of leaving the government to the most able individual led to favoritism. Elections engendered disputes, revolts, and coups, and election results, instead of being guided by the merits of the candidates, depended on intrigues, vested interests, and political cliques, as we shall see when we turn to the Inca successions according to the traditional chronology. Sinchi Roca did not designate his oldest son, Manco Sapaca, as lord of Cusco but, rather, Lloque Yupanqui. The latter's selection caused no disturbance, whereas that of Maita Capac was followed by fratricidal conflicts. An Inca by the name of Tarco Huaman was deposed in favor of Capac Yupanqui. Something similar occurred at the end of the reign of Capac Yupanqui, which was disrupted by internal strife in which Quispe Yupanqui, son of the Inca, was killed and the ruler himself fatally poisoned by one of his concubines.

To ensure the ascent of his designated heir, Inca Roca, the ruler of Hanan Cusco, associated his son Yahuar Huacac with his government, a means adopted to eliminate struggles for power. The government of Yahuar Huacac was continually shaken by insurrections and conspiracies; his heir, Pahuac Gualpa, was assassinated, and shortly afterward the Inca himself died at the hands of the people of Cuntisuyu, who considered his expansionist tendencies dangerous.

Under these circumstances, the principal lords met and elected Viracocha as ruler, at the suggestion of a woman of Hanan Cusco (Cieza de León, *señorío*, chap. 28). This Inca, in turn, following the example of Inca Roca, associated his son Urco with his government as his co-ruler.

The appearance of Cusi Yupanqui as defender of Cusco has been discussed along with the beginnings of Inca expansion and the wars against the Chancas. His repeated victories over his enemies demonstrated his ability and therefore the right to assume power. With this individual, who took the name Pachacutec Inca Yupanqui upon assuming power, began the grandeur and territorial expansion of the Incas. After many years of rule he decided to assure his succession by associating his son Amaru Yupanqui with his government as his co-ruler, an act he hoped would avoid the chronic conflicts that followed the death of an Inca (Cabello de Valboa; La Casas; Santa Cruz Pachacuti Sarmiento de Gamboa). Years later, the ruler reversed this appointment after concluding that Amaru did not possess all the qualities he sought in his successor. Apparently the heir was not a warrior, but a gentle individual who preferred to devote himself to agriculture and the construction of hydraulic canals. It was then that Tupac Yupanqui, youngest son of the ruler, was elected successor (Rostworowski, 1960a).

Before continuing with the successions, let us briefly examine Amaru and references to co-rule elsewhere in the Andean world. Although this prince was removed from command, he continued to play an important role in the government. One of his responsibilities was to visit the *huacas* and sanctuaries of Collasuyu in the company of Huayna Yanqui Yupanqui, his brother (Sarmiento de Gamboa, chap. 37). In the triumphal festivals celebrated when Tupac returned from his northern campaigns, Amaru occupied a place of honor next to the Inca. He also enjoyed a private palace where he could live apart from the other members of his *panaca*. Cobo tells us the name of his palace was Amaru Huasi. It was located on the road to the Andes, along with many small farms such as Chaquaytapara, in Carmenca, and Callachaca and Lucrichullo (Cobo, vol. 2, book 13, chaps. 12 and 14; Santa Cruz Pachacuti, 1927:191).

The removal of Amaru Yupanqui gave rise to another intentional source of confusion by Garcilaso, who inserted an Inca Yupanqui between the rule of Pachacutec and that of Tupac. Garcilaso's error was not one of citing one more Yupanqui in the *capaccuna* or list of rulers, but of having him rule alone and naming him as father of Tupac Yupanqui (Rostworowski, 1953).

We find a typical case of co-rule in the small *señorío* of Lima at the time of the founding of the city of Los Reyes in 1535. The chief then was the elderly Taulichusco, who, to ensure his succession, had associated his son Guachianamo with his government. When the old lord died, shortly before the assassination of Francisco Pizarro, his son automatically assumed the office (Rostworowski, 1981–82).

Many sources maintain that the custom of marriage of the heir or co-ruler with a sister was introduced with Tupac Yupanqui. We note that the term "sister." does not necessarily indicate a sister by the same mother and father, but also might refer to a half-sister, cousin, or woman of his lineage (González Holguín). Undoubtedly the Inca rulers were trying by this means to diminish the struggles for power by adding the support of traditional maternal rights to those of co-rule with the father. At first glance, naming a son as co-ruler appears to follow a patrilineal inheritance. The rights of the heir were further ensured, however, by royal incest – that is, by the marriage of the prince with his sister – which maintained the Andean right of the son of the sister (Hernández et al., 1987). Also, given the numerous descendents of an Inca, it was hoped that this practice might reduce the number of pretenders.

According to Toledo's informants (Levillier, 1940, vol. 2), Tupac Yupanqui did not reach an advanced age. He was said to be neither young nor old at the time of his death. The chroniclers do not mention a co-ruler, and in any case, his death was surrounded by mystery and contradictory information. Cabello de Valboa reports that Tupac died in Cusco from poisoning, but adds that his heir went to Cajamarca to mourn for him. Murúa insists that he was wounded by an arrow. Equally confused are the accounts surrounding Tupac's succession.

Sarmiento de Gamboa (chap. 34) says that Tupac Yupanqui was in Chinchero, on his lands and estates, when he fell ill and called together his lords and kin to designate as his heir Tito Cusi Gualpa, son of his sister and wife, Mama Ocllo. Nevertheless, the same chronicler says that shortly before this the Inca had named Capac Guari, his son by a secondary wife named Chuqui Ocllo, as his successor.

In spite of the secrecy that surrounded the death of an Inca, news of Tupac's demise quickly reached Cusco thanks to Curi Ocllo, a relative of Capac Guari, whose supporters then hurriedly began preparations for the Sun to confer on him the *mascapaycha*, ignoring or feigning ignorance of the change in designation of the heir.

On his part, Guaman Achachi, brother of Tupac Yupanqui and Mama Ocllo, convened the members of his *panaca*, who quickly armed themselves and rushed to find Tito Cusi Gualpa to proclaim him Inca. Fighting broke out between the factions of the two candidates, and Capac Guari was killed in the encounter. Other informants said that he was taken prisoner and sent to Chinchero, never to return. Cieza de León (*Señorío*, chap. 61) provides no details concerning these events but refers to rivalries among the Inca family members, and efforts to claim royal power by various sons of Tupac Yupanqui by different women.

Tito Cusi Gualpa was the name of Huayna Capac before being elected

ruler. It was customary for the ruler-elect to change names during the ceremony of the transfer of the tassel. There is a consensus among the sources
that Huayna Capac was too young to govern and therefore needed a regent.
Now, in the Andean world underage children were considered neither capable of serving in office nor eligible to do so. It appears that Gualpaya, the
apparent "co-ruler," seized the royal tassel upon the death of Tupac Yupanqui. He was deposed and killed, however, by Guaman Achachi, lord of
Chinchaysuyu and an uncle of Huayna Capac's, who had been instrumental
in eliminating Capac Guari and now finally succeeded in putting his
nephew on the throne. Then Huayna Capac, after ascending to power,
erased all memory of his predecessor (Murúa, 1962, chap. 29; Sarmiento de
Gamboa, chap. 57) and, to avoid further pretenders and conflicts, ordered
two of his brothers killed (Guaman Poma, 1936, folio 113).

Huayna Capac wed his sister Cusi Rimay in a solemn ceremony. The
roofs of the city were covered for the occasion with the finest cloths woven
with brilliant feathers of tropical birds. The young ruler left the palace of
his grandfather Pachacutec in his litter, while the princess took her own
from the palace of Tupac Yupanqui, and they proceeded to tour Cusco in
separate litters (Cabello de Valboa; Cobo Santa Cruz Pachacuti). It is likely
that their departure from different palaces reflects the *panaca* to which their
respective mothers belonged: Hatun Ayllu for Huayna Capac and Capac
Ayllu for the *coya*.

According to Santa Cruz Pachacuti, Cusi Rimay died giving birth to a
son named Ninancuyochi, while other chroniclers say that the *coya* had no
children. Huayna Capac then wished to take another sister as his principal
wife, but the princess did not accede to his wishes, preferring instead to
enter the *aclla huasi* as *mamacona*. According to Cieza (*Señorío,* chap. 62),
Huayna Capac then married another sister by the name of Chimbo Ocllo.

Although a ruler possessed numerous concubines from throughout his
realm, only the women belonging to the royal *panaca* were considered potential mothers of future candidates for rulership, owing to the custom of
double descendency and because the *panaca* were exogamous and matrilineal.

This analysis of the royal successions in Cusco demonstrates that the
panaca played an important role in the political life of the capital. If we add
to this the possible exogamous and matrilineal structure of the royal lineages, it is understandable that the candidates for power turned to advantage
their rights by their maternal *ayllus*. This situation encouraged the formation
of alliances among the lineages to which the mothers of the aspirants belonged. In addition, the maternal *ayllus* ranked the numerous sons of an
Inca. Obviously, not only was a mother's social status important, but so was

the size of her family. Large families were highly esteemed in the Andes, where an individual lacking an extended family was considered a *huaccha*, or orphan. For these reasons, research on the rulers of Cusco should take into account the female affiliations of each Inca. Polo de Ondegardo (1917: 117) claims that the women held in highest esteem for marriage, who were considered "wealthy," were those who counted on extensive kinship groups, since the system of reciprocity depended on having many relatives.

To understand the events that took place in Cusco after the death of Huayna Capac, we have to consider the identities of the mothers of Huascar and Atahualpa and review the available information regarding these two *coyas*. In view of the matrilineal rights of the *panaca* it is important to determine whether the mothers of the candidates belonged to royal lineages or were of "provincial" origin.

The Confrontation between Huascar and Atahualpa: The Mothers of the Pretenders to the Throne

According to most chroniclers, the mother of Huascar was Raura Ocllo, sister of Huayna Capac and member of the Capac Ayllu *panaca* of Tupac Yupanqui. This is of great importance for understanding the events that unfolded around the rivalry of the two brothers. Murúa (1962, vol. 2:122) confirms this version when he says that Huascar's mother belonged to the house of Tupac Yupanqui, and therefore her son was considered a member of that lineage and not of the Tumipampa *panaca* of his father.

The sources of controversy are the identity of Atahualpa's mother and that prince's place of birth. Cieza de León (*Señorío*, 1943, chap. 69) says that he made "strenuous inquiries" in Cusco to obtain information concerning the place of birth of Atahualpa. According to the nobles he consulted, Atahualpa had been born in Cusco and was older than Huascar. Cieza notes that his mother, Tupa Palla, belonged to a lineage of Upper Cusco or of Quillaco, and he denies that she was a Quiteña princess.

Sarmiento de Gamboa, always well informed through his consultations with Inca nobles, tells us that the mother of Atahualpa was called Tocto Coca and belonged to the lineage of Inca Yupanqui, that is to say, of Pachacutec. Santa Cruz Pachacuti (1968:308) contends that the mother of Atahualpa was called Toctollo, while Cobo refers to her as Tocto Coca (1956, vol. 2). Both chroniclers, without mentioning her place of origin, contend that Atahualpa was born in Cusco.

Murúa (1962, vol. 1) and Cabello de Valboa (1951:364) limit themselves to indicating that the mother of Atahualpa had already died when Huayna Capac left Cusco on his last voyage with the prince. Betanzos's *capaccuna*, or list of the rulers of Cusco, with which he opens his account, includes Atahualpa but not Huascar. This is a typical omission in Inca historiography, as we have seen, following the practice of interpreting events so as to avoid displeasing the following ruler. I have already mentioned the close relation between Betanzos, married to a relative of Atahualpa, and the relatives of the Inca. The suppression of Huascar from the *capaccuna* confirms the tie between Atahualpa and Hatun Ayllu, the *panaca* of Pachacutec.

In his discussion of the end of Huayna Capac's regime, Esquivel y Navia (1980, vol. 1:61) refers to the northern origin of the mother of Atahualpa. His list of Huayna Capac's descendants, however, contradicts this conclusion. Among the sons of the Inca he names "Thupa Atahuallpa, his mother was Tocto Ocllo Cuca Coya, this family is from Hatun Ayllu" (that is, of the lineage of Pachacutec). The origin of this information is not known, but it may be the version of the Inca nobility.

Now let us examine the controversy surrounding the northern origin of Atahualpa, for which Garcilaso de la Vega is the principal source. For several centuries his Royal Commentaries were the principal source for the history of the Incas and his account was accepted as accurate. A good part of the existing confusion surrounding the Incas and their achievements can be attributed to this author, whose chronicle contains many serious "mistakes."

This Inca historian belonged on his mother's side to the lineage of Tupac Yupanqui, and therefore, from the native point of view, to the *panaca* of Capac Ayllu. Huascar also belonged to this *panaca*, through his mother Raura Ocllo, which is why Garcilaso was his staunch supporter. The long domination of his chronicle, because of the absence of other publications and sources for the critical study of Andean customs, led to a blind acceptance of the *Garcilasista* version of history. In his favor, it is conceded that he worked with the purest indigenous spirit, manipulating events according to his pleasure. His hatred for the person and *panaca* of Atahualpa caused him to change the course of history without considering that the Inca's right to power was based on his being capable and adequate.

The erroneous points in Garcilaso's account are many. He makes every effort in his chronicle to diminish the image of Pachacutec, who was a prominent figure of rival Hatun Ayllu. For this reason, in his account of the victory of Viracocha over the Chancas, Garcilaso makes no mention of Uscovilca, the Chanca idol found by Polo de Ondegardo together with the mummified corpse of Pachacutec. Adrede confuses the mummies of the deceased Incas that he saw in Cusco before leaving for Spain. He adds to his history an Inca Yupanqui, between Pachacutec and Tupac, in order to omit Prince Amaru, who, as we have seen, was for a time co-ruler with Pachacutec and later deposed in favor of Tupac Yupanqui. Such circumstances made Garcilaso uncomfortable because they were unlike any in European history. Finally, he could not explain according to the traditions of the Old World the relationship between the sons of Huayna Capac or the importance of maternal ties. Both would be incomprehensible to the seventeenth-century European mind imbued with primogeniture, illegitimacy, and paternal rights.

For these reasons, Garcilaso promoted a version of history in which Huayna Capac divided the Inca realm between Atahualpa and Huascar, leaving the chiefdom of Quito to the former and the rest of the Inca state to the latter. This kind of partition resembled the division of a medieval European kingdom among a king's sons, and was therefore intelligible for the Spaniards of the sixteenth and seventeenth centuries. Besides, the Conquistadores were concerned with taking control of Peru and its precious metals, and not with learning about foreign customs of inheritance.

Garcilaso did not wish, or know how, to explain the different native customs, and so preferred to distort his account in order to accommodate his history to the European masters. It was to be a model piece, laudable in every way for his Spanish reader. He painted the Incas as whining and cowardly, instead of as a warrior people, conquerors who implanted their policies and defended their interests harshly and violently.

The chroniclers who hold that the mother of Atahualpa was from Quito, in addition to Garcilaso and Vásquez de Espinoza, who follows Garcilaso in all matters, are Pedro Pizarro, Zárate, Gutiérrez de Santa Clara, and López de Gómara. They refer to her as the widowed queen of the lord of Quito, while Guaman Poma (folio 114) gives her a Chachapoyano origin.

Juan de Velasco, in his *Historia de Quito*, cites Fray Marcos de Niza as his principal source for the legendary history of the Scyris, who ruled before the Inca conquest in the mythical kingdom of the Caras, Scyris and Puruhua. According to Niza, Huayna Capac had married the last descendant of these lords, and from this union was born Atahualpa.

In Ecuador, the work of Velasco and of his supposed informant, Niza, was regarded with great suspicion. Such was the opinion of the Archbishop González Suárez and of Jijón y Caamaño. According to Porras Barrenechea (1986), both the *Historia* of Velasco and the nonexistent chronicle of Niza have little credibility. Nevertheless, an Ecuadorian intellectual current has revived the myth of the Scyris for nationalistic purposes, but with no historical basis.

According to some chroniclers, neither Atahualpa nor Huascar was designated by Huayna Capac to succeed him. When the ruler was asked who he selected as heir, he named Ninancuyuchi, provided the augury were favorable. A commission of high-level dignitaries sought the prince, only to find that he had succumbed to the plague. When they returned to consult with Huayna Capac, they found that he, too, had expired.

It is at this moment that the palace intrigues around the next heir began, and the factions and supporters of the two candidates swung into action. Although the reader may find it boring, it is important to indicate the chroniclers who mention the selection of Ninancuyuchi. They are: Cabello de Valboa, Cobo, Murúa, Santa Cruz Pachacuti, and Sarmiento de Gamboa. On the other hand, the chroniclers in favor of the thesis that Huayna Capac ordered a division of Tahuantinsuyu before dying are the following: Diego de Molina, Estete (both in Fernández de Oviedo, 1945, vol. 12), and Garcilaso, followed by Vásquez de Espinoza. According to the rest, Atahualpa rebelled against Huascar.

Diego de Molina, Estete, and López de Gómara (the last named never stepped on Peruvian soil, but received information from the first Conquistadores) support the version of a partition of the Inca realm ordered or recommended by Huayna Capac, as well as the existence of a Quiteña princess who was the mother of Atahualpa. This is a result of their lack of knowledge of the Andean world, and of their judging circumstances according to their own sixteenth-century Spanish perspective. They could understand the fratricidal war only in terms of a partition analogous to European rights and historical experience. That is, the right of primogeniture favored Huascar, whereas the high nobility supported Atahualpa, thus justifying the latter's rebellion and explaining subsequent events. Otherwise, Atahualpa had to be considered a bastard with no possibility of justifying his right to power.

The chroniclers provided a European explanation for the struggle between the two brothers. On the one hand, they regarded Huascar as having a clear right, as the eldest son, to succeed Huayna Capac. On the other, Atahualpa's rebellion was explained as his prerogative as heir to a nonexistent kingdom of Quito. So it was that the Spanish invented a completely erroneous situation based on mistaken concepts and rights. If we analyze the data from an Andean point of view, the same events can be explained very differently.

Among the Incas, the right to rule was based on the matrilineal exogamy of the *panaca*, which gave preference to the son of the sister. In order for the succession to pass from father to son, an important first measure was co-rule, the association between father, while still alive, and son, chosen to succeed him. A second option was matrimony between the heir and his sister, to justify the Inca's wish to leave his power to his son.

Nevertheless, these precautions were not enough to eliminate or diminish the wars, intrigues, and conflicts that broke out at the death of a ruler. Such chronic problems were aggravated at the death of Huayna Capac by the tremendous territorial expansion of the Inca state, the distances, and the ease of remaining far from the capital and administrative center of Cusco. These circumstances gave the old local quarrels state dimensions with ample resonance and repercussions.

By reviewing the information gathered in the chronicles, we can discern two opposing "histories" of the war between Huascar and Atahualpa, both supported by statements by the chroniclers. In the face of such confusion of contradictory information, it is impossible to give an opinion concerning the "truth" of the events. Rather, to interpret them we must examine the unfolding of events surrounding the death of Huayna Capac carefully and with a critical spirit. I try to analyze the references supplied by the chronicles, when possible from an Andean, rather than European, perspective. In doing so, I am not taking an anti-Spanish position but simply recognizing that the Spanish and Andean traditions were very different. It would be equally absurd and mistaken to judge European history from an Andean perspective.

The Struggle for the Royal Tassel

We pick up the thread of events at the beginning of the last voyage north of Huayna Capac. While the Inca was inspecting his estates in Charcas, news arrived of the outbreak of an insurrection among the northern chiefdoms. He quickly returned to Cusco, formed a war junta, and enlisted a great army to march on Quito. In his retinue and among the lords who accompanied him were his two sons, Ninancuyuchi and Atahualpa. Remaining in the capital as governors were Hilaquita, Auqui Topa Inca, Topa Cusi Hualpa, called Huascar, and Tito Atauchi. We note there were four principals in charge of state business in the capital (Sarmiento de Gamboa, chap. 60).

The Inca remained more than ten years in the northern regions, dedicating himself, as we have seen, to many conquests. When he was not fighting against some rebel ethnic group, he stayed in Tumipampa, his place of birth and preferred residence. From there, Huayna Capac went forth to visit Pasto and Huancavilca. When he arrived in Quito, an epidemic broke out, possibly of smallpox and measles, that decimated the population of the Inca state. These diseases made their appearance in the land as a result of the first voyages of the Spaniards and caused terrible havoc among the inhabitants of the Andes, foreign to such evils and without genetic defenses against them.

The news from Cusco was also alarming. In the capital, the two rulers named by the Inca to administer his estates had also fallen victim to the epidemic, while the populace made sacrifices and supplications to drive away the diseases. Stricken by disease, Huayna Capac convened his lords and kin and named Ninancuyuchi as heir, provided that the sacrifices of the *callpa* were favorable. Sarmiento de Gamboa (chap. 62) contends that his second choice was Huascar, but that both auguries were negative. Disturbed, the priest returned to where he had left the Inca so that he could select another successor, but he was already dead.

At the death of Huayna Capac, a crucial historical moment, the realm of the Incas was so peaceful that, according to Cieza (*Señorío*, chap. 69), there was no one who would dare rebel or resort to war, and the will of the Inca was accepted as law. Nevertheless, this tranquillity was only apparent, like the calm before the storm. This peace could last only while the regime – which refused to admit the least initiative by its subjects – remained in firm hands. Thus, when the old ruler died, all was effervescence and political conspiracies. Parties and enemy factions were formed and previously contained passions flourished.

A group of noblemen led by Cusi Topa Yupanqui set out for Tumipampa to inform Ninancuyuchi of the will of his father, but he had also succumbed. It is possible that Atahualpa was the brother considered as the double of Ninancuyuchi, and in which case had the latter lived, he would have become the lord of Antisuyu. This was likely the case with Amaru Yupanqui during the government of Tupac Yupanqui, in accordance with the traditional dual and quadripartite system.

Extraordinary preparations were made for the posthumous travel of Huayna Capac from Quito to Cusco. Santa Cruz Pachacuti reports that the death of the Inca was kept secret for fear of uprisings and the mummy was taken to the capital as if it were still alive. Nevertheless, Raura Ocllo, Huascar's mother, left precipitously for Cusco accompanied by several nobles to bring the news to Huascar and prepare him for his election. It is possible that this *coya*, who according to the chroniclers took an active role in the naming of Huascar, persuaded the *panaca* and the high-ranking lineages to confirm his election as Sapa Inca.

The lord charged by Huayna Capac with carrying out his last will and making the preparations for the designation of the new Inca was Cusi Topa Yupanqui, who belonged to the *panaca* of Pachacutec and was kinsman of the mother of Atahualpa (Santa Cruz Pachacuti, 1927:218; Sarmiento de Gamboa, chap. 63). While that individual accompanied the mummy of the deceased ruler on the road to Cusco, another group of lords remained in Quito, among them Atahualpa, who passed unnoticed in the ceremonies that preceded the departure from Quito.

When the funeral procession arrived in the capital, the nobles responsible for the voyage were soundly scolded by Huascar for not having brought Atahualpa with them. He accused them of favoring his brother and of preparing to betray him. The surprised nobles protested their innocence, but an incredulous Huascar ordered them tortured. Knowing nothing of Huascar's accusations, they were unable to confess anything. The new ruler, however, ordered them killed, reasoning that if they were pardoned, they would always be dangerous enemies.

According to Cabello de Valboa (1951:396), as the funeral procession neared Cusco a group of lords went ahead to Urcos Calla to meet the Coya Raura Ocllo. Among them was Chuquis Guaman, who convinced several of them to attempt a coup by killing Huascar and replacing him with Cusi Atauche. Fearing disaster, however, Chuquis Guaman headed directly for Cusco in search of Tito Atauchi and informed him of the intrigue to eliminate Huascar and his mother. Tito Atauchi, faithful to Huascar, seized Chuquis Guaman, Cusi Atauchi, and the other conspirators and ordered their execution. According to the same chronicler (p. 398), Huascar did not wait for the arrival of his father's mummy in Cusco before punishing the principal lords for having left Atahualpa in the north. He also indicates that the events in question took place in Limatambo.

These events and the punishment inflicted on those responsible for bringing the body of Huayna Capac displeased some of the members of the funeral entourage, several of whom resolved to return immediately to Quito. Huascar's actions aggravated the hatred of the *panaca* toward him, above all among the members of Upper Cusco, who were kinsmen of the executed nobles. It seems likely, however, that Huascar was hoping to receive the tassel of rulership from the hands of the high priest of the Sun before turning against the lords who were bringing the remains of his father, since he would not want to risk his election not being confirmed.

While these events transpired in Cusco, and after the departure of the funeral train of Huayna Capac, Atahualpa set out for Tumipampa to order the construction of new palaces for Huascar. His attitude displeased the chief of Tumipampa, by the name of Ullco Colla, who found no better outlet for his anger than sending secret messengers to Huascar, complaining about the works undertaken and hinting at the possibility of an attempted uprising by Atahualpa (Cabello de Valboa: 407).

When Huascar received this news from Ullco Colla, he became furious with his mother and sister for their carelessness at having left Atahualpa in Quito. In addition, several of Huayna Capac's principal generals had remained in the north, and Huascar knew the great esteem in which these men of war held his brother (Cieza de León, chap. 70).

Atahualpa, to ingratiate himself with Huascar, or to comply with established custom, sent rich gifts to Cusco, but Huascar flew into a rage and killed the messengers, ordering drums to be made from their remains. Then he dispatched his ambassadors to Quito, sending with them women's clothes, jewels, and cosmetics as gifts for Atahualpa. These actions resulted in the final break between the two brothers. In the face of his brother's fury, Atahualpa could not return to Cusco as ordered, since by doing so he would be going to a certain death (Santa Cruz Pachacuti, 1927:219).

According to Cobo, it was Huayna Capac's generals who had remained in the north who pushed Atahualpa to rebel against his brother, judging, with good reason, that if they went to Cusco to put themselves under his command, they would not find themselves in the same position they held with Atahualpa, with whom they had enjoyed close ties for many years.

Under these circumstances, the Cañaris took advantage of Atahualpa's carelessness to rise up and take him prisoner (Cieza, *Señorío,* chap. 70). Other chroniclers relate different versions of these events. According to Pedro Pizarro, Huascar sent an army against Atahualpa while the latter was in Tumipampa, where he was taken prisoner while fighting for the principal bridge of the city. During the night, he was locked up in a *tambo,* but he succeeded in making an opening in a wall with a copper bar provided by a noblewoman, and escaped without being heard by the troops celebrating their victory (Cobo, vol. 2, book 12, chap. 18; Zarate, chap. 11; López de Gómara, chap. 116).

Later, Atahualpa would tell of being transformed by his father, the Sun, into a serpent and fleeing through a small hole. A touch of magic was useful to explain the prince's escape. One of the Inca's ears was cut during his capture, requiring that a cape be put over his head, tied underneath his chin, to hide the wound (Pedro Pizarro, 1978). Cabello de Valboa (1951) rejects Atahualpa's imprisonment, assuring us that if he had fallen into enemy hands, he would have been killed. It is likely that the Cañaris were responsible for these actions and, for that reason, Atahualpa held a special hatred for them.

Once freed, Atahualpa set out for Quito, where he quickly gathered a strong army to march on Tumipampa. His victory there was followed by cruel punishment of the entire population, and the destruction of the flourishing city founded by Tupac Yupanqui and the cradle of Huayna Capac.

In these early days of Atahualpa's insurrection, the Inca could not count on total support for his cause in the north. Only the continual blunders of Huascar succeeded in forming a consensus in favor of Atahualpa among the local lords and the Inca *panaca.*

After his triumph in Tumipampa, Atahualpa marched on the coastal region, devastating all that opposed his rule. He thus arrived in Tumbes with the intention of defeating the rebellious islanders who were loyal to Huascar. For this purpose he gathered a great number of rafts, on which his troops embarked for the island. The ruler of the island, meanwhile, prepared to repel the attack. He armed his people, gathered a fleet of rafts, and set out on the open sea to give battle to Atahualpa. In the naval encounter that followed, the rafts of La Puná got the upper hand and Atahualpa, badly wounded in the leg, decided to return to the mainland (López de Gómara, vol. 2, chap. 112).

We have seen that such naval encounters had occurred during the reigns of Tupac Yupanqui and Huayna Capac. They must have followed the coastal traditions, especially in the northern regions, where there were abundant trees suitable for building such craft. This information, together with the sea voyages undertaken by the Chincha, demonstrate the existence of an ancient coastal maritime tradition along the entire littoral (Rostworowski, 1977, 1982).

While Atahualpa embarked on his rebellion, Huascar established his government in the capital. At first he could count on the support of the nobles of Cusco and the leadership of Tahuantinsuyu. He did not, however, know how to maintain or was not interested in preserving his prestige among them, nor did he try to secure the friendship and respect of the generals who had faithfully served the deceased Inca. Of a cowardly, violent, cruel, and foolish character, Huascar did not give the nobles of the royal *ayllu* the attention to which they were accustomed from the previous rulers. As we have seen, Andean tradition demanded the attendance of the Inca together with the members of the *panaca* and the important *ayllus* at the great feasts in the public plaza to strengthen the ties of reciprocity among kinsmen. This ruler, however, did not attend such gatherings.

Another cause for anger and resentment toward the Inca was the removal from his guard of the *ayllus* that traditionally surrounded the Sapa Inca and protected his person. After the intrigues and attempts at rebellion by Chuquis Guaman in favor of his brother Cusi Atauchi, Huascar lost confidence in the Cusco nobility and decided to surround himself with foreigners of Cañari and Chachapoya origin, an act taken as an offense by the noble caste.

Such quarrels and disputes continued and were further aggravated by Huascar's declaring on a public occasion his intention of stripping the *panaca* of their vast private domains, of their possessions and haciendas, and of burying the mummified bodies of the previous rulers. According to Inca tradition, the mummies of the deceased were preserved as if they were still alive, surrounded by their wives and servants. Theirs were the best fields on the outskirts of Cusco. Thus, the dead enjoyed greater riches and privileges than the living. Around the bodies of the former rulers gathered numerous retinues sustained at the expense of the *panaca*, which kept the capital busy with reciprocal festivals, drunken parties, and gluttonous feasts.

Huascar's threats provoked fear and anger among the members of the *panaca* and their many servants and dependents. In the face of worsening relations with his kin, Huascar threatened to abandon the upper moiety, to which his brother Atahualpa also belonged, in favor of the lower moiety (Sarmiento de Gamboa, chaps. 47–48). This demonstrates the extent to which his differences with the nobility of Cusco, those who had been the principal supporters of his election, had reached. Their goodwill was essential to his remaining in power; without it, his cause was already lost.

If such was the situation in which Huascar found himself, that of Atahualpa was quite different. His long absence from Cusco, more than ten years, had disengaged him from the capital and its court intrigues. The distance separating the northern regions from the metropolis permitted him to avoid playing a direct role in the conflicts among the lineages. Atahualpa could count on the support of his father's old captains and soldiers, and therefore on the backing of part of the army. Cieza makes this point repeatedly, regarding the attitude of the northern troops as well (*Señorío*, chaps. 69, 71, 72).

Huascar's disrepute permitted the members of Hatun Ayllu *panaca*, to which Atahualpa belonged, to undertake their intrigues for supreme power. Little by little this lineage attracted followers, convincing Huascar's generals to change sides and pledge allegiance to his brother. The continual defeats suffered by Huascar's military chiefs, in spite of the significant manpower at their disposal, may reflect this circumstance. The open confrontation between the two brothers requires closer analysis of its dynamics and the circumstances that surrounded these events. Cieza says that the natives related the events in many ways, and adds that he always follows the opinions of the oldest nobles because the common people were uninformed in this regard (*Señorío*, chap. 71).

From Cusco, Huascar ordered the formation of a splendid army, which he sent to Tumipampa under the command of General Atoc. According to the native tradition, the troops always carried with them a *huaca* of some importance, in this case the statue of the Sun, by which they hoped to persuade Atahualpa to lay down his arms (Cabello de Valboa, 1951).

For his part, from Quito, Atahualpa made a call for support from the

Matched Inca-style ceramic bowls with modeled puma effigy handles, from the Island of Coati, in Lake Titicaca, Bolivia, 6" diameter at base. Photo by Robert E. Logan, Neg. No. 299281, courtesy of Department of Library Services, American Museum of Natural History.

people, and designated Chalcochima, Quizquiz, Rumiñaui, and Ucumari as his generals. Also, cautious messengers were sent to probe Atoc's intentions.

The two armies had their first encounter on the plain of Chillopampa, with Huascar's troops defeating those of Atahualpa. Nevertheless, Atahualpa's generals, reacting quickly, regrouped their scattered troops and, with fresh reinforcements from Quito, were able to recover. According to Cabello de Valboa, this first encounter took place in Mullihambato, near the river, and in a second battle, luck favored Atahualpa's captains. Cieza maintains that only one battle took place (Señorío, chap. LXXII).

In this fighting, Ullco Colla, lord of Tumipampa, was killed. Atoc was taken prisoner and fell victim to the cruelty of Challcochima, who, according to some versions, had a gold-incrusted chicha cup made of his skull. Other chroniclers say that he was left alone in the field with his eyes torn out (Santa Cruz Pachacuti). Sarmiento de Gamboa maintains that drums

A cloth bundle consisting of a miniature wool mantle in which were wrapped an Inca-style gold male figurine 2-¼" high, a miniature poncho shirt (on the left), and a miniature coca bag (on the right). Photo by Lee Boltin, Neg. No. 329852, courtesy of Department of Library Services, American Museum of Natural History.

were made from the skins of Atoc and Hango, the second general of the army. Cieza de León adds that, passing by the old battlefield, he saw quantities of bones scattered about the place. According to the same chronicler, Atahualpa then headed for Tumipampa, where he accepted the tassel and assumed the title of Sapa Inca.

News of Atahualpa's victory struck terror in Huascar, who feared the end of the war from that moment on. His advisors recommended raising new troops among the Collas, Canas, Canchis, and Charcas, as well as gathering forces on the road to Chinchaysuyu. Great supplications were made to the *huacas* in all the sanctuaries. Offerings were made to the gods and the oracles were consulted.

For his part, Atahualpa marched slowly south, and from Huamachuco

Inca-style silver alpaca, 9-7/16" high. Photo by Lee Boltin, Neg. No. 322739, courtesy of Department of Library Services, American Museum of Natural History.

sent two lords as emissaries to consult the famous *huaca* Catequil to question him concerning his future. The oracle responded that the Inca would come to a bad end. Furious, Atahualpa strode with a gold halberd in his hand to the place where the *huaca* was to be found. An ancient priest more than a hundred years old came out to meet him. He was

Inca-style silver female figurine, 6⅛" high. Photo by Lee Boltin, Neg. No. 323437, courtesy of Department of Library Services, American Museum of Natural History.

dressed in a long tunic that reached his feet and was covered with seashells. Atahualpa, recognizing that it was Catequil who had predicted such a destiny for him, gave him a blow to his head that destroyed his skull. Then he ordered the temple razed and burned (Sarmiento de Gamboa, chap. 64).

Inca-style llama of silver with cinnabar and gold inlay, 9⅛" high. Photo by Rota, Neg. No. 327112, courtesy of Department of Library Services, American Museum of Natural History.

The new supreme commander of Huascar's army was Guanca Auqui, who marched north accompanied by generals Ahuapanti, Urco Guaranca, and Inca Roca. Atahualpa, informed of the advance of enemy troops, sent against them Quizquiz and Challcochima, and the two armies confronted each other in Caxabamba. Guanca Auqui was defeated and fled as far as Cajamarca, where he found a new contingent of troops.

Santa Cruz Pachacuti (1927:221) recounts that Guanca Auqui entered into a secret agreement with Atahualpa and from that time on, only feigned his battles against him. It is difficult to explain otherwise the continual defeats of this general in spite of his command of many constantly replenished armies.

Atahualpa took no part in these battles, but observed them from nearby heights. The Inca did not pursue Guanca Auqui in his continuous retreat toward Cusco, but remained in Cajamarca. Perhaps Atahualpa feared how the fighting might unfold, preferring to retain his refuge in the north in case of some disaster. Cieza (*Señorío,* chap. 73), however, maintains that he did not march on the capital because he had learned of the appearance of Pizarro's forces.

Guanca Auqui's defeats continued one after another, in spite of his receiving reinforcements from various parts of the Andean world for each new encounter. Cabello de Valboa relates the locations of the battles in greatest detail of all the chroniclers: Cocha Guailla between Huancabamba and Huambo, then Pumpu, and Jauja, where Guanca Auqui found troops composed of Soras, Chanca, Aymaras, and Yauyos. There, a company of Cusco nobles reached him, led by Mayta Yupanqui, who transmitted a strong reprimand from Huascar. Guanca Auqui, angered by Mayta Yupanqui's harsh words, answered that he would test his own strength against that of Atahualpa, then spent the next days in drinking bouts with his kin in the valley of Jauja instead of preparing for combat.

In order to ingratiate himself with the god Pachacamac, Guanca Auqui sent many gifts to the coastal *huaca,* asking for his support. The oracle replied that victory would be his, and the other *huacas* consulted said that he would triumph in Vilcas (Santa Cruz Pachacuti:223).

In spite of these favorable auguries, the generals of Cusco were defeated. The bulk of the army retreated to the pass of Angoyacu, where Mayta Yupanqui remained, while Guanca Auqui continued almost alone to Vilcas. Sarmiento de Gamboa (chap. 63) relates that Mayta Yupanqui was ready to switch to Atahualpa's side, had he not been prevented by the other generals. Led by a noble from Cusco, new reinforcements arrived in Angoyacu to try to prevent Atahualpa's army from crossing the river, but the rivalry among Huascar's generals was greater than the danger of such disunity, and Guanca Auqui refused to provide the necessary help to the recently arrived forces, preferring to retreat to Vilcas (Santa Cruz Pachacuti:224). After the loss of Vilcas Huaman, Huascar's troops continued retreating, first to Andahuaylas, then to Curahuasi. Meanwhile, Huascar increased his sacrifices for the support of the *huacas*, but the oracles predicted a bad outcome for him, which must have even further weakened this Inca's already fearful and unwarlike spirit.

The uncontainable advance of the armies of Atahualpa forced Huascar to the conclusion that the moment had arrived for him to take personal command of his troops, as was the tradition among earlier rulers. His spies informed him that Atahualpa's troops in Curahuasi had abandoned the direct route to Cusco by way of Limatambo and the bridge crossing at the Apurímac River (perhaps finding it defended), and instead were heading southwest toward Cotabamba.

Huascar divided his armies into three groups. The first, composed of troops from Cuntisuyu, Charcas, Collasuyu, and Chile, and commanded by General Uampa Yupanqui, followed the route through the heights of Cotabamba. A second army, led by Guanca Auqui, Agua Panti, and Paca Yupanqui, was to turn one of the enemy's flanks, while Huascar himself led the third army (Sarmiento de Gamboa, chap. 64).

Santa Cruz Pachacuti (1927:226), narrating the same events, describes the troops that accompanied the ruler. He mentions the role of the nobles of Lower Cusco as the Inca's special guard, in addition to the Chachapoyas and Cañaris. It was the members of the lower moiety who were held in greatest confidence by the ruler. This further indicates that Huascar distrusted the members of Upper Cusco, the moiety allied with Atahualpa, who belonged to Hatun Ayllu. Is this not a clear indication of the participation of the *panaca* in the conflict between the two brothers? This is further evidence that the conflict reflected exclusively internal Cusco rivalries and not the abstract concepts of north against south. Analyses of Inca history have always appropriated European ideas, without taking into account the very different native sensibilities.

The day of the decisive encounter between the two armies had arrived. Huascar's troops communicated among themselves by lighting fires and sounding trumpets, while spies came running with the news that a squadron commanded by Challcochima was advancing along a ravine that led to a place called Huanuco Pampa. Huascar then gave the order for the first army, led by Uampa Yupanqui, to move to the front, initiating a fierce battle. A captain of Atahualpa's named Tomay Rima was killed in the fighting, encouraging Huascar to commit his remaining troops to the battle. His two brothers, Tito Atauchi and Topa Atao, stood out among the generals (Sarmiento de Gamboa, chap. 64). Although it lasted all day, the battle proved indecisive, and when night fell the armies of Challcochima and Quizquiz retired to a hill near Huanuco Pampa covered by tall grass.

Seeing this, Huascar ordered the dry grass set on fire. It burned voraciously, fanned by the wind. The rapidly advancing flames caught many of Atahualpa's troops, who, left with no escape, died in the conflagration. His generals, however, succeeded in retreating safely across the Cotabamba River.

Huascar, however, militarily inexperienced, did not take advantage of the disorder produced among the enemy troops by pursuing his adversaries, rather preferring to celebrate, prematurely, his victory. When Challcochima realized that they were not being pursued, he regrouped and encouraged his soldiers. The spies that he sent to Huascar's camp brought back information of the ruler's strategy, which consisted of dividing his forces with the intention of attacking Atahualpa's army from several sides (Sarmiento de Gamboa, chap. 64).

The following day, Huascar charged Topa Atao with advancing a squadron of men along a ravine in order to determine the maneuvers and intentions of the enemy. Challcochima discovered Topa Atao's advance and, as an experienced general in the wars of Huayna Capac, divided his army into two parts, with the order to post themselves silently on either side of the ravine and await the advance of their adversaries. When these had entered well into the deep ravine, Challcochima attacked forcefully, taking Topa Atao prisoner and decimating his troops.

Meanwhile, the improvident Huascar left his third army in Huanuco Pampa and set out in the footsteps of Topa Atao without waiting for word from the latter. Challcochima, seeing Huascar's carelessness, sent word to Quizquiz to come with his army to attack the ruler's rearguard when he entered the ravine.

Huascar quickly discovered the remains of Topa Atao's squadron and realized that he had fallen into an ambush. He tried to retrace his steps, but came up against Quizquiz's men. Sensing all was lost, the Inca tried to flee. Challcochima, following Andean tactics, searched for him, since, according to ancient tradition, when the head of an army fell prisoner, the battle was ended. Therefore, spotting Huascar in his litter, he quickly attacked, knocked him down, and took him prisoner. Then, employing an ingenious ruse, the general climbed into the ruler's litter and, with the curtains lowered, ordered his men to head in the direction of the plains of Huanuco Pampa, where Huascar's third army was waiting. Joined by Quizquiz and his men, all of Atahualpa's troops marched together as if they were Huascar's victorious army. Approaching Huascar's soldiers, who were awaiting orders, Challcochima freed a prisoner to inform them of the disaster. The news threw the third army into complete confusion, and most of the soldiers, fearing Challcochima's wrath, took to headlong flight.

The attack by Atahualpa's generals ended by smashing what was left of Huascar's troops, who were pursued up to the bridge of Cotabamba. Many died trying to cross the river. Once Challcochima's troops reached the opposite bank, they fell on Huascar's soldiers and seized Tito Atauchi. The triumphant troops advanced on Cusco, since by then nothing could stop them, and marched as far as the heights of Yavira, where they encamped before making their entry into the capital. Huascar had remained well guarded in Quiuipay (Sarmiento de Gamboa, chaps. 64 and 65).

Santa Cruz Pachacuti narrates these episodes with some variations. For example, the events mentioned by Sarmiento de Gamboa as occurring on the first day of battle are attributed by Santa Cruz Pachacuti to the fourth day. These differences, however, do not significantly affect the unfolding of events, and both chroniclers are in agreement that the final battles took place in the environs of Huanuco Pampa, district of Tambobamba, province of Cotabamba (Stiglich, 1922).

The cries and screams of the inhabitants of Cusco resounded to the hill of Yavira. To calm the population, the victorious generals sent messengers and ordered the principals to come to Yavira to venerate the statue, or double, of Atahualpa, called Ticsi Capac (Sarmiento de Gamboa, chap. 65; Santa Cruz Pachacuti:230).

On the appointed day, the *panaca* and important lineages arrived, organized by *ayllus*, and sat according to the established order, those of Hanan on one side and Hurin on the other. When they were all gathered together, they prostrated themselves before the *huauque*, or "brother," of Atahualpa, facing in the direction of the distant location of the new Inca, in compliance with the Mocha ritual.

On this occasion, Huascar's principal generals, including Guanca Auqui, were taken prisoner, as were the two priests of the Sun, Apo Challco Yupanqui and Rupaca, for having awarded the tassel of rulership to Huascar. (We will not enter into the details provided by the chroniclers concerning accusations and other things said at this time.) Meanwhile, messengers left to bring news of the events to Atahualpa, and they awaited his orders.

After a time a relative of the new Inca by the name of Cusi Yupanqui arrived in Cusco, with powers to execute the punishments and exact the revenge of Atahualpa. The chroniclers are in agreement in describing the cruelties ordered against Huascar's kin, women, and children. All were hanged, and in the houses of the deceased Incas those of the lineage of Huascar were sought out. The greatest punishment was reserved for the *panaca* of Tupac Yupanqui. All of its members who could be found were killed, including the servants and *mamacona.* Even the mummy of this Inca

Reed boat, or *caballito de totora*, on Late Titicaca, similar to those used on the coast in pre-Hispanic times for fishing, hunting, and transport. Photo by Bennett-Bird, Neg. No. 600993, courtesy of Department of Library Services, American Museum of Natural History.

was taken and burned in an isolated place. To destroy the body of an ancestor was the greatest possible punishment.

Atahualpa's anger extended as well to the Cañaris and Chachapoyas, who were Huascar's bodyguards. We can imagine that Atahualpa remembered that some time back the lord of this ethnic group had taken him prisoner and had him at his mercy.

The revenge exacted against the *panaca* of Capac Ayllu, to which Huascar belonged, shows that the confrontation between the two brothers was a struggle between rival *panaca*. Only from this Andean perspective can we understand Atahualpa's ordering the burning of the mummy of his own paternal grandfather. This act is further proof that kinship ties were not determined by male descent, as in Europe, but through the *ayllu* or *panaca* of the mother.

During these events in Cusco, Atahualpa remained in Huamachuco, celebrating the triumphs of his generals and preparing his departure for the capital. Under these circumstances, there arrived some messengers sent by the *curacas* of Payta and Tumbes advising him of the appearance of some strange people who lived in floating houses and rode enormous animals. It was not the first time they had appeared, since in the time of Huayna Capac they had been seen on the coast, only to disappear without any more being known of them.

Perhaps through curiosity, Atahualpa delayed his march to Cusco in the hope of seeing the recent arrivals, and he ordered his generals to take Huascar to Cajamarca, where he would meet them. The Spaniards, however, remained on the plains, where they were occupied with learning about the land and founding a town in Tangarará that they named San Miguel. There, Pizarro learned of Atahualpa, of the war between the brothers, and of the victory of Atahualpa's generals (Mena, in Porras, 1937).

According to Mena, Atahualpa sent one of his captains, disguised as a man of low birth, to spy on the Spaniards. After carefully observing them, he returned to tell Atahualpa what he had seen. This military chief wanted to return with an army and fall on the Spaniards, but Atahualpa would not permit it, since he preferred to do so where he was located, that is, in Cajamarca.

Meanwhile, Pizarro, after leaving his new neighbors in the recently founded town of San Miguel, left for Piura – Mena is the first to refer to the native town of that name. There Pizarro found his brother Hernando, who had gone ahead with forty men to scout the land and obtain information.

Pizarro, informed that the native captain continued marauding through the region, learned of the importance of a town called Caxas. Not wanting to send his brother there, he instead sent Hernando de Soto with a group of men, while the rest waited for their return in Serrán (Mena, in Porras, 1937). In Caxas they found good buildings partly destroyed by the recent fighting, since the local ethnic chief had opposed the troops of Atahualpa. The storehouses were filled with maize and wool, and five hundred *mamacona* were engaged in weaving and the preparation of beverages.

Mena recounts that the lord of the region gave five or six *mamacona* to the Spaniards so that they might prepare their meals. Diego Trujillo who accompanied de Soto on the expedition, reported that the soldiers demanded that the women be divided among them, and that Atahualpa's captain became indignant and threatened future punishment by the Inca. Pizarro's orders during these early days were strict, and forbade any excess or pillage that might provoke the natives.

At that moment, a messenger sent by Atahualpa arrived with gifts for the Spaniards, which greatly frightened the local chief. He was reassured by Hernando de Soto, who invited him to sit at his side. The gift consisted of gutted ducks filled with straw and a message that the same would happen to the Christians. In addition, the messenger had brought two clay models of sturdy fortresses to warn them of what they would find ahead.

De Soto left with Atahualpa's emissary to meet with Pizarro. The latter, good diplomat that he was, appeared pleased to be with an envoy of the Inca and presented him with a very fine shirt and two glass cups for his master. He also indicated his desire to meet with the Inca, assured him of his friendly intentions, and offered his assistance in combating any of the ruler's enemies.

With these instructions, Atahualpa's envoy departed to report to his master, and two days later Pizarro and his men began their journey to meet the Inca. From Serrán they took a walled road, along which they found shelters every two leagues where they could rest. Most of the towns were deserted. They passed through a village called Cala, or Tala, and Hernando Pizarro together with de Soto went ahead to observe the route, swimming across a swift river that, according to Porras, must have been the Saña (Trujillo, 1920:15). There they received word of a town of great wealth, and arrived in Cinto, which was deserted.

The following day, Francisco Pizarro and the rest of his men crossed the river and captured two men to obtain information concerning Atahualpa's movements. One of them said that the Inca controlled two difficult mountain passes. No amount of torture could elicit further information from the prisoners.

After resting for two days, the Spanish forces marched on, leaving the principal road to head directly for the mountains. Arriving at the foot of the sierra, Pizarro divided his forces, one group departing earlier to climb the steep flanks while a second climbed more slowly. They passed a walled fortress and continued climbing until they reached a town a league beyond the fort. They chose the stone house of the chief in which to rest, while the rear guard remained in the fortress.

The following day they left before sunrise, since the road led through the two difficult passes and Pizarro wanted to be certain that the natives did not reach them ahead of him. Their efforts were successful, and they crossed the mountain passes without being attacked, after which the rear guard rejoined the rest of the troops. When they were reunited, two messengers arrived from Atahualpa with presents of camelids, and Pizarro returned the gesture with many gifts.

For five days they continued along the mountain road, and before they arrived at Atahualpa's encampment, the Inca sent them presents of roast meats, maize, and *chicha* to drink. Meanwhile, Pizarro had dispatched a friendly lord to the ruler's camp, but the posted guards would not let him pass, in spite of the chief's protests. Pizarro's messenger had no alternative but to return to the waiting Spaniards, and after recounting his experiences, he advised them not to eat the food sent by the Inca (Mena, in Porras, 1937:82–83).

By nightfall, after a day's march, the Spaniards arrived at Atahualpa's camp, where white tents extended for more than two leagues. Hernando Pizarro, going on ahead, reached a large town, where he was surprised by a heavy hailstorm. Few people were to be found that afternoon in Cajamarca, no more than 400 to 500 men guarding the houses of the *mamacona*, who were occupied with preparing *chicha* for the Inca army. Pizarro's forces entered the town fearfully, knowing there were no reinforcements to aid them in that critical situation.

Hernando Pizarro and de Soto requested Francisco Pizarro's permission to go to Atahualpa's camp with only five or six mounted men and an interpreter, to observe the camp at close hand. They marched a little more than a league, the distance that separated the city from the place where the Inca was encamped with his army. As they proceeded to walk past the troops, they could see the variously armed squadrons along either side of their path, without anyone making the slightest gesture to prevent their passing.

The Inca was seated on a *tiana* or seat, in the door of his house, surrounded by his principals and many women. De Soto approached, wheeling his horse so close to the ruler that Atahualpa's tassel moved with the snorting of the animal without his making the slightest sign or smallest gesture of surprise or fear. Hernando Pizarro, who had fallen behind, appeared with the interpreter behind him on his horse, and without showing concern for having crossed a field filled with the Inca's troops, asked the ruler to raise his head, which he had kept lowered with a contemptuous attitude, as he neither looked at them nor answered their questions directly but, rather spoke through one of his principals as intermediary.

The version of this historic encounter related by Diego Trujillo differs from those of Jerez and Mena. According to the former, de Soto marched ahead to meet with Atahualpa, and Pizarro, delayed and fearing something bad would occur, sent Captain Hernando Pizarro ahead to inform him of what was happening. On arriving at the Inca's camp, Hernando found that the ruler had not yet made his appearance. Impatient, the Spaniard sent a messenger, who returned with the same response: Wait. As time passed, a second native went to see what was happening, and Hernando raised his voice to show his impatience.

At last Atahualpa appeared and ordered that two gold cups be filled with *chicha*. He offered one to Pizarro, and both of them drank. Then he had two of silver brought to drink with de Soto. Hernando protested, saying that both were captains and that there were no differences between them. At the repeated requests of the Spaniards, Atahualpa promised to go the next day to Cajamarca. Before departing, de Soto wheeled his horse, frightening some of the natives, who were later punished for showing their fear (Porras, 1937:17).

The Spaniards spent the night on guard in constant fear of a surprise attack, but no one bothered them. The following day, during the morning, messengers were coming and going between the two camps, with the Inca in no hurry to meet with Pizarro. Shortly before sundown, and at Pizarro's repeated insistence, Atahualpa decided to enter the town. Some four hundred men preceded the Inca, all dressed the same, whose mission was to clear the road of stones and straw.

Meanwhile, Pizarro divided his forces into four groups, which hid in the buildings that surrounded the great plaza. In the first waited Hernando Pizarro with fourteen or fifteen horsemen; in the second, De Soto with fifteen or sixteen horsemen; in the third, another captain with more soldiers; and in a shed lay hidden Francisco Pizarro with twenty-five foot soldiers and two or three horsemen. In the middle of the plaza, in a fortress that was probably an *usnu*, or throne, waited the rest of the force, consisting of Pedro de Candia with eight or nine harquebusmen and a small cannon (Mena, in Porras, 1937).

Pedro Pizarro, narrating the events in Cajamarca, indicated that up to that point the Spaniards had not fought against the natives and did not know their battle tactics, since the encounters at Tumbes and La Puná had been mere skirmishes. According to this chronicler, Pizarro divided his horsemen in two groups, commanded by Hernando Pizarro and de Soto, respectively. Pedro de Candia and a few men were placed in the small structure in the middle of the plaza.

Slowly and hesitantly the Inca entered the plaza after his soldiers had partially occupied it, surprised to find it empty. When he asked for the Spaniards, they told him that because of fear they remained hidden in the sheds. Then, with great solemnity, the Dominican Valverde came forward with a cross in his hands, accompanied by Martinillo, the interpreter, and formally requested, as he handed him the Gospel, that Atahualpa embrace the Catholic faith and serve the king of Spain. The dialogue that followed is recounted differently by each of the witnesses. Possibly the tremendous anguish of those moments prevented them from remembering the exact words exchanged among the various actors in the tragedy.

Behind the Inca, carried in another litter, was the lord of Chincha. In that moment, Pizarro hesitated, not knowing which of the two was the ruler. Nevertheless, he ordered Juan Pizarro to move toward the latter, while he and his soldiers advanced in the direction of the Inca.

At Pizarro's signal, the menacing silence that enveloped the plaza gave way to an immense roar. Thunder broke loose, the crash of the cannon, and the trumpets sounded, which was the signal for the horsemen to gallop from the sheds. The bells tied to the horses rang and the deafening harquebuses were fired. The shouting, screaming, and moaning were everywhere. In this confusion the terrified natives, in their efforts to escape, knocked down a wall of the plaza and succeeded in fleeing. Behind them hurtled the horsemen, overtaking and killing all those they could, while others were crushed to death in the human avalanche.

Meanwhile, Juan Pizarro rushed in the direction of the lord of Chincha and killed him in his litter. Francisco Pizarro and his soldiers, for their part, massacred the natives who desperately held up the litter of the Inca, while those who fell were replaced by others. Seeing this situation, a Spaniard drew his knife to kill Atahualpa, but Pizarro prevented him, and was wounded in the hand in doing so, ordering that no one touch the Inca. Finally, the Spaniards succeeded in tipping over the litter and seizing the ruler.

By nightfall of that fateful sixteenth of November, 1532, the Inca realm had ceased to exist forever. The Sapan Inca was held captive, and with his imprisonment the autonomy of the indigenous state came to an end. From that moment on, transcendental changes transformed the Andean world, changes that had profound consequences in Europe as well.*

Pedro Pizarro indicates in his chronicle that until that memorable day at Cajamarca, the Spanish had not fought the natives, with the exception of the skirmishes at Tumbes and La Puná. Not once during their march from the coast to Atahualpa's camp had the Spaniards encountered the slightest obstruction. On the contrary, at all times they were offered guides and produce from the state storehouses. Atahualpa did not fall in open war; rather, what befell him was a fearless and audacious ambush.

That fateful late afternoon, Atahualpa, in his blindness, underestimated the technology and power of the foreigners. The danger he ran by letting them advance to his camp, instead of wiping them out in a narrow pass,

---

* The European economy was affected by the impact of the arrival of enormous quantities of Peruvian gold, and later by the introduction of the potato, which permitted European population growth and ended the periodic famines that threatened the continent whenever the wheat crops failed.

never crossed his mind. The Inca believed he could suppress them at any moment and chose first to satisfy his curiosity.

In the court of Huayna Capac, Atahualpa had heard stories of mysterious bearded men who arrived by sea in floating houses, and on land mounted enormous unknown animals. But much as they unexpectedly arrived, one fine day they disappeared and nothing more was heard of them. Perhaps the Inca thought that the same would happen again, and he did not wish to miss the opportunity of meeting such strange people. It was a dangerous desire that would cost him his kingdom and his life.

Once taken prisoner, the Inca, knowing the Spaniards' thirst for precious metals, hoped to obtain his freedom by offering in exchange a room full of gold and silver. The proposal would make the foreigners tremble from greed, and Pizarro rushed to have the promise confirmed in writing in the presence of a scribe.

Atahualpa fulfilled his commitment. In a few months the famous "ransom room" was filled with gold. It remained for Pizarro to fulfill his part of the bargain. Having met his obligation to fill the room with glistening gold, however, Atahualpa ceased to be of interest and began to cause problems. Although the Inca had kept his side of the bargain, Pizarro had no intention of fulfilling his, that is, to set the ruler free. The danger that freeing Atahualpa would represent for the Spaniards was obvious. The Inca's prestige as Son of the Sun alone would suffice to rally his generals and his armies behind him.

For the Spaniards, it was best to get rid of him as quickly as possible; so rumors were spread of a supposed meeting of native armies. Pizarro had no desire to continue on with Atahualpa, since this would expose him to a surprise attack by Inca troops desiring to free him. Hernando de Soto, who had developed a certain friendship with the Inca and was considered his protector, was sent to Caxas at the head of a group of soldiers to verify the rumors, whose falsehood was subsequently demonstrated. Francisco Pizarro, with his officers, including his principal captains, charged the Inca with the death of Huascar and with gathering an armed force against the Spaniards.

In fact, Pizarro had learned that Huascar was being held prisoner, and indicated to Atahualpa his interest in meeting him, asking that he order Huascar to be brought to Cajamarca. The Inca, fearful that Pizarro intended to replace him in power with Huascar, secretly sent a message to his generals, ordering them to kill Huascar immediately, a deed accomplished in Antamarca, near Yanamayo.

On the basis of these accusations and the rumors of impending war against the Spaniards, Atahualpa was immediately condemned to be burned alive, with the sentence commuted to strangling on the condition that he agree to be baptized. There was nothing worse in the Andean world than to suffer the destruction of one's body, since that would make mummification and continuity after death impossible. Thus, the Inca accepted baptism. Jerez tells us that Atahualpa "died in good spirits, without showing emotion."

The following morning, with great solemnity, he was buried in the church, from which several days later his corpse mysteriously disappeared. His faithful subjects took his body and hid it, and guarded his mummified remains somewhere in the mountains. From there, he continues to guard his domains and his people. With his mummy preserved, according to popular belief, he could be expected to return some day.

The last ruler of the Inca state became mythicized in spite of the certainty of his historical existence. Doubts and controversies woven about his personage have endowed his memory with an even more legendary character. So it is that his final destiny remains in the mists of the magical, and perhaps his ever vigilant mummy is still hidden in some wild corner of the Andes.

By an irony of destiny, the date of Atahualpa's execution is not known with certainty, which has contributed to historical errors and confusion. We can review the information that Jerez provides in his chronicle, since it is the most detailed and precise and gives the dates of the principal events. From the month of November 1532, when Atahualpa fell prisoner, his ransom slowly arrived in Cajamarca. On May 13, 1533, Pizarro ordered that certain pieces be melted down, while others were simply marked to indicate the weight of the precious metals. A month later, on June 13, there arrived from Cusco another shipment, containing two hundred loads of gold weighing more than 130 carats, as well as twenty loads of silver.

Still according to Jerez, by July 25, Santiago's day, the entire treasure had not only been melted and marked but had been distributed as well. There was no longer any reason for Pizarro to remain in Cajamarca, and it became urgent for him to continue his march toward Cusco. Jerez's chronicle terminates on July 31, 1533. On the other hand, we know that Pizarro wrote the king two letters relating the latest events, one dated June 8 and the second July 29. The loss of this correspondence is unfortunate, but a missive from Carlos V to Pizarro acknowledges receipt of the letters and mentions the dates indicated. In one of the letters, Pizarro had sent word of the trial of the Inca (Porras Barrenechea, Cedulario del Perú, 1948).

The king's reply indicated his displeasure with the sentencing and execution of Atahualpa, ordered by one of his subjects, since the action represented a threat to the institution of monarchy. Years later, Philip II would express similar displeasure to Toledo on the death of Tupac Amaru, based on the same principle of a threat against royalty.

Based on the dates we have, it is logical to assume that the death of Atahualpa took place after June 8 and before July 29, 1533. The Spaniards remained some days longer in Cajamarca preparing for their departure, which took place toward the middle of August. By August 26 they were already in Andamarca, and by September 2 they were in Huaylas. It is important to clarify the date of Atahualpa's death and correct the totally unfounded assertion that it occurred on August 29.

It remains to explain why these events did not produce an immediate reaction from the natives, why they did not rise up to liquidate the Spaniards. How did a small group of Spaniards conquer the Inca state so easily? The question is an important one. Pizarro's achievement did not include an encounter or military confrontation between Spaniards and Andeans. The foreigners had no need to be cautious toward the natives because no one attacked them. At no time did Atahualpa order an attack against or attempt the extermination of the Spaniards. On the contrary, he facilitated their access to his camp without placing anything to block their way.

The Spaniards were able to seize possession of the Inca realm as a result of cunning, daring, the exploitation of circumstance, and a good deal of diplomacy. The natives, on the other hand, underestimated Spanish technology, were ignorant of the power of firearms and of military tactics different from their own, and above all were unprepared for the psychological impact of the ambush.

Atahualpa committed the mistake of underestimating the Spaniards, believing that he could numerically overwhelm them at a time of his choosing. His desire to see the strange beings firsthand prevailed over any wariness or precautions.

After the events of Cajamarca, the disorder among the Cusco nobility must have been considerable. With Huascar and Atahualpa dead, and in the absence of fixed rules for the succession to power, the Inca state was left adrift and leaderless. To resolve this situation, Pizarro quickly named a new ruler in the person of Tupac, a brother of the deceased Incas who had come to see Atahualpa when he was a prisoner and did not want to leave his quarters for fear of being killed (Pedro Pizarro, 1973:71). This Inca lived only a few months after his appointment and died of poisoning in Jauja. In his place, the Spaniards named Manco II, half brother of the former Incas. Manco, subject to the orders of Pizarro, could not act on his own until free from Spanish control, and only then began the struggle against the invaders.

As for the Andean macroethnic groups, the majority, after overcoming the first moments of stupor after the events of Cajamarca, joined the Spanish, motivated by a desire to free themselves from Inca hegemony. The local lords were decidedly on the side of the foreigners, providing them with food supplies, porters, and support troops, without which the Spanish undertaking would likely have ended in disaster.

Pizarro, as a great politician and diplomat, knew how to take advantage of the desire for independence on the part of the ethnic lords in order to win their cooperation. The Spaniards, far from being alone in a hostile country, counted from the beginning on the help of the natives, who could not know the state of subservience and dependence in which they would later find themselves.

PART TWO

Organizational Aspects

4

The Social Structure of the Inca Realm

To investigate the organizational system of the Inca state, one must first study its social structure. We will begin with the highest levels of the social hierarchy, by distinguishing among various types of lords.

Before the Inca expansion, the Andean region was divided among macroethnic groups whose chiefs were the *hatun curaca*, or great lords. The lands under their jurisdiction varied according to their power and ethnic components. These lofty rulers governed, in turn, various subordinate chiefdoms of lower rank, some of them quite small. The sociopolitical model of the Andean world consisted of a mosaic of diverse chiefs grouped under the hegemony of greater chiefs. Such appears to have been the situation at the beginning of the Inca expansion.

With the Inca conquests, these arrangements changed as the great lords recognized the preeminence of the Sapa Inca and accepted the requirements of reciprocity. As the power of the Inca state became more secure, new categories of lords were added, such as the lords by privilege, non-nobles whom the Inca wished to reward with a chiefdom. There were also cases of chiefs of the social category of *yana* (literally, servants), who offered the advantage of depending directly on the will of the Inca rather than on their *ayllus* of origin.

With territorial expansion came a vast new class of lords of very different ranks and attributes. To this entire "provincial" elite was added the innumerable state administrators responsible for the smooth functioning of the government.

Also included among the elite of the Inca realm were the priests, who formed a very diverse category of dignitaries filling a variety of functions. Finally, the "merchant" lords of Chincha and those of the northern regions were influential figures in coastal society.

On lower steps of the social ladder we find the artisans, the commoners, the *mitmaq*, the fishermen, and the *yana,* forming the popular classes of the Inca realm. The commoners were divided according to a decimal system into domestic units of 10, 100, 1,000, and 10,000, each population group with its own chiefs.

In addition, the population formed subgroups by age, according to the labor service they were able to render. Above this multitude rose the person of the Sapa Inca, surrounded by the *panaca* and royal *ayllus* constituting the Cusco aristocracy, to which were added the Incas by privilege. In the beginning, however, the lords of Cusco were the same as the other chiefs of the region. As their domains increased, however, so did their power. We might ask to what extent the conquest of the Chimor, with their culture and refinement, influenced the rude Inca warriors by introducing them to the habits of luxury and to the solemnity with which the great Lord of the North presented himself. The mythical retinue of dignitaries who surrounded and accompanied the legendary Naymlap on his arrival in Lambayecana lands shows the refinement of his court.

We next analyze the structure of fifteenth-century Andean society, beginning with the highest classes.

THE ELITE

The social structure of the earliest Incas could not have been very sophisticated. The uppermost hierarchy consisted of the sixteen *panaca*, from among whose members were elected the rulers of Cusco; the *ayllus* of the most recent Incas possessed the greatest prestige, while the *panaca* of the oldest chiefs tended to be forgotten. These were followed in importance by the ten "guardian" *ayllus* – so named by Sarmiento de Gamboa – who were responsible for the care of the city and of the Inca. When Huascar took this ancestral privilege away from them to surround himself with newly arrived peoples such as the Cañaris and the Chachapoyas, his act was taken as scandalous and insulting and brought the Inca the rancor of the displaced members of the elite.

The Lords

With the territorial expansion of the Incas, each *señorío* annexed to the domain of Cusco sent a lord to live in the capital as a way of ensuring its fidelity. This lord could serve as hostage in case of a rebellion in his place of origin. An example of this is the case of Caxapaxa, chief of one of the two moieties of the *señorío* of Lima, who lived in Cusco, while Taulichusco, the second lord in the dual system, resided in Lima. The lords whose lands had been annexed earliest to the Inca state resided closest to the center of the city. They also preserved as individuals the spatial relationships of the various zones that constituted the Inca territory by occupying the geographically appropriate quarter within the city.

From the Spanish administrative documents, we know of the existence, during the fifteenth and early sixteenth century, of a variety of great *señoríos*, throughout the length and width of the Inca state, who possessed dual chiefs, one of whom was preeminent. The Spaniards proceeded to divide these macroethnic groups into *repartimientos*, or allotments of land and labor, to increase the number of *encomiendas* that could be awarded, thus upsetting the traditional Andean organizational system. In this way some subservient chiefs found themselves in superior positions, while formerly higher-ranking lords saw themselves stripped of their prerogatives. This situation led to innumerable lawsuits among the natives during the viceregal period.

Fray Domingo de Santo Tomás, in a letter addressed to the king, mentions the dismemberment of towns and macroethnic groups in order to increase the number of *repartimientos*; places that formerly constituted a single unit were divided into two or three *encomiendas* (Lisson y Chávez, 1943, vol. 1:196–98).

Under the Inca state, the lords of macroethnic groups governed several *guaranga* (one thousand domestic units). Examples are the great Guzmango, lord of the seven *guaranga* of Cajamarca; the lord Contar Huacho, female ruler of the six *guaranga* of Huaylas; and Nina Vilca, lord of the *guaranga* of Huarochirí.

In the central sierra, the great lord of the Atavillos also governed the natives of Canta, Huamantanga, Piscas, and Socos, in addition to his own group (Rostworowski, 1978a). On the south-central coast, Chincha was a rich and prosperous *señorío*; and in the northern region the *señorío* of Callanca, whose pre-Inca name was Chuspo, formed, in the beginning of the sixteenth century, a unit with Reque and Monsefú. Later on, Pizarro divided the *señorío* between two *encomenderos*, Callanca going to Francisco de Alcántara and Reque to Miguel de Velasco, thus creating two independent *señoríos* where there was formerly only one (Rostworowski, 1961). Vaca de Castro, in 1543, divided the valley of Chimor between Alonso de Alvarado and Alonso Gutierrez (AGI – Justicia 398, suit of Doña Francisca Pizarro against Diego de Mora).

The religious center of Pachacamac comprised the low valleys of Lima and Lurín. This macroethnic group comprised a series of small *señoríos* that submitted to its hegemony. In Lurín we can identify the chiefdoms of Manchay, Huaycan, Sisicaya, Quilcay (a fishing center), Caringa, and Pacta, located in the desert hills.

In the lower valley, in the basin of the Rímac River, were the *señoríos* of

Surco, Guatca, Lima, Maranga, Gualcay, Amancaes, and Callao. Each retained its own local chiefs, even in number, representing the two halves of each small political unit (Rostworowski, 1978a).

In each of the places just mentioned, we find a great lord ruling a considerable area, with a series of lesser chiefdoms, some of them extremely small, under his control. This appears to have been the pan-Andean pattern at the beginning of the sixteenth century (see Rostworowski, 1990).

The dictionaries of Fray Domingo de Santo Tomás and Diego González Holguín contain various terms used to describe pre-Hispanic society. Many of these native words fell quickly into disuse because the Spanish administration preferred to employ other terms, such as *cacique* (chief or boss), brought from the Caribbean region, which came into use beginning with the first voyage of Columbus (López de Gómara, 1941:44).

The following are the terms that are found in the dictionary of Fray Domingo de Santo Tomás (1951/1563) relating to the various kinds and hierarchies of lords:

Capac or Capac Capa	king or emperor
Capac Apo	sovereign ruler
Appo	great lord
Appocac	great lord
Yayanc	lord, generic
Curaca	lord, principal of subjects
Atipac	powerful
Appocta, Sayani, gui	to be standing before a great lord
Appo Ayllon	lineage of lower nobility
Appoycachani, gui	to outrank
Mussoc Capac or Mosso Cappo	newly crowned emperor (young)

This list of terms provides useful information concerning Andean social structure. There are a number of terms that refer to the various lords who constituted the elite of that time. Terms that come from the word *yayanc*, from *yaya*, father, suggest an evolution in the kinship system toward social stratification. Other terms, such as *appo* or *curaca*, lord of subjects, allude to categories within a differentiated social scheme.

In the second Quechua dictionary consulted, we find the following terms for lords (González Holguín, 1952/1608):

Çapay Apu	
Çapay Auqui	the principal of or noble gentlemen
Hatun Curaca	the highest-ranking lord, best known, oldest, richest man

Stone-walled storehouses on steep terraces at Ollantay Tambo (Tambo), a fortified Inca city in the Urubamba valley, northeast of Cusco. Photo by Edward Ranney.

Hatun o Akapac Curaca	great lord
Auquicuna	the lower nobles, lords
Rinriyoc Auqui	*orejón* nobles
Curaca	the lord of the people (*pueblo*)
Curaca Cuna	the principals or those who execute what he orders
Llactayoc Apu	the lord of the people
Llactacamayoc	deputy *curaca* or one who executes his orders
Llactayok	lord or owner of camelid herds
Michini Runacta	govern or rule men or be of higher rank
Ccoripaco Ccoririncri	the *orejón* captains
Pacuyok	commoners who were made *orejónes* in war
Huaranga Curaca	lord of 1,000 families
Pachaca Curaca	lord of 100 families
Chunca Curaca	head of a faction

In this long list of terms for the diverse levels of status within the nobility, a considerable range of conditions, occupations, and power can be clearly seen. We find the *Capac Apu*, the supreme lord, followed in rank by the

Hatun or *Akapac Curaca*, the *Orejón* captains, who earned that distinction through bravery in war, unlike the *CCoripaco CCoririncri*, or *orejones* by birth, something similar to the Incas by privilege.

Terms such as *Llactayoc Apu*, lord of the town, and *Llactacamayoc*, his deputy, of lower rank, disappeared very quickly from the Spanish documents. The title of *Llactayok*, an owner of large herds, indicates that there were distinctions based on wealth as well as on blood.

González Holguín discusses the various terms for the nobles of lower status. According to him, the *Pachaca* was nothing more than a *mayordomo* of the Inca. In the chronicles and *relaciones*, there are many references to the establishment of the system of *guaranga* and *pachaca* by the Inca Tupac Yupanqui following his conquests. These terms refer to categories of chiefs: the *pachaca* exercised control over what were supposed to be one hundred families, while the *curaca de guaranga* commanded ten *pachaca* lords, or a hypothetical thousand domestic units. That Tupac Yupanqui established this system in Tahuantinsuyu appears to be a reasonable conclusion supported by the chronicles.

It is likely that the Incas tried to reorganize the local administrative hierarchy by installing a decimal system to facilitate population estimates and the organization of the labor force. The new arrangements, however, did not affect the traditional internal ways of the local *señoríos*. We do not know if this decimal system originated in Cusco, or if the Incas imposed it after conquering some region that had used the model earlier.

Although we have discussed the Inca realm as a whole, we cannot ignore the terms used among the Aru or Jaqi speakers. For these we have Bertonio's Aymara dictionary, which is rich in terminology for the noble hierarchy:

Hakhsarañani apu	lord of great majesty
Ccapaca Suti	royal name or great ruler
Ccapaca cancaña	king or lord, an ancient term no longer used with this meaning
Ccapaca	wealthy
Apu	lord, *corregidor*, prince
Apu Cancaña	*señorío*, domain
Auqui	father or lord
Taani	fieldmaster, provider of something, such as a banquet
Pachpa marcani mayco	rightful and natural lord of the people (*pueblo*)
Cchamani, Sinti, Ataani	captain
Hilacata	the principal or head of the *ayllu*

Hisquiquiri	rich or noble gentleman
Huallpani	captain, or the one in charge of banquet preparations and other aforementioned
Laa Mayco	intrusive chief, or one without the right to the position
Mallco vel. mayco	*cacique*, lord of subjects
Maycoña vel. mayco	domain, royal authority
Tataña	one who plays the role of lord

Among these terms, we note a difference between *ccapaca cancaña*, the equivalent of kingdom, and *apu cancaña*, which refers to a domain – that is, a distinction between the hegemonic power exercised by the chief of a macroethnic group as compared with that of a simple *curaca*. We also find reference to the economic condition of a notable in the term *hisquiquiri*, which indicates a wealthy or noble individual, as distinct from *mayco*, the natural lord of a people. There is also a term, *laa mayco*, for an intrusive chief.

The objection is sometimes made that these dictionaries contain certain Spanish concepts. But they appear to be secondary, especially if we consider the overwhelming documentary evidence for the presence in the Inca state of great lords who governed vast lands. Below these lords were the subordinate chiefs of diverse rank. Such appears to have been the sociopolitical structure in the Andean world. In this sense, native society offers a more complex pattern than what has been generally thought. With colonial domination, the multiple terms to designate different categories of lords were simplified, the language impoverished, and the complex terminology that described native social organization lost.

If we accept the evidence of the documentary sources concerning the existence of great *señoríos* in the Andean world, it is appropriate to ask how they functioned internally and what ties held their members together.

When the forces of Tupac Yupanqui made their appearance on the coast, they met with the armed resistance of the Colli Capac, who was aided by the chief of Quivi and his warriors. In this instance, we are made aware of two kinds of obligations on the part of this chief toward his lord, the first being the provision of food, and the second, of military support.

A similar close subordinate relationship existed between the chief of Chaclla and the great lord of Huarochirí. The chief of Chaclla stated that when he visited the lord of all the *guaranga*, he took ears of corn, coca, chile, and other things. These "gifts" came from the fields held by the lords of the macroethnic groups in Quivi. When I deal with land tenancy, I will clarify the data on this, which come from a long lawsuit carried on by the natives of Canta against those of Chaclla over some lands suitable for the cultivation of coca (AGI – Justicia 413; Rostworowski, 1988b).

Dual Rulership

It is necessary to examine the various forms that dual rulership might take in different *señoríos* and the various kinds of evidence regarding this phenomenon. This information generally takes an implicit form in the chronicles and is confirmed in many archival documents. Until now, little attention has been paid to Andean duality, primarily because the data are dispersed in Spanish administrative documents such as those relating to inspections, assessments, lawsuits, and wills.

I emphasize the importance of duality in the exercise of power because many scholars who limit themselves to a stereotyped vision of the indigenous world are afraid to break with the established scheme of things and refuse to accept new approaches based on ample documentary evidence. We are far from having resolved the mysteries of the Andean world and must remain open to constant reexamination of our conclusions in the light of new research.

Every chiefdom within the Inca state was divided into two moieties corresponding to the native concept of *hanan* and *hurin* (upper and lower) or of *ichoq* and *allauca* (left and right). Each moiety was governed by a chief, concerning which numerous documents provide detailed information. One of the chiefs of the two moieties was always subordinate to the other, although this dependence might vary, sometimes the upper half (as in Cusco) being more important and in others, the lower (as in the case of Ica).

Although the chronicles, and especially that of Sarmiento de Gamboa, make no specific reference to duality, the lords of the various regions of the Inca state are always mentioned in pairs. This insistence on naming two individuals together joined in power permits the inference that they represented the opposite halves of their organizational system. During the earliest period of Cusco, Tocay Capac and Pinahua Capac were dual rulers, although each of the parts comprised many *ayllus* (Rostworowski, 1969–70). Another example in the same region was the Choco-Cachona, insistently described as a single unit although they were two separate groups, each comprising several *ayllus*. Their presence in Cusco was sufficiently ancient for them to possess *huacas* in the *ceque* system.

In some administrative documents, such as the colonial *Visitas*, or inspections, the dual character of the lords is clearly demonstrated, as in the case of the Lupacas (Garci Diez de San Miguel, 1567, 1964/1972) and in the *Visita* to Acarí in 1593. Information concerning other regions comes from additional documentary sources, as in the case of the *señorío* of Lima and the data contained in the legal testimony of its chief, Don Gonzalo (Ros-tworowski, 1978a, 1981–82).

In the south, the Collaguas were divided into Yanqui Collagua of Han-ansaya and of Hurinsaya. The Lari Collaguas also had different lords for each moiety, and in the same way the Cavana Condes were divided into two halves with their respective lords (Relaciones Geográficas de Indias, 1885, vol. 2:38–59).

There are many data, then, concerning the duality of the lords. A differ-ent kind of example concerns the women who exercised power, as in the case of the *capullana* of the region of Piura. In Colán, in the sixteenth century, Doña Luisa and "her second person," of the same sex, by the name of Doña Latacina, governed jointly (Rostworowski, 1961:32). Under vice-regal pressure, the female chiefs lost their effective power to their husbands.

The Andean organizational model was not limited to this, however, but showed itself to be a more complex piece of machinery. In a *Relación* con-cerning the city of La Paz (Relaciones Geográficas de Indias, 1885, vol. 2: 72), there is an interesting reference to the classic dual division. Not only did each moiety have a principal chief, but each principal had a subordinate chief of lower social status as well. This individual was the *yanapaq*, "helper" or "companion." This information might be considered somewhat odd were it not confirmed by another piece of evidence: the *Tasa Toledana de Ca-pachica* (1575; AGI-Patronato 140, Part 4; Rostworowski, 1985–86), an excellent document for understanding the organization of power. It is our principal source for the following analysis of the roles of the chiefs of Ca-pachica.

There were eight lords of Capachica, four of them Aymaras, two govern-ing the Urus, and another two subordinate chiefs ruling on the island of Amantani. The most interesting information concerns the existence of two lords in each of the moieties, that is, two for Hanansaya and two for Hurin-saya. The "second person," the term used by the Spanish for the dual companion, was referred to as the "double" of the chief of each half. The *Tasa* indicates that the internal structure of the *señorío* was not merely dual but quadripartite in form, which represented the fundamental configuration of the Andean system. Is this situation in Capachica and La Paz a special case, or does it represent the system prevalent in the region in pre-Hispanic times? To remove any doubts, let us consult the *Tasa General de Toledo (Tasa Toledana)* directly (Cook, 1975).

This document, published by Cook, begins on page 6 – the preceding pages are missing – with the *repartimiento* of Aullaga and Uruquillos. Four lords are named in the document, two Aymaras for Hanansaya and two for Hurinsaya. In the other *repartimientos* in La Plata listed in the *Tasa Tole-dana*, we count more than ten *encomiendas*, each with four lords for the

Aymara population, in addition to the Uru ethnic chiefs. It appears likely that some *repartimientos* had fewer than four lords because of the fragmentation of territory in order to increase the number of *encomiendas* that could be awarded.

The divisions determined by the Spanish authorities were carried out arbitrarily, without taking into account native sociopolitical conditions. Under these circumstances, the colonial system did not favor the native quadripartite tradition but, on the contrary, proceeded to name only those local leaders who appeared to be necessary, eliminating the rest as dispensable.

In analyzing the *Tasa Toledana*, we find the same to be true for the regions of La Paz and Cusco, indicating that the ancient capital of the Inca state underwent further territorial divisions, translated into smaller *repartimientos* to satisfy the Spaniards. Four lords each, however, are noted for Arequipa and Guamanga. All of which shows that at the end of the sixteenth century traditional Andean sociopolitical structures were still in place, but that they were being gradually transformed and simplified as the colonial regime became stronger. Indigenous customs gradually fell into disuse, also weakened by persistent demographic decline and the flight of the natives from their *ayllus* and *señoríos* of origin.

With the disappearance of the *yanapaque* or "helper," and with him the quadripartite structure, the Spanish term *segunda persona* ("second person") was transformed and applied to the chief of the second moiety, creating, from that time on, a principal chief and governor of a *señorío*, and a "second person," often without even mentioning the existence of the two moieties.

Santillán (1927/1563, para. 24) complained of the large number of local bosses and a need to solve what he considered a serious problem. The demographic decline mentioned above and the flight of the natives from their places of origin made more evident the substantial numbers of ethnic chiefs. Seen from the perspective of the Spanish administration, a desire to simplify the organizational structure and limit what appeared to be an excessive number of lords was entirely justified.

With the disappearance of part of the sociopolitical structure, it becomes difficult to trace the extent of the quadripartite tradition or to determine if it existed in other regions as well. By means of early documents, we have been able to find a similar model for Lurín (or Urin) Ica in 1562. At that time, Hernando Anicama the Elder had been principal *cacique*, and in a testate clause had left the office to his brother, Guaman Aquixe, with whom he had long shared rule of the lower half. Later, when Hernando Anicama the Younger succeeded Guaman Aquixe as *cacique*, his second person was Andrés Mucay Guata. All this occurred without the participation of the nobles of Anan Ica (Rostworowski, 1977a).

When we study the names of the *guaranga* of Lurín Ica, we find that they appear to be related to the group of languages known as Aru or Jaqi, rather than to Quechua. It is possible that the inhabitants of Ica spoke a dialect influenced by this language group, and that theirs was a linguistic border region with the coastal Runi Simi of Chincha.

Perhaps the quadripartite tradition was the norm during the period of Inca rule as an institution imposed by the government in Cusco. There is also the possibility that it came from the highland region, where the group of Ayar Mango originated, and that it was he who established the system in Cusco.

Frank Salomon (1985) studied the dual model in Ecuador and concluded that it was an imposition of Inca origin. More research is needed to improve our understanding of what was happening in the northern region of ancient Peru, for which we lack information regarding this and other subjects. There are still many questions concerning Andean political structures, and it is possible that the Incas superimposed their quadripartite tradition on various preexisting local models.

The Lords by Privilege

The lords by privilege are not related to the traditional nobles, since their existence dates only to the period of Inca expansion and the appearance of the state. During the travels of the rulers through their territory, they came into contact with the local people. Royal travel, whether to visit lands or undertake military expeditions, involved passing through many towns, from which local inhabitants were selected either to join the retinue of the ruler or to perform specific tasks. Sometimes a group of individuals would be required to perform such tasks. These were not the massive population transfers that are discussed later in this chapter but, rather, the somewhat capricious selection of individuals for certain official tasks. In any case, this practice illustrates the great social mobility that existed in Andean society at the end of the fifteenth century.

The *Informaciones de Toledo* (Levillier, 1940, vol. 2) contain direct references to natives who reported having served the Inca, or remembered their fathers or grandfathers having done so. Such accounts possess the advantage of having been lived and experienced by the informants, which, of course, makes them extremely valuable for research purposes.

One example is the account of Don Juan Puyquin, chief of four towns near Cusco. According to the informant, his father was from "towards Quito" and as a child was taken into the retinue of Tupac Yupanqui after the conquest of the region, in which all his relatives were killed. In this way he entered the service of the Inca, who later appointed him lord of some villages near the capital (Levillier, 1940, vol. 2:55). There are many instances of chiefdoms being given as awards for faithful service or for the affection linking a superior and his good servant. Some of these selected individuals belonged to the local nobility of the region, while others were of *yana*, or servant, status (Levillier, ibid.:107).

From the considerable material on this subject contained in the *Informaciones*, let us examine the case of Pedro Astaco, from the town of Cache. His father was a servant of Tupac Yupanqui, who appointed him chief of a town near Cusco. Sometime later, the ruler revoked the appointment on the pretext that the *huacas* and the Sun found him unsuitable for the position. He and his relatives then returned to their previous condition as commoners in their town of origin (Levillier, ibid.). The rulers named in this manner formed a special category of chiefs, whom we will call lords by privilege or appointment. Their condition, which was not necessarily hereditary, led to a new governing class created by the Inca rulers. The advantage of such lords to the central government is evident, since only their loyalty to the Inca and their ability kept them in their positions. They were necessarily staunch supporters of the regime and could be easily removed from office should they prove incapable.

These examples illustrate the Inca's practice of making local lords of individuals loyal to him. The possibility of revocation demanded of them permanent loyalty and efficiency. It was important for an Andean chief to be able to carry out his responsibilities effectively. The *Informaciones* refer to lords who were said to have left their positions because of old age. In such situations, their younger brothers or nephews would inherit their positions (Levillier, ibid.). Such was the case of Don Pedro Cutinho, of Chucuito de Hurinsaya, who was said to have been chief of the Lupacas. In 1567, however, he no longer held that office, although he continued to enjoy the same rank and prestige.

For the same reasons of ability and efficiency, those who were underage were excluded from holding office. During the Colonial Period, this tradition was modified to permit the inheritance of political power by children under the regency of a relative. This new system encouraged innumerable lawsuits, which abound in the archives, among claimants to the position of *cacique*.

The *Yana* Lords

One of the more surprising facts to emerge from research in the archival documents concerning the status of the lords of the Inca state is the existence of *yana*, or servant, lords. The first such data come from testimony concerning the lords of Chachapoyas (Espinoza, 1967). According to the proceedings, when the office of lord of Leimabamba and Cochabamba became vacant, Huayna Capac awarded it to a servant in his service.

We found a similar case for the *señorío* of Collec (Collique), in the valley of the Chillón River, near Lima. During the conquests of Tupac Yupanqui on the central coast, the Colli Capac opposed him with his armies and was defeated and killed. In his place, the Inca appointed a *yanacon yanayacu* as chief (Rostworowski, 1977).

It is important to analyze the term *yanayacu*. According to Torero (personal communication):

yana	*ya*	*cu*
to help or serve	(suffix) continually	(suffix) for me

This information broadens the already extensive range of the governing class in Andean society during Inca rule.

A third piece of evidence regarding *yana* lords is found in the testimony of the native witnesses presented by Don Gonzalo, lord of Lima, in 1555. The *cacique* of Surco testified that the two lords of Lima were Taulichusco, who was *yana* of Mama Vilo, a secondary wife of Huayna Capac; and his "cousin" Caxapaxa, lord of the second moiety, who was in the service of the Inca himself. Both belonged to the social category of *yana* (Rostworowski, 1981–82). While such evidence appears reliable, we might ask what might be the advantage to the Inca of naming a *yana* to the office of lord.

The *yanacona* held positions of "servants in waiting," whether of the Inca, the Sun, the *coya*, the *panaca*, or the most important *huacas*. Also, a limited number of high-ranking individuals in Cusco and the great lords of the macroethnic groups might hold such servants (Murra, 1966, vol. 2).

Given the Inca's unlimited power, he could replace the natural lord of a region with a loyal servant who enjoyed his confidence. This would be a way to reward a servant, and at the same time serve as a warning to difficult and disloyal chiefs, who could be removed from office. Such a policy provoked anxiety among the nobles, who had to show themselves to be submissive to the wishes of the ruler or be replaced by *yana*.

The advantage of appointing a *yana* as lord consisted in his finding himself, by his very condition, separated from his origins, with no ties of kinship or reciprocity with his birthplace. With the *yana*, the Inca had no need to recur to the mechanism of reciprocity, and could give orders directly without having to apply the formula of the "request" and solicitude inherent in the system.

I have already analyzed the early forms of reciprocity, when the Inca lacked sufficient power to order the execution of a task. The institution of *yana* lords under the last Inca rulers was a means of obviating the request, and thereby increasing the power of the Inca. Later, when I return to the subject of the *yana*, I discuss this point further.

The Obligations of the Lords

Little is known about the obligations of the lords in the Inca state. It appears likely that certain religious and agricultural ceremonies were the responsibilities of the ethnic lords, although we still cannot define their limits.

In colonial documents that deal with the eradication of idolatries, the local lords are mentioned as officiating in rites dressed in their ancient fine wool *cumbi* garments, with their plates and jewelry of gold and silver. Possibly such chiefs had some responsibilities regarding the cult, but the evidence is limited by the clandestinity of post-Conquest Andean religion. Later I take up the subject of the priests, and we will see the surviving evidence.

Martínez Cereceda (1982) has emphasized the investiture in office of a lord and his symbols of authority. Every Andean lord had his special seat, which he occupied for any ceremony of importance. In addition, he possessed a litter carried by his bearers. In documents referring to Chimor, there is evidence that the number of bearers indicated the status of the lord. Also on the north coast, trumpets formed part of the pomp of a lord, along with the *tavernas*, as the Spaniards called the bearers of large jars of beverages that accompanied a chief whenever he left his residence. Whenever his litter was set down, the public could come and drink at the expense of the *cacique*. The more important the lord, the greater the number of drinking vessels to distribute among the people (Rostworowski, 1961).

The dress of the nobles also corresponded to their social status, and their clothes and adornments varied by region. The luxuriousness of the garments of the lords of the north coast must have been especially impressive. They wore their rich apparel not only for funerary rituals, but also in the great ceremonies when they presented themselves in all their splendor before the masses. Our museums contain examples of rich ornaments, such as nose rings, crowns, necklaces, medals, and ear spools of gold and silver, in addition to the exquisite textiles used for the *uncu* or men's shirts, cloaks, headdresses, and featherwork of the mummies.

Probably as a result of the conquest of Chimor, the Incas learned to surround themselves with the luxury of the northern lords. It appears likely that before the Inca expansion, the investiture ceremony of an Inca was similar to that of the great lords, and that the ostentation of Atahualpa noted by the chroniclers had been introduced only with the last Inca rulers.

The lords of the macroethnic groups constituted the foundation of the Andean system. The Spanish recognized this, for which reason in the early years of colonial rule the lords were left in their positions. Viceroy Toledo initiated the reorganization of the viceroyalty, which led to a reduction of power in the hands of the chiefs and the Cusco elite. The power of the native elite continued to diminish during the seventeenth century and finally disappeared in the nineteenth.

From documentary evidence, we can see that despite the formation of the Inca state, local society – that is, the *señoríos* – maintained its internal structures, preserving regional traditions without the intervention of the Incas. The brief duration of the Inca state did not permit the consummation of the integration of the ethnic lords with the metropolis.

The internal organization of the *señoríos* continued to function according to their ancestral traditions. We find, then, the chiefs of the macroethnic groups acting on two levels, on the first as lords of their *señoríos*, governing their subjects and subordinates, occupying themselves with local matters; and on the second, maintaining relations with the state, facing the demands for labor services ordered from Cusco.

In this chapter I deal only with the chief's local responsibilities, leaving for later their relations with the state. The Inca state has been classified as redistributive, and as such it received the surplus production that it redistributed according to the needs of the government, in conformity with a state rationale (Murra, 1978:198).

As we have already seen, in the beginning the Incas were mere local chiefs, like many others in the vast Andean region. For this reason, with the formation of the state, its internal structure rested on what already existed, that is, on the model of the *señoríos* of the southern region of the realm. In other words, the macroethnic groups functioned as redistributive nuclei at the local level.

The lords enjoyed the benefits of the lands accompanying the title of *cacique*, which were worked by a local labor force. The products of these lands served the ends of governing the chiefdom, since the ethnic chiefs were responsible for supporting the elderly, orphans, and widows. An example of this redistribution by minor lords is found in the *Visita* to the Guancayos, the inhabitants along the Chillón River in the central coast region (Rostworowski, 1977). This document indicates that the responsibility for picking coca leaves fell to the elderly, who were unable to perform more arduous tasks. The chief, in return, was obliged to provide them with food, drink, and clothing.

If we compare the highland elite with that of the coast at the beginning of the fifteenth century, we find a great difference between them. By that time, the ancient splendor of the Middle Horizon Wari hegemony had long since disappeared, and we do not know how much of that culture remained among the highland ethnic lords. Among the possible causes for the decline of the Wari state may have been the arrival of wild mountain groups such as the Chancas.

In the beginning, the Incas must also have been rude warriors, with few refinements, concerned only with extending their domains. What impression would the conquest of the wealthy *señorío* of Chincha have made on them? We cannot doubt that the great lord of Chincha enjoyed considerable prestige among the Incas, since he was the only lord in the entourage of Atahualpa carried in a litter on that fateful day in Cajamarca. To have seized the sanctuary of the most important god of the lowlands, Pachacamac, the god of earthquakes, must have caused a profound impact on the Incas. We can perceive this special sentiment in the accounts of the chroniclers relating the arrival in Pachacamac of the triumphant Tupac Yupanqui as a simple pilgrim, prostrate before the coastal idol.

The greatest impact on the Incas, however, came from the conquest of Chimor. The luxury and majesty with which the great Lord of the North surrounded himself, his overwhelming display of jewels and objects of gold and silver, must have impressed the rustic highland conquerors. It seems likely that they later attempted to emulate the opulence of the nobles of the coast and the pomp of their court. This desire must have been one reason for transferring large numbers of artisans from the coast to Cusco, to be able to satisfy their new masters' need for magnificence.

It was probably not only the sumptuousness of the ruler and court of Chimu Capac that influenced the Incas, but also the despotism and absolutism of the coastal lords. With the conquest of the north, the authority and political power of the ruler of the Inca state were greatly increased.

How many cultural loans did the Incas receive from the lowlands? This is difficult to answer, but one such borrowed custom was probably the creation of lords of the social category of *yana*, and resulting greater facility of deposing ethnic lords who were not sufficiently compliant to the wishes of the Inca.

As for land ownership and agrarian policy, we know that on the coast all land belonged to the ethnic lord, and that he then granted it to his subjects in return for a portion of the harvest. This might be the origin of the colonial practice of *yanaconaje*. Coastal customs may also have influenced the inception of private property among the last Incas.

Between coastal and highland inhabitants there was an extended exchange of loans and influences in the linguistic as well as technological and ideological spheres, and at times the boundary between the two becomes difficult to identify.

The Administrators

The enormous territories acquired by the Incas lead us to consider the problem of the administration of such a vast area. We may ask ourselves who initiated the tasks of government and who was responsible for carrying them out. There was a whole world of functionaries to carry out the multiple tasks and manage the business of the state. It seems likely that the positions of greatest responsibility and status were in the hands of the members of the Cusco elite, that is, of the *panaca*, of the "guardian" *ayllus*, and of the Incas by privilege. Perhaps each ruler also appointed his favorite kinsmen to positions of confidence, producing, on the death of an Inca, a great change among the personnel closest to the ruler.

With the formation of the state, a new governing class was created, composed of administrators responsible for the smooth functioning of the state machinery. Its numerous responsibilities included controlling state income, effective storage of accumulated goods, and planning work teams supplied by the lords for a great variety of tasks, in addition to determining the availability of manpower in each region for service in the armies. The administrators ordered the construction of roads, bridges, *tambos*, and administrative centers, the achievement of which was a huge task accomplished with the means of communication provided by the *quipu* and the oral messages of the *chasqui* runners. This represented an enormous effort and a test of the organizational abilities of the ruling class.

Among the individuals of various ranks who occupied positions in the administration of the state are found, at the first level, the *Inca Rantin* or *Capacpa Randicac*, as they were called, in charge of inspecting the regions under their responsibility (Guillén y Guillén, 1963). Santillán (1927, para. 14–15) calls them the "inspectors throughout the land" (*visitadores por toda la tierra*). Other principals were sent to count the inhabitants of a region, which they divided into *pachaca* and *guaranga*, while still others, known as *Runaypachacac*, counted the commoners by age or stage in the biological cycle (Santillán, 1927, para. 15).

Each kind of activity was supervised by someone responsible for its execution, such as the lord who supervised the cultivation of crops, or another, known as the *Apu Panaca* who selected the "chosen women" for the *aclla huasi*.

An important office was that of the lord sent to judge or punish special offenses. In a file dated 1558 in the *Archivo de Indias* (Justicia 413; Rostworowski, 1988b), we find the case of the lowland chief from Quivi, in the valley of the Chillón River, accused of conspiring against the health of the Inca through a *huaca* at Acupayllata. News of this reached the ears of the ruler, who sent a nobleman by the name of Apar Yupanqui to conduct an inquiry and report on what had transpired there. As a result, the chief, Chaumecaxa, was brought as a prisoner to Cusco, together with various others accused of taking part in the plot, and executed for treason. The punishment in Quivi was bloody, with most of the male population killed, leaving only the women and children.

With territorial expansion and the growth of the Inca state, government pressure on the population increased, which translated into increasing state intrusion into the lives of individuals. The labor force was the principal productive factor in the Inca economy, which led the ruler to intervene by ordering marriages and forbidding people to remain single. For this purpose a special inspector toured the country arranging the marriages of young men and women, which were performed in the town plazas in the presence of the Inca's representative.

The state accountants deserve a special section. It can be assumed that all the state storehouses had their *quipucamayoc*, who maintained a rigorous count of the incoming and outgoing agricultural and manufactured products. It seems likely that this information was collected together in Cusco for all regions by a principal lord, who was then able to inform the Inca regarding accounts anywhere in his realm. In the same way, each high lord kept his *quipu* accounts; the lord of Hatun Huanca demonstrated this in the Real Audiencia by presenting his *quipu* with accounts received by Pizarro for payment of his troops.

Also mentioned by Guaman Poma were those officials in charge of guarding the major roads. They oversaw the roads and *tambos*, at the head of which was an *Ynga Tocricoc* (Inca official). When a *señorío* was annexed to the state, whether by war or peacefully, a group of officials was assigned to it to establish the Inca form of organization. The first thing they did was construct a clay model of the area. Sarmiento de Gamboa mentions that such models were presented to the ruler, who before dispatching his representatives, indicated the changes he wished them to introduce. They would go on to mark the boundaries of the lands that were to be the Inca's and those of the governor of the region, and continue with the installation of the rest of the Inca organizational scheme.

At a lower level than these officials would be the *Tocricamayoc* (AGI, Escribanía de Cámara 501-A, folio 62) or supervisor of the artisans of any craft that was transferred from one region to another for the purpose of carrying out certain tasks. Craftspeople had the status of *mitmaq* or of *yana*, and performed work for the state within their specialties. They could be sent to the most distant locations, wherever the output of their craft was needed.

Priests, Witches, and Oracles

The religious intolerance so common in Europe in the sixteenth century, especially among the Spaniards, who had recently fought the Moors for the peninsula, made it impossible for the natives of the New World to preserve their own cults. The destruction of the *huacas* and sanctuaries was automatic, and their priests became clandestine, regarded from then on as witches possessed of evil powers. Satan himself roamed the country and could tempt the most sainted. The terror that the idea of this diabolical presence inspired in the Spaniards can be glimpsed in the chronicles, and in the accounts of the conquerors.

For these reasons, the information we have concerning the Andean priests at the time Pizarro's forces arrived is poor. In the letter Hernando Pizarro addressed to the Real Audiencia of Santo Domingo (Fernández de Oviedo, 1945, vol. 12:87), referring to the sanctuary of Pachacamac, he writes that its "bishop" was found in Cajamarca and had sent Pizarro "another roomful of gold, such as that ordered by Atahualpa." This is the only reference we have concerning a high priest of the most important temple on the entire coast.

When Hernando, accompanied by a small group, reached Pachacamac in January 1533 to arrange for a shipment of gold to be made for the ransom of Atahualpa, they were received by the principal lord of the place, named Taurichumbi. The sources for Cusco are more explicit. The high priest of the Temple of the Sun was named Villac Umu, or Vilaoma, as the Spaniards called him.

Given the dual character of the Andean world, and that the rulers of Lower Cusco resided in the Temple of the Sun, it is likely that the high priest belonged to the lower moiety. Molina, *el Chileno* (1943:37), indicates that the Vilaoma was the second person of the Inca and was called "servant or slave of the Sun." Elsewhere we have affirmed the priestly character of the lineage of the Incas of Lower Cusco within the dual system (Rostworowski, 1983).

An aspect of special importance in relation to the priests of Cusco is Cobo's (1956, vol. 2 book 14, chap. 6) contention that the Inca religion had undergone many changes from its inception until the Spanish Conquest. In the chronicles there are references to religious changes that occurred over time in support or to the detriment of one cult or another.

An account by an anonymous author (Biblioteca de Autores Españoles, 1968:161, 167) relates how in the time of the Inca Viracocha the priests fomented rebellions and riots. After these events, which coincided with the attack on Cusco by the Chancas and their subsequent defeat, the priestly

The Sicán site of Batán Grande, a ceremonial city in the valley of Lambayeque on the north coast. Photo by Billy Hare.

caste lost much of its previous power. With the enemy defeated, it seems likely that the priests became subject to punishment, which would have facilitated religious changes. After that time, the solar cult rose to preeminence over those of the other *huacas*.

Guaman Poma (1936:109) recounts that the ninth Inca named new priests and condemned the old, false priests to death. These changes are in agreement with the innovations introduced by the Inca Pachacutec in the Temple of the Sun and the splendor achieved by that sanctuary.

With the formation of the state, the position of religious inspector was created. These inspectors were charged with establishing and eliminating *huacas* and naming new priests. Both Sarmiento de Gamboa and Cabello de Valboa name Amaru Yupanqui and Guayna Auqui as individuals who held this office.

In the Andean world, oracles enjoyed great followings, and the future was predicted in many different ways. No important action was taken in Cusco without first consulting the *callpa*. This consisted of extracting the palpitating heart of a camelid, in which the augury was read. The most famous oracles were those of Pachacamac and Apurímac, the oracle Chinchaycamac of Chincha, Mullipampa of Quito, and Catequil in Huamachuco. Most of the *huacas*, however, had their own oracles.

Special priests called *guacarimachic* spoke with the *huacas* and the *ayatapuc* communicated with the dead (Cabello de Valboa, 1951:287–88). The *caviacoc* drank potions before giving their oracles. It is curious to note the similarity to the name of the princess-*huaca* called Cavillaca, who may have been a priestess or prophetess (see Avila; Salomon and Urioste, 1991).

The *Relación Anónima* (1968, Biblioteca Autores Españoles: 164) includes as oracles the *huatuc*, who would drink a beverage and then, in a disturbed state, emit their prophecies. The *hamurpa* examined the entrails of sacrificed animals for their auguries. Avila's (1966, chap. 18) informants related an augury concerning the end of the adoration of the god Pariacaca. We are told that, following their conquest of the region, the Incas, wishing to honor the *huaca*, installed fifteen priests from Upper Yauyos and a similar number from Lower Yauyos dedicated to his cult. One day, all of them having convened to read the augury of a sacrificed llama, one of the priests, who belonged to the Llacuace ethnic group, exclaimed: "What misfortune! The auguries are ominous; brothers, our father Pariacaca will be abandoned." Furious, the other priests insulted him, but a few days later news arrived of the events of Cajamarca. Under these circumstances, the priests dispersed and returned to their *ayllus* of origin.

The same *Relación* distinguishes between two groups of priests. The principal function of the *yañca*, who belonged to the Cacasica *ayllu*, was to observe the movement of the sun's shadow against a wall, to determine the most propitious time to celebrate certain festivals. In addition, each *ayllu* had a *huacasa*, or *huacsa*, who was responsible for the ritual dances held three times a year (Avila, chap. 9). Obviously, the priestly functions and hierarchies of the *yañac* and the *huacsa* were different. When the Incas conquered the region, the ruler visited the sacred place of the *huacsa* and took part, as one of them, in the rites in honor of Pariacaca, a gesture that flattered all the Yauyos.

Arriaga (1968), writing about the eradication of idolatries, mentions different kinds of *hechiceros* (witches), the term used by the Spaniards for the ancient priests. According to him, it was the *huacapvillac* who spoke with the *huaca* and enjoyed the highest status among the priests. The function of the *malquipvillac* was to communicate with the mummified ancestors. Similarly, the *libiaopavillac* worshiped lightning; and the *punchaopvillac*, the sun. Each priest had his *yanapac*, or helper, a supremely Andean concept, as we have seen in the case of the lords.

The *aucachic*, called *ichuri* in Cusco, performed the functions of confessors. This was a pan-Andean custom followed in the great ceremonies or festivals, when fasts were practiced in which chile, salt, and women could not be touched. The *azuac*, or *accac*, who were charged with preparing the beverages consumed during these rites, were men on the coast, while in the highlands they were women. During the Inca period the preparation of sufficient beverages for state and ritual purposes was an obligation of the chosen women.

The *socyac* were able to predict the future by means of maize grains. The *pacharicuc*, or *pacchacatic*, foretold future events using large spiders. According to documents on idolatry, the spiders were kept in hollow human bones, and the predictions would be based on how they fell to the ground. The importance of spiders on the coast is also evidenced by their presence in Nasca and Mochica iconography. In addition, among the geoglyphs of the famous Nasca lines there is represented a spider that may be related to this kind of prediction. To these diverse priests and oracles must be added the healers, known as *macsa* or *viha*.

There were many ways to enter the priesthood. One could enter by inheritance, but first one had to demonstrate aptitude for its functions. There were *ayllus* dedicated to certain priestly offices, such as the *yañacs* of Cacasica, previously mentioned, and the *tarpuntay* of Cusco, who were responsible for agricultural rites. A second way to enter the priesthood was by election. The convened priests named a successor to a vacant position. When an unusual event occurred to an individual, such as being injured by lightning and surviving, it was considered a form of predestination.

Women as well as men filled these positions. There were famous priestesses, such as that of the idol of Apurímac, who preferred to throw herself into the abyss rather than fall into the hands of the Spanish (Pedro Pizarro, 1978). In general, the rites and ceremonies in honor of the moon and the earth were in the hands of the *coya*, or queen, and of the women of the Inca

An aerial view of the valley and religious center of Pachacamac, on the south coast. Photo by Shippee-Johnson, Neg. No. 334837, courtesy of Department of Library Services, American Museum of Natural History.

elite (Santillán, 1927). One of the greatest festivals in Cusco was the Coyaraimi, which took place during the September equinox and coincided with the arrival of the first rains. During these days they celebrated the festival of the Citua, which consisted of acts of purification to free the city of all its evils. The celebrations lasted several days, of which the fourth was dedicated to the moon and the earth (Molina, 1943).

THE "TRADERS"

In the coastal region, there was a social class that specialized in barter and exchange. There were several categories of these traders, according to the items they traded.

In the sixteenth-century documents the term *mercader* is used for native specialists in exchange. The word must be understood in its indigenous context, however, within an economy that did not use money, but only practiced the barter of goods.

The pre-Hispanic Ascope acqueduct, in the Chicama valley, on the north coast. Photo by Edward Ranney.

The Chincha Traders

In 1970, I published a valuable document from the Biblioteca del Palacio Real in Madrid, by an anonymous author, which made reference to the existence of six thousand traders in Chincha. They carried out exchange over two routes, a northern sea route, using rafts as far as Puerto Viejo and Mantas, in present-day Ecuador; and a land route using caravans of camelids and carriers toward the Peruvian-Bolivian altiplano and Cusco.

These traders carried copper for maritime exchange with the north and brought back *mullu* shells from the warm northern waters. These red shells were of great importance, since they constituted the favorite offering of the *huacas* and were used in rites related to rainfall and springwater. Archaeologists have found *Spondylus* at sites dating to the Chavín period, long before the Late Intermediate Period, about which we have the references in question regarding the great apogee of the *señorío* of Chincha.

We will not deal here with the issues of the existence of the traders, of the evidence for trade in the Andean world, or of raft navigation along the Andean coast (Edwards, 1965; Hartmann, 1971; Rostworowski, 1970, 1977). We will only take note of the long-distance trade in *mullu* mentioned in the 1549 *Visita* to Atico and Caravelí (Galdos Rodríguez, 1977). In the document in question, the chief of the region of Chincha Pula testifies that the inhabitants had received red shells called *mollo* from Huancavilca, in Ecuador, with which they had specialized in carving statues. The skill of these craftspeople was such that Huayna Capac ordered fifty of them to be brought to Cusco. The same Galdos Rodríguez finds that this information is proof of the control exercised by the Incas over the trade in *mullu*, from which he concludes that there were neither traders nor a coastal commerce in these shells.

If his conclusion were accurate, the Inca monopoly would be an extremely late development at best, since only at the end of Huayna Capac's rule were the Huancavilcas conquered and dominated by the Incas. It has already been shown that a possible motive for the conquest of Ecuador was the desire of the Inca to control access to the source of *mullu*, which was of great magical-religious importance. Since the use of *Spondylus* in the Andean world is very ancient, however, Galdos Rodríguez's hypothesis would appear to be incorrect. The skill of the artisans of Atico also evidences a long artistic tradition.

Hence, it would appear that the references to the use of *mullu* in Atico, rather than negating the possibility of coastal exchange, confirm it. We can suggest two means by which Atico may have obtained the precious shells. The first is that the Chincha traders supplied the artisans of Atico with the *mullu* they required for their sculptures; the second, that the latter were themselves navigators who conducted long-distance trade at their own expense. Since it is more plausible that only the Chincha traders possessed the necessary means to organize such expeditions, we are inclined toward the first alternative. We know they had many rafts, knew the course, and had the navigation skills required for such difficult and dangerous voyages. There is additional evidence in the name of the lord of Atico, Chincha Pula, which connects him to the *señorío* of the same name.

I have tried to discover the native term for *mercaderes*, that is, the name that the Chinchanos themselves gave to the traders in *mullu*, as Frank Solomon was able to do for Ecuador. On a list of the functions performed by the coastal people prepared by Francisco Falcón in 1571 (Rostworowski, 1977), there is a reference to the *mollo chasqui camayoc*, literally, the messengers that bring the *Spondylus* shells. Falcón's account, however, appears to have been based on a Cusco lexicon, in which case it would not correspond to the coastal terminology.

The *Lexicón* of Fray Domingo de Santo Tomás (1951) contains Spanish synonyms of terms in coastal Quechua. The Spanish word *mensajero* (messenger), which corresponds to the word *chasqui* in highland Quechua, is translated in coastal Quechua as *cachac*, or *ñanguincha*. If we substitute these for *chasqui* in the above sense, we obtain *mollocachac camayoc* or *mollo ñanguinha camayoc*, terms closer to the speech of the lowlands of the south-central coast. Although it appears likely that the Cusco term for those who transported the *Spondylus* was *mollo chasqui camayoc*, we still cannot be certain of the term used in the *señorío* of Chincha.

The use of the Spanish terms does not, of course, change in any way the activity carried out by the traders, which consisted of transporting the shells to distant places to exchange them for other objects. The Spanish terminology does, however, imply a different cultural context from that which would be conveyed by the native terms. The northern coastal traders themselves asserted that their exchange was carried out "the Indian way," which confirms that the central idea that motivated their business was different from "the Spanish way." This is further proof of the danger of translating Andean concepts with erroneous terms.

The Northern Traders

Later, when dealing with the coastal economic model, I discuss at greater length the subject of exchange in the northern region. Here, I indicate only that there were two levels of people involved in such tasks, apart from local barter to obtain subsistence products. On the first level, groups of specialized fishermen traded in dried and salted fish, exchanging their products in their own valleys and with the neighboring highlands. On the second level, the "lords" who possessed neither lands nor water – as they themselves assert – devoted themselves to trade in "wool clothing, pearl beads, cotton, beans, fish, and other things," while others of more modest means traded salt (AGI – Justicia 458, folios 1917, 1922, 1929, 1926, 1930, 1931; Justicia 461, folios 1454v, 1456v, 1957, 1463r, 1464, 1466). The early data, from the *Juicio de Residencia* of Dr. Cuenca in 1566 and 1567, are extremely valuable because they antedate the establishment of acculturated trade.

Information regarding traders can be found elsewhere as well. In a lawsuit between Spaniards, one of the parties introduced as evidence two natives who were said to be *mercaderes*. Neither had a Christian name; one was named Chuquen, from Motupe, and the other Yancop, from Pacora (Rostworowski, 1977).

We should not be surprised by the presence of specialists in trade on the north coast. In Ecuador there were traders called *mindalá* (Salomon, 1980), and it is easy to demonstrate the close relationship, in pre-Hispanic times, between the Peruvian coastal region and the Ecuadorian, a relationship maintained well into the nineteenth century.

THE COMMONERS

Several categories of commoners can be distinguished, according to their status and the functions they performed.

The Artisans

Artisans had an important role on the coast, where labor specialization formed part of the organizational model. In the highlands, there were *ayllus* of silversmiths and potters living in villages, but these were not full-time specialists as were those on the coast. Elsewhere, for example, in Canta, all the communities of a chiefdom would meet at specified times to engage in the production of ceramics and fine textiles.

In the list compiled by Falcón in 1571 Biblioteca National Madrid, Ms. No. 3042; see Rostworowski, 1977) we see that many tasks were classified as crafts that today are not considered as such. This is probably due to differences over time in the way various crafts are practiced.

Craftspeople enjoyed a special status in the Inca state. Although they worked for the state, they did not take part in the agricultural or war *mita*. The coastal artisans also occupied privileged social positions before the advent of Inca hegemony; although they worked for their ethnic lords, they were able to barter part of their production and retain the benefits of such exchange. Later, with the establishment of Inca power, they retained their special status but came under the control of the state. We do not know if they continued to retain the benefits of their surplus production.

When the Inca rulers began to require greater amounts of sumptuary goods, they initiated the practice of sending groups of *ayllus* of full-time artisans to Cusco and the other principal administrative centers in order to improve state access to their products.

The craftspeople in greatest demand were the artisans in silver and gold. There are documents in the archives that indicate the places of origin of the *ayllus* of craft specialists who resided in Cusco. Among them were workers from Ica, Chincha, Pachacamac, Chimu, and Huancavilca, in distant Ecuador (Rostworowski, 1977). These last named are listed as residents of a zone near Cusco, Zurite, at the end of the sixteenth century, on lands of the Tumipampa *panaca*. The Huancavilcans were brought from the north by Huayna Capac to produce objects of precious metals for the Inca (AGN – Títulos de Propiedad, cuad. 431, 1595–1710).

In colonial times, native silversmiths were in much demand by Spaniards desiring rich silver tableware. In Peru, unlike in Mexico, prohibitions against the native silversmiths' plying their trade were not enforced. In the

Chanchán (Chan Chan), the capital of the Chimu, on the north coast, which reached its apogee during the Late Intermediate Period. Photo by Shippee-Johnson, Neg. No. 334900, courtesy of Department of Library Services, American Museum of Natural History.

document concerning the *Juicio de Residencia* (an evaluation required of Spanish colonial officials) of Dr. Cuenca when he was *corregidor* in Cusco, we find complaints by coastal silverworkers who were not paid for their wares. These artisans worked in private houses or in their huts without applying the required government marks to their silver products, for which reason marks are rare on Peruvian metal objects of the sixteenth century. In 1575, Viceroy Toledo again tried to eliminate this kind of fiscal fraud, but without any great success, as the *corregidores,* priests, and *encomenderos* continued to avoid payment of the royal tax.

Another example of the transfer of artisans to another location to carry out their craft is that of the coastal pottery makers of Xultin, who were sent to Cajamarca to make pottery for the administrative center of the region. After the fall of the Inca state, the ethnic lords fought among themselves for control over such valuable artisans (Espinoza, 1970).

Among the many coastal artisans practicing special crafts, I can mention

A massive adobe-brick ceremonial platform at the Chimu site of Túcume in the valley of Lambayeque, on the north coast. Photo by Billy Hare.

the cloth painters, who painted garments and traveled through the valleys plying their craft. In the *Juicio de Residencia* at the completion of Dr. Cuenca's term in the north, we find several natives requesting relief from obstructions to the practice of their crafts in the various villages to which they traveled (AGI – Justicia 456 and 458). This pictorial tradition, of remote origin, clearly permitted the emergence during the viceroyalty of continuous artistic traditions in colonial painting and popular art (Macera, 1979). The *ordenanza* for the coast dictated in 1566 by González de Cuenca prohibited artisans from changing or abandoning their craft occupations (Rostworowski, 1977).

We lack data concerning the artisans of the highlands during the fifteenth and early sixteenth centuries. In the *Visita* to Huánuco (Ortiz de Zúñiga, 1967, 1972), there is information regarding the presence of diverse crafts-people such as *cumbicamayoc* (weavers), salt makers, potters, and specialists in building litters for the Inca and in making rope for hunting deer. These craftspeople did not, however, form specialized groups, but lived among the agriculturalist majority. In addition, they were considerably fewer in number than the coastal artisans, whose organization by crafts resembled a guild system.

The *Hatun Runa*

The *hatun runa,* or adult males, called *atun luna* in the dialect of the coast, constituted, with their families, most of the Andean population. These were the peasant farmers and herders from among whose ranks the state derived the enormous labor force indispensable for the functioning of government.

According to most of the chroniclers, Inca Tupac Yupanqui reorganized the Andean population, dividing it into units of 10 (*chunga*), 100 (*pachaca*), 1,000 (*guaranga*), and 10,000 households (*unu*). The representatives of units of 10 were low-status *caciques;* those of 100, lesser chiefs; and the others, lords of higher rank.

From among the *hatun runa* were selected the soldiers who formed the armies that would go to do battle in distant lands, the *mitmaq* of different kinds and functions that were sent to various regions, and the *yana* that were selected to labor for the Inca, the *coya,* the Sun, or the *huacas.*

The great demand for manual labor led to the creation of other demographic units, in addition to the decimal groups, based on the biological cycle. The advantages of this system of computation were enormous, since the *quipucamayoc,* or accountants, were able, with their *quipu,* to indicate with great precision the number of inhabitants of a given age in each location.

In the Spanish administrative documents, it can be seen that the natives were totally ignorant of their own ages. Although they observed and used various systems for computing time, they did not employ this knowledge to determine the ages of individuals or to count years, as in the Old World.

The date of the death of Huayna Capac, so close to the Spanish Conquest, is the subject of debate among the chroniclers, which indicates that the natives did not possess a means of computing time that would permit them to provide an absolute chronological placement for such events. Probably they were guided by other concepts and focused on events from a different perspective. When Rowe (1958:503, 519) investigated individuals' ages in the Inca censuses, he realized that the Incas did not calculate their ages by years, and that individuals were classified not by chronological age but according to their physical condition and capacity for work.

In many sixteenth-century *Visitas* it can be observed that the tributaries and their wives are mentioned as all having the same age. In the Andean realm, individuals kept record of their ages by biological cycles, based on the development and decline of the human body. This information is found in the "*calles*" or "*visitas*" of the chronicler Guaman Poma and in the age categories listed by Castro and Ortega Morejón (1974). I shall analyze carefully the information provided by both chroniclers: first that of Guaman Poma, then that of Castro and Ortega Morejón.

What attracts our attention in the *calles* of Guaman Poma is that the ages do not follow chronological order, do not begin with infancy and advance through life. Rather, instead of what would be a logical sequence for us, Guaman Poma emphasized, above all, the most important age in the Andean world, the age of maximum labor potential for humans, from twenty-five to fifty, when they attain the height of their faculties. For men, this age was called *auca camayoc*, a term that comes from the word *auca*, or warrior. To this class were assigned not only soldiers but also agricultural workers, *mitmaq*, and *yana*. These were the people who provided the most labor, rendered the greatest service.

To this first male age category corresponded a female category, *auca camayoc huarmi*, the wives of the warriors. In his accompanying drawing, Guaman Poma represents a woman seated before a loom, a "tribute woman" at work. The chronicler repeats for her the same phrase found in the manuscripts, saying that "these women as well as these men are of the same reproductive age."

The obligatory laboriousness of the Indian is demonstrated in his appreciation of this important vital stage in the human biological cycle, to which must be added its being the stage of human reproduction. By saying that the couple was of the same age, he was indicating they were of an age appropriate for reproduction.

Guaman Poma divided his *visitas* or *calles* into years for the benefit of his European readers, but an individual's belonging in a particular *calle* and passing to another meant that he was entering another biological stage. Following the *calle* of *aucacamayoc* came the categories belonging to the various stages of old age.

The second *visita* was called *puric macho*, and included men aged sixty to seventy-eight, who carried out light work such as gathering firewood and straw and such tasks as those of gatekeeper or *quipocamayoc*. The women were the *payacona* of fifty years of age, who wove coarse cloth, baskets, and rope, and might be dispensers of food or cooks, according to their social status.

The third category included the very old, eighty years of age or more, who were called *rocto macho*, the old deaf ones. Guaman Poma illustrated this stage with an old man leaning on a cane; he only ate and slept. Some might weave blankets or rope or raise rabbits or ducks. The women of at least eighty were the *puñocpaya*, those who slept, who might also sew bags, make rope, or raise some small animals.

In the fourth *visita*, Guaman Poma departs from the established pattern to mention a sector of the population consisting of the disabled, mentally ill or deficient, and dwarfs of both sexes. He indicates that these married among themselves according to their deformity in order to increase the population. It can be seen that the women remained productive longer than the men. According to their ability, they made fine garments or might be expert weavers or cooks.

The following *visitas* included the rest of the population in order of diminishing age. The young people of eighteen to twenty were the *sayac payac*, youths who paid half tribute. From the most agile were selected the messengers, or *cachacona*, who were called *chasqui* in Cusco. Others guarded the community or state herds. The young women were called *zumac cipa*, from among whom were chosen those dedicated to the Sun, the temples, the gods, and the Inca, with the rest marrying the young men.

The sixth *calle* was that of the *mactacona*, boys twelve to eighteen years old who served the community and hunted birds for the preparation of dried meat. Their female counterparts were the *corotasque,* that is, the young girls. They helped their parents in various activities, in light work, learning to sew and weave, guarding the herd and keeping watch over the fields.

The seventh *calle* included the young boys nine to twelve years old. They also helped their elders and hunted birds. The young girls picked flowers to prepare dyes and various edible wild plants. Perhaps the most interesting information is that from among these girls were chosen those destined for the *capaccocha*, the most important sacrifice in the Andean world. There is copious information about these human sacrifices, which took place only on occasions of great importance, in honor of the Inca, a queen, or a *huaca* (Duviols, 1976b; AGI – Justicia 413).

The eighth *visita* corresponded to children five to nine years of age. Those of both sexes were considered *puellacoc*, those who played. Even at that early age, however, they began to help their parents with light work, such as watching the herd, gathering firewood, and taking care of their younger brothers and sisters. The girls learned to sew. The final two age categories consisted of the youngest children, those who crawled and those who nursed. Guaman Poma notes of both that they are "useless" or "good for nothing" because they require "others to care for them and serve them." These reflections of the chronicler are very significant, because they illustrate a practical and utilitarian spirit and underline the importance with which the natives regarded work-related effort.

Traditional highland dress worn in Cusco. Photo by Charles H. Coles, Neg. No. 288577, courtesy of Department of Library Services, American Museum of Natural History.

The chronicle of Castro and Ortega Morejón, written by Spaniards, loses certain Andean values in its information. For example, the decimal system used by the natives and unknown among sixteenth-century Europeans is replaced by a count by dozens, the Spanish custom at that time. More than half of the description of the classificatory system is devoted to the categories of children and nursing infants, based on concepts that are not indigenous, as we have seen, since these were not productive age groups.

The first age category is that of *poño loco,* from the terms *puñuc,* to sleep, and *roco* or *rucu,* old. The Quechua used in the chronicle is a coastal dialect spoken in the central coast region, in which the "r" is changed to an "l." The second age category is *chaupi loco,* or middle age; then *auca pori,* the virile warrior, twenty-five to forty years old, who has his equivalent on Guaman Poma's list. The fourth age category is that of *micho guayna,* one who is becoming a young man; the fifth, *coca pallac,* or one who picks coca leaves, from the existence of numerous fields on an appropriate coastal strip (Rostworowski, 1976, 1977). The sixth is the *pucalla guamara,* or *puclla guamra*, the child who plays. Several additional age categories comprise the children from six years of age to the newborn.

On the *quipu* presented by Don Martín Cari, chief of Anan Saya, to the *Visitador* Garci Diez de San Miguel, in Chucuito in 1567, we find concepts regarding age categories similar to those of Guaman Poma. Similar sensibilities are demonstrated in the statement of the lord of Urinsaya underlining the Andean concept of calculating the available human energy. We have already seen the importance of the age of maximum human production in the native tradition.

Reaching adulthood was further confirmed with marriage. It is with marriage that the couple takes their place in the *ayllu* and assume their responsibilities within it. The new home, considered a domestic unit, would receive a *tupu* of land for its subsistence. The *tupu* was determined as the amount of land necessary to maintain a single couple, and would be increased according to the number of children they had. It was a measurement of distance and also of area. Its peculiar characteristic is that it was a relative unit of measurement, which took into account not only the quality of the soil but the amount of fallow it required. This meant that the *tupu* given the couple could vary in its dimensions according to these factors (Rostworowski, 1960, 1981d).

The *hatun runa* were not only peasant farmers but also herders, who cared for the flocks of the Inca, the Sun, the *huacas*, the ethnic lords, and their *ayllus*.

The Fishermen

The fishermen inhabited the length of the extensive Peruvian coast and formed a social class distinct and separate from the others, especially from those who farmed the land (Rostworowski, 1981b). They lived near their coves and ports, in the vicinity of the coastal lagoons that existed in all the coastal valleys in those times. In the Andean world, beaches were not open to all, as in Europe; rather, each *ayllu* or group had a zone on the coast that belonged to it exclusively.

In 1566, the *Licenciado* and *Visitador* González de Cuenca, during his stay in the north, ordered that the beaches be common to all. This declaration caused such confusion, disturbance, and protest among the chiefs of the fishermen that Cuenca decided to revoke his order and retain the ancient practice, for lack of a better solution (AGI–Justicia 458, folio 205v).

Probably the ownership of the beaches, as of the lands, was based on a kind of discontinuous tenancy that obeyed special native concepts. We know that in 1549, on the occasion of the *Visita* to the coast of the chiefdom of Maranga in the valley of Lima, the Spanish found that people from the neighboring *señoríos* of Lima and Pachacamac would fish there even though they possessed their own coves. Perhaps we are dealing with horizontal, rather than vertical, enclaves based on the type of coast, since some beaches were of sand and others of pebbles or rocks. Naturally, the fish available at each of these would have been different, and there may have been arrangements among the fishermen so that all would have access to the various products of the sea.

A noteworthy characteristic of the fishermen is that they did not possess land for cultivation. Only well into colonial times can we observe a change in this situation. Besides, their beaches included their own lagoons, where they not only fished for *lisa (Mugil cephalus)* but also hunted birds and harvested reeds with which to build their boats and huts. To preserve the supply of rushes, they would plant them on the margins of their lagoons.

The kinds of vessels used varied according to region. On the north coast, they used rafts built with logs; farther south, they used the *caballitos,* or tuba boats, made from bundles of *totora* reeds; while in the south they used sealskins.

As already mentioned, the fishermen lived in settlements on the margins of the farming villages. In pre-Hispanic times, in the case of Chincha, they resided on a long street, at the edge of the sea. Their numbers are estimated at ten thousand, which can be explained only if an evident surplus catch was used for trade. The fishermen dried the fish for barter with the inhabitants of the highlands (Rostworowski, 1970, 1977).

We have other references to fishermen in the village of Quilcay, bordering the sanctuary of Pachacamac, which disappeared in the tidal wave that followed the devastating earthquake of 1746. We know from documents that the fishermen were not obligated to join the *mita* in the town of Lurín but, rather, had their own *mita* by which they took turns in going to sea.

They were endogamous by tradition, that is, they married only among other fishing families. When in Quilcay during the viceroyalty there were too few men, the women, instead of marrying the men of Lurín, sought husbands among the fishermen of Chilca or distant Santiago de Cao.

The division between agriculturalists and fishermen was accentuated in the north, where it was reflected in different dialects: the *muchic,* or *yunga,* was spoken from Huarmey to the north (Mogrovejo, 1920/1593) in the *señorío* of Chimu Capac, while the fishermen spoke their own dialect, called by the Spaniards "*la pescadora.*" Possibly this dialect was a kind of lingua franca whose function was to facilitate trade and navigation all along the coast.

The fishermen of Sechura, near Paita, also had their own way of speaking, perhaps similar or related to *la pescadora*. The fact that the fishermen had their own language is consistent with the socioeconomic condition of these groups, marginalized by the agriculturalists and in longitudinal communication among themselves. The exercise of a particular occupation, limited to certain members of society, conforms to the pattern of the division of labor on the coast.

The various villages of fishermen, near the sea and surrounded by lagoons, maintained close relations with the agricultural towns of each valley. While the fishermen had their own lords, it can be seen that in the sixteenth century, before the upheavals created by the Toledano reductions, they were dependent to a considerable extent on the principal lord of each chiefdom. There was a complementarity and reciprocity between the settlements of fishermen and farmers along the coast.

The *Mitmaq*

The *mitmaq* were more or less numerous groups sent, with their families and under their own subordinate ethnic chiefs, from their places of origin to other regions to fulfill specific tasks or missions. Though separated from their places of origin, they maintained ties of reciprocity and kinship with them. This was the fundamental difference that distinguished them from the *yana*, whose ties with their places of origin were lost. When the Inca state reached the peak of its expansion, however, and thousands of miles might separate the *mitmaq* from their original homes, this reciprocity, while not eliminated in principle, was in practice considerably weakened or lost.

The *mitmaq* were not permitted to change the dress or headwear of their native villages, and when they received the order to move, they did so with all their household goods, seeds, and other belongings, preserving all their own customs (Cieza de León, *Señorío* 1943, chap. 22). Retaining their distinctive customs permitted state administrators to distinguish rapidly between newcomers and long-time residents.

The origins of the *mitmaq* were no doubt pre-Inca. *Mitmaq* had long been used by the macroethnic groups to obtain from other ecological zones products that were unavailable in the core zone. The geographical distribution of the Lupacas was such that they possessed colonies in environments different from that of the altiplano, with enclaves on the coast and some in the jungle. Possibly a similar system was practiced during the time of the Wari hegemony.

Although in its beginnings the *mitmaq* provided labor for lands more or less distant from their places of origin, the practice underwent a transformation during the reigns of the last Incas, when massive population movements were carried out to serve the economic interests of the state.

During the final phase of the Inca state, the power of the ruler was such that he utilized *mitmaq* on a vast scale to carry out expansionary state works. This is the case of the *mitmaq* of diverse ethnic groups sent by Huayna Capac to the valley of Cochabamba to work the lands (Wachtel, 1980–81). From this perspective, the *mitmaq* became an important source of power in the hands of the rulers of Cusco, who learned how to utilize it to increase the production of the state.

Mitmaq could vary considerably and served a wide variety of purposes. In some cases, *mitmaq* status could be considered a reward or a show of confidence and distinction, in others, as punishment for an ethnic group that had earned such punitive action. The documentary sources provide information about various kinds and functions of *mitmaq*.

The first category of *mitmaq* might be considered a form of deference, as when a group of Inca ancestry was sent to teach the *Cusqueño* language, defend borders, or pacify rebellious zones. In such cases the *mitmaq* would receive honors, gifts, luxury objects, and women in appreciation and compensation for their absence from the capital (Cieza de León, *Señorío*, 1943, chap. 22).

An example of this kind of *mitmaq* would be Tupac Yupanqui's sending noblemen to the zone of the Chupaychos of Huánuco to defend against the jungle-dwelling Panataguas (Ms. Ministerio de RR.EE.s/n, 1782; Ortiz de Zúñiga, 1972, vol. 2:50, 185). The *mitmaq* sent during the reign of Tupac Yupanqui to Cochabamba would have served the same purpose as a military rear guard against the border incursions of the Chiriguanas (Wachtel, 1980–81).

On some occasions, people loyal to the Inca would be sent to try to break remaining resistance in recently conquered enemy regions, or following the pacification of rebellious groups. In such cases, the government would proceed to evacuate a region of its original inhabitants and replace them with others loyal to the Inca. Such was the case of the conquest of Guarco (Cañete) after several years of war. The lands on the left bank of the river were given to *mitmaq* of Chincha origin, who, as neighbors, wished to expand their own chiefdom while the Coayllos, old enemies of the Guarcos, were installed as *mitmaq* on the fields on the right bank of the river (Rostworowski, 1978–80). On this occasion the *mitmaq* served to consolidate an Inca conquest and benefited from their cooperation with the Inca. This practice of expelling rebellious natives from their lands and homes caused ethnic lords who wished to oppose the Inca troops to further consider the consequences. In such cases the institution of *mitmaq* had an essentially political objective.

When we discussed the rebellions and unrest during the period of Inca rule, I mentioned the uprising of Chimu Capac and the resulting transfer of most of the population to various locations in the Inca state. Among these *mitmaq*, various occupations were represented: fishermen, silversmiths, and perhaps specialists in hydraulic technology; in any case, these *mitmaq* were created for punitive reasons because of the attitude of the Chimu lord.

We do not know the purpose of an entire *guaranga* of *mitmaq* in Cajamarca, composed of Quechua, Cañari, Guambo, and Colla peoples. Possibly in lightly populated regions a larger supply of labor was needed to intensify agricultural production, and contingents of *mitmaq* were sent to cultivate untilled land. This is what happened in the valley of La Convención, near Cusco, where people from Chachapoyas were sent as *mitmaq* (Rostworowski, 1963).

The colonists at the entrance to the jungle region, most of whom returned to their places of origin when the Spaniards arrived, constituted another variety of *mitmaq*. There were also *mitmaq* who worked in the Inca's mines – who should not be confused with those who worked in the mines in carrying out a *mita*, that is, temporary labor in the mines belonging to the macroethnic groups or the *ayllus* (Relaciones Geográficas de Indias, 1885, vol. 2, appendix 3, p. 39).

Finally, there were the *mitmaq* who had religious responsibilities, such as *camayoc* who honored and served the various important sanctuaries, such as that of Copacabana. There might be large numbers of *mitmaq* performing such functions, which could include the cultivation of the fields belonging to *huacas* whom the Inca wished to thank for services rendered (Duviols, 1967).

After the Spanish Conquest, there was agitation among *mitmaq* and *yana* to return to their places of origin. The Spaniards, however, prohibited such movements, which, had they continued, would have caused chaos in the colonial administration (Cedulario del Perú, 1534–38:263–64; Porras Barrenechea, 1948, vol. 2).

The *Yana*

There are many questions about the *yana* (literally, servants) that still cannot be answered. We do not know, for example, if the institution had a single origin or more than one. According to some chroniclers (Cabello de Valboa, 1951; Sarmiento de Gamboa, 1943), during the reign of Tupac Yupanqui, a noble plotted rebellion against the Inca, but the plot was discovered and the guilty party brought to justice. The population of the region would have suffered a similar fate had not the queen intervened, suggesting to the Inca that the rebels be sent as *yana* to serve the state and the Sun. On the other hand, in the Mochica language, the term *yana yanaho* means "servant," so this may be a case of linguistic influence in one direction or another.

Whatever their origin, the *yana* became a significant institution during the regimes of the last Incas. It is likely, however, that, as with the *mitmaq*, this institution had previously existed on a limited scale among the lords of the macroethnic groups. When I discussed the status of the lords and their various social categories, I mentioned lords who are *yana* and who enjoyed a high social status. It seems likely that only the last rulers were permitted to appoint *yana* as chiefs, since by that time Inca power had become so secure as to be nearly absolute. Not only could wellborn individuals become *yana*, but lords might pass that status on to their sons. All of this shows that the *yana* cannot be considered as slaves. Rather, this was an institution that included a complex set of Andean social categories (Falk Moore, 1958).

Many authors have dealt with the subject of *yana*, but numerous questions remain. The term *yana* contains two fundamental concepts: one, of help, of lending services; the other, of being a servant. Unlike the *mitmaq*, the *yana* lost all communication with their *ayllus* of origin. For the ruler of the Inca state, the *yana* represented a source of labor that did not have to be requested according to the ancient forms of reciprocity. The Inca expressed his will and his orders were obeyed without discussion.

Who had the privilege of enjoying the labor of *yana* as servants? In the first place, the reigning Incas and their *panaca* held *yana*. The last Incas possessed extensive lands, which constituted their own private property. When I analyze land tenure, I will examine the landholdings of the rulers. Here I mention only that they were cultivated by large numbers of *yana*. At the death of an Inca, his *panaca* continued to enjoy all the benefits of his property, which remained as if he were still alive (Rostworowski, 1962, 1970a). When Damián de la Bandera carried out his *Visita* to the valley of Yucay, he found fifty *yana* under the orders of one Apu Yanacona, dedicated to the care of the mummy of Huayna Capac, to which they offered sacrifices (Ms. AHC, book 2, ind. 4: 154, 155v). Surely not just anyone could be *yana* of a deceased ruler, and these must have enjoyed very special privileges.

The Sun and the principal *huacas*, such as that of Huanacauri, also had *yana* in their service (Cieza de León, *Señorío*, 1943:152). If the Inca wished to honor one in particular, he assigned it a number of servants, as occurred in Huarochirí with the idol of Pariacaca.

On the day that the Inca received the tassel of rulership and married he granted a number of *yana* to serve the *coya*. Finally, on a lower level, we know from the *Visita* documents that the lords of the macroethnic groups also held such servants, although in smaller numbers. It appears that if an Inca wished to reward an ethnic lord he would grant him some *yana* (Diez de San Miguel, 1964; Murra, 1975).

The *Mamacona*

The female counterparts of the *yana* were the *mamacona*, or young girls taken in large numbers from their places of origin to occupy the *aclla huasi*, or "Houses of the Chosen Women." Other than the daughters and sisters of the Incas, who enjoyed a privileged status, to the state, women represented a source of labor for the production of textiles, for the preparation of ritual beverages, and as wives, when such were needed to fulfill the obligations of reciprocity.

The girls selected for the *aclla huasi* were eight to ten years of age. They were brought to Cusco from throughout the Inca realm and divided into various categories according to their social origins, beauty, and aptitudes (Cabello de Valboa, 1951; Guaman Poma, 1936; Murúa, 1946). The *yurac aclla* mentioned by Santa Cruz Pachacuti (1927) were always of Inca blood. They were consecrated to the cult of the Sun, and one was selected as his bride. These were followed by the *huayrur aclla*, generally the most beautiful girls, from among whom the Inca selected his secondary wives. The *paco aclla* eventually became the wives of the chiefs whom the Inca wished to reward. The *yana aclla* were not considered of exceptional rank or beauty, and became servants to the others. Murúa also mentions the *taqui aclla*, who were selected for their ability as singers and entertained in the fiestas of the court with their drums and *pincullo*, or flutes.

Pedro Pizarro (1977) indicates that only those of the first category remained virgins, after being consecrated to the Sun. Those belonging to the other categories were not permanently secluded in the *aclla huasi*, and could come and go during the day. The Spaniards likened this institution to the Christian convents, but in reality their functions were quite different (Murra, 1975).

The *Piña*

The *piña* or prisoners of war were at the bottom of the social scale of the Inca state. We know of their existence only because they are mentioned in the dictionaries of *runa simi*, but the chronicles and the documents provide no information concerning them. Might not the origins of the institution of *yana* be found in this group? This is another question we pose for future research.

DUAL RULERSHIP AND THE POWER OF THE INCA

To this point we have dealt with the hierarchy of social classes in the Inca realm. Let us now turn to two closely related subjects: (1) dual rulership as an Andean model and (2) the development of the power of the Inca. When I analyzed the functions of the ethnic lords, I discussed the duality of rulership at the chiefdom level, including the specific cases of La Paz, Capachica, and Lima, concerning which we have documentary evidence.

In the first two cases, power was shared between the lords of the upper and lower moieties, each accompanied by his "helper." One of the two principal lords, however, held the power and was considered the chief of the ethnic group. With the creation of the Inca state, this existing sociopolitical structure, including the dual system, was preserved.

It was difficult for the chroniclers, our primary source for Inca history, to understand and accurately interpret the information sought and received from the natives. Moreover, as men who shared a sixteenth-century Western mode of thought, they were not receptive to ways of thinking different from those of the Iberian Peninsula. For this reason their accounts contain so many contradictions: They frequently refer to customs similar to those of Europe, only to reverse themselves later and describe something quite different.

Thanks to many documents published in recent years, we can eliminate certain points of confusion in this "history" that are constantly introduced by those who do not compare these older interpretations with the new sources. For example, many chroniclers asserted mistakenly that the commoners paid tribute to the Inca and to their chiefs. Murra, however, has made it clear that this so-called tribute consisted of labor and not the transfer of products from their parcels of land. The valuable contributions of Murra (1975) have established the basis for a firmer understanding of the native organizational system.

Other inaccuracies on the part of the chroniclers are in their descriptions of customs relating to the inheritance of the cargos or offices, succession to power, and the absence of a chronological unit for calculating the ages of individuals (as opposed to age categories based on stages in the human biological cycle, as already described). Nor did the Spanish understand the tradition of dual command in the armies, the chiefdoms, or the rulership of the Inca state. The repeated dual element became a quatripartition, a ubiquitous indigenous social model. For this reason I proposed in a previous work that the Inca government was a dual structure composed, as were the *señoríos*, of two double personages, two of Upper Cusco and two of Lower Cusco.

The information we possess concerning the quadripartite tradition is not always explicit. The subject is not dealt with directly in the chronicles, but only incidentally when an author describes an indigenous situation. Such is the case when Molina, Cristóbal el Almagrista (1968:68) reports that in certain ceremonies the Inca ascended a structure accompanied by three lords, apparently providing further confirmation of quadripartite rule.

Previously in this book I discussed the evident Andean need to divide space into four parts. In early times, when Manco Capac arrived in Acamama, the future Cusco, there were four sectors that, following their permanent settlement by Manco and his siblings, became the four principal *señoríos* of the Incas. Then, with Inca expansion, the quadripartite scheme could no longer be limited to chiefdoms, which were too restricted in space, but had to be expanded to comprise the vast regions of the *suyu*. Thus was created the Inca state, or *Tahuantinsuyu* in Quechua, which means the four united regions, from *tahua*, four; *ntin*, plural suffix meaning internal union; and *suyu*, "land" in the sense of region. We cannot be certain, however, if this is a native term used before the Spanish Conquest or is of later origin. This demarcation of space was a prerequisite for the establishment of the sociopolitical system; with the creation of the state, the original quadripartite governmental structure continued to be used.

When discussing dual rule, I indicated the difficulty of re-creating the chronology of Inca rulers because of the confusion in the colonial sources. If we develop a double list with the rulers of the upper moiety functioning simultaneously with those of the lower, as proposed by Duviols (1979), we obtain an extremely short duration for the Inca state, which corresponds only to its apogee. This results in part from our ignorance regarding the number of local ethnic lords before the period of Inca expansion, when Inca chiefs such as Tocay Capac and Pinahua Capac shared the territory with chiefs of other ethnic groups.

The acceptance of this proposal of a dual political order would cast doubt on everything referring to Inca rulers before the war against the Chanca, and Inca "history" would begin with the Chanca conflict. There have been few archaeological excavations in Cusco, and these do not give us a good picture of the development of the Inca groups in the valley. In the future, there should be an effort made to penetrate the mystery surrounding the beginnings of the capital.

There is no lack of researchers who claim that all of Inca "history" is merely a myth, but in that case, who created the state that the Spaniards saw, conquered, and destroyed? Was all of that also a myth?

The existence of the Inca state cannot be denied. There are numerous accounts of natives who knew and served Huayna Capac, whose parents, in turn, knew Tupac Yupanqui (Informaciones de Toledo, Levillier, 1940, vol. 2). To preserve memories over three generations is not a difficult or impossible task, especially with the aid of *quipu*, paintings, and songs. Another factor to take into account is the absence of a native preoccupation with chronology and exactness regarding the events of the past; this need appears to be an Old World concept not shared by the peoples of these latitudes.

As already indicated, it was the native custom to erase the existence of a ruler whose memory was considered unnecessary by his successors. The memory of such individuals would remain only with the members of his own *panaca*. This would explain the ferocity of Atahualpa's generals against Huascar, the destruction of the mummy of Tupac Yupanqui, and the murder of Huascar's wives and children.

While in principal we can accept that the two Inca moieties functioned simultaneously, this does not help us re-create an adjusted chronology of Inca rulers. Although we have the example of a long-lived ruler, Pachacutec, who must have governed with several successive individuals of the other moiety, as a general rule, life expectancy was short for the native chiefs as well as the general population. (See Rostworowski, 1978a, on the *señorío* of Canta.) As the Incas were in their beginnings simple chiefs, we can apply data from elsewhere in the region to the lords of Cusco. In the documentary data, we find that a new lord would be named to fill the vacancy resulting from the death of the previous chief without removing from office the lord of the other moiety (see Rostworowski, 1978a; and 1977 on the curaca of the Lurín Ica, Hernando Anicama).

We can now turn to the subject of the development of the power of the Inca and the mechanism by which his influence increased. In the beginnings of the government of Pachacutec, the ruler did not have sufficient power to order the neighboring lords to provide labor services for the construction of storehouses. Nor did he possess the agricultural and manufactured products to bestow the appropriate benefits on them. To further his accomplishments, Pachacutec had to resort to reciprocity, to the great favors granted to the nobles, in addition to eating and drinking with them (Betanzos, 1968). By the arrival of the Spaniards, however, the situation had been transformed and the Sapa Inca exercised absolute power. What had occurred in the lapse between the defeat of the Chancas and the appearance of Pizarro? How had the rulers of Cusco achieved this dramatic change?

The principal factor was the intimidation of the lords of the macroethnic groups, which was accomplished by various means. In the first place, the appointment of each new local chief had to have the approval of the ruler. Also, an uncooperative lord who showed signs of disobedience was removed from office and replaced by a more submissive individual.

During the period of expansion, when the Inca found himself forced to use arms instead of reciprocity, the defeated chiefs would be taken to Cusco for the triumphal celebration and then executed. In some cases, an individual of the social category of *yana*, more obedient to the authority of the Sapa Inca, would then be designated to replace him as lord.

Some chroniclers mention that every chiefdom had to send one of its dual chiefs to reside in Cusco in the geographical zone of the city that corresponded to the location of his region within the Inca state, in accordance with prevailing vision of the cosmos. The nobles of greater seniority belonged to the inner circle of Cusco and resided closest to the center. An example of this, already mentioned, is found in the *Probanzas* of Don Gonzalo, lord of Lima. At the time of the founding of the city of Los Reyes, the elderly Taulichusco was its chief, while the second lord, called Caxapaxa, resided in Cusco (Rostworowski, 1981–82). The residence of the "provincial" chiefs in the capital was a way of holding them hostage in case of rebellion, using their lives as a guarantee against an attempted uprising.

The methods for intimidating the masses were different from those applied to their lords. In an insecure or rebellious region, the Inca would proceed to deport a part of the population, sending them as *mitmaq* to distant zones, where they would find themselves surrounded by foreign peoples, hostile toward them for having displaced part of the original population, removed to make a place for them.

At other times, perhaps in cases of prisoners of war or rebels, the people to be transferred belonged to the status of *yana*, that is, they lost all contact with their *ayllus*. At the peak of Inca expansion, however, the status of *mitmaq* was confused with that of the *yana*, owing to the enormous distances that the *mitmaq* were of necessity taken from their *ayllus* of origin. This eventually led to the entanglements found in the colonial documents involving these two social categories.

There is also the case of a town accused of having conspired against the health of the Inca by means of witchcraft. Reprisal was quick in coming, as all the male inhabitants of the town were killed, leaving alive only the women and children (AGI – Justicia 413).

The power and prestige acquired by the Incas permitted them to dominate and exercise control over the subordinate lords linked to them by kinship and reciprocity. But this dominion, however great, was fundamentally insecure and inevitably short-lived because it was not based on a true integration of the macroethnic groups with the Cusco regime.

A final means of subjugating the chiefs and the people was psychological and consisted of sending to Cusco their most important *huacas*. When towns rebelled, their populace knew that punishment could also be applied to their idols.

The Inca state did not create feelings of solidarity among the macroethnic groups, nor did it integrate the population of the Inca realm, owing to the persistence of local and regionalist loyalties. The *ayllus* coalesced around their own *huacas* and their lords, with whom the common people identified rather than with the great, distant, and terrible Inca rulers.

5

The Economic Wealth of the Inca Realm

It is important to understand, as we take up this subject, that in the absence of money, wealth in the Inca state had to be based on the possession of certain resources that could be measured and calculated. With such resources the government could undertake plans for the future and meet its current needs. What resources could serve as the basis for economic and political domination and control?

It is my view that Inca economic power was based on three sources of income: the labor force, the possession of lands, and the state herds. The result of these three forms of wealth took the form of goods accumulated in the state storehouses. These goods in the possession of the state provided economic and political advantages, chief among them the control over reciprocity, the key to the entire Andean organizational system, which permitted the functioning and expansion of the Inca regime. If a government found itself, for any reason, without great quantities of accumulated goods, it would not be able to meet either administrative requirements or the constant demand for "gifts" required by the institution of reciprocity.

The chronicles testify to the astonishment of the Spaniards at the storehouses filled with a great variety of manufactured products, as well as preserved consumables, all duly recorded on the *quipu*. The Spaniards, with incredible irresponsibility, wasted all that the natives had gathered and preserved with so much effort.

I have discussed the limited power of the lord of Cusco when the Chancas attacked the city. The Inca lacked sufficient control over the neighboring lords to require them to build storehouses and fill them with goods. It was the booty seized from the Chancas that permitted the Incas to begin their drive for conquest, and to satisfy the neighboring lords with gifts that established reciprocity and, consequently, Inca superiority.

THE LABOR FORCE

The enormous interest of the Inca state in having access to a large labor force is illustrated by the population counts based on the biological cycle. When I dealt with the *hatun runa*, or commoners, I discussed the Andean custom of classifying the population by age and according to the tasks carried out during each stage in the human biological cycle. The most important stage in this classification system was the *auca camayoc* and *auca camayoc huarmi*, corresponding to men and women, respectively, which provided the greater part of the labor force in the Inca realm.

The second method of facilitating the rapid calculation by the *quipucamayoc*, or state accountants, of the number of inhabitants of a *señorío* was the division of macroethnic groups into *pachaca* and *guaranga* (divisions of 100 and 1,000 households). It is amazing that this regime, in the absence of a writing system, could possess sufficient demographic statistics to achieve its objectives. The *quipucamayoc*, with their *quipu* and abacus, could calculate the numbers of inhabitants by age groups. This enabled them to determine how many individuals could be taken from a particular region for administrative purposes, such as sending *mitmaq* from one zone to another, covering the needs of the war *mita*, or constructing great administrative centers. This entire organizational system demonstrates the importance of the workforce and the solutions developed to measure and exploit it.

Murra (1975) proposes that what has been called tribute, as understood in a Spanish context, did not exist in pre-Hispanic Peru; everything produced on a commoner's parcel of land belonged to him. The equivalent of tribute in the Andean world was the labor force, organized by the *mita* on a rotational basis, whether for the benefit of the *ayllu*, the local chief, the lord of the macroethnic group, the *huacas*, or, during the period of Inca rule, for the state. The amount of labor provided increased according to the status of the beneficiary.

The Incas satisfied the ethnic lords with great gifts, and they, in turn, were obligated to provide the state with manpower and the best lands in a *señorío*. To what extent did the gifts compensate for the sacrifices in land and manpower made by the lords? Was this simply a pretext to satisfy them? Were they actually satisfied?

It is seems probable that there was latent discontent among the chiefs of the macroethnic groups. What had they gained from the expansion of the Incas? All these factors must have created unrest among the "provincial" ruling class and were likely among the causes of the rapid collapse of the Inca state.

The *Mita,* Regulator of the Labor Force

The *mita,* or system of rotational service, is a very old Andean concept, employed to carry out projects at determined times on an orderly cyclical basis. All such labor contained the idea of *mita,* of repetition in time, such that very different tasks could be carried out under the *mita.*

This Andean form of labor services was carried out at various levels within the same *ayllu*: for communal tasks, to work the fields of the chief and the local *huaca,* and also to help the chief of the macroethnic group. During the Inca hegemony, the lands of the state and those of the Sun were worked by means of the *mita* and the *minka* in a festive atmosphere, with music, song, and food at the expense of the beneficiary, which lightened the tasks.

The agrarian *mita* was distinct from the fishing *mita,* and these labor groups never intervened in each other's occupations. In the *señorío* of Chincha, the fishermen numbered ten thousand, and went to sea in turns, the rest of the time enjoying themselves by dancing and drinking. The Spaniards criticized them as lazy drunkards because they did not go to sea daily and all at once.

I have mentioned on several occasions the war *mita,* which took men from their *ayllus* to serve in the state armies. All labor in the Andean world was performed as a rotational service, whether for maintaining the *tambos,* roads, and bridges or for guarding the storehouses or other such tasks.

The mining *mita* was also fulfilled at the level of *ayllus,* of the local lord, and, in the last instance, of the state. The significance of the term *mita* goes beyond that of a system for organizing labor. It contains a certain Andean philosophical concept of eternal repetition. The constellation of the Pleiades, called the Cabrillas or Little Goats by the Spaniards, were known as *oncoy* – disease – during the rainy season *mita,* and as *colca* – storehouse – during the season of harvest and abundance. The seasons were divided into the dry *mita* and the rainy *mita.* The day *mita* succeeded the night *mita* in a repetition that reflected an ordering of time that the natives conceptualized as a cyclical organizational system of order and chaos.

THE LAND

The land was one of the most prestigious forms of property, and its ownership followed the Andean pattern of possession. The chroniclers contend that the lands were divided among the Inca, the Sun, and the common people, but this explanation is too simplistic for concepts that are much more complex and diverse, as we shall see shortly in some detail.

Lands of the Inca or of the State

The lands of the state in general could be found throughout Inca territory, the lands of the royal *ayllus* and of the *panaca* were around the capital, and other lands belonged to a particular ruler as his private property, whose products constituted the personal income of the Inca separate from the income of the state. There are clear distinctions among these various categories of land tenure. Before discussing the state lands, however, I must clarify the nature of land tenure among the macroethnic lords before the advent of the Incas.

I have already noted that tribute consisted in giving not the products of the parcels of the commoners but their labor. In other words, in the absence of money, manpower was employed on the lands of those who would have received tribute, whether the Inca, an ethnic lord, or a *huaca*.

By means of the archival documents we know that all lords had fields assigned according to the function they served, and that these were cultivated by *mita* by the local inhabitants. Examples are the small chiefdoms of Macas and Guarauni, subjects of the Collec macroethnic group. When the natives were asked by the Spanish *Visitadores* in 1571 concerning the lands of the *señorío*, they answered that the lord of the place received the products of five fields, one of maize, others of *camote* (*Ipomea batata*), *yuca* (*Manihot esculenta*), chile peppers (*Capsicum sp.*), and coca (*Exytroxylum sp.*), all of them worked by turns (Espinoza, 1963:64).

Not only did the subordinate chief of a *pachaca* of a hundred families hold such lands, but the great lords of the macroethnic groups also enjoyed the privilege of lands distributed throughout the territory under their jurisdiction, according to their rank and power. Evidence of this can be seen in the possession by the lord of all the *guaranga* of Huarochirí of lands in Quivi, in the middle valley of the Chillón River, at a considerable distance from the capital of the ethnic group (Rostworowski, 1988b). The same occurs in the case of the *señorío* of Collec, whose lord, the Colli Capac, enjoyed landholdings in the small coastal chiefdom of Quivi, which came under his jurisdiction and rule. This form of landholding should not be confused with enclaves and archipelagos. The presence of people of Huarochirí in Quivi as *mitmaq* was the result of the defeat of the lord of Collec by the Inca.

When Inca domination was imposed, one of the first measures taken was the designation of state lands to be worked by the local people in turns. It was the responsibility of the local lord to provide the necessary labor and oversee the cultivation of the land. Officials were sent from Cusco periodically to supervise the storage of the products of the land, and decide whether they should be sent to the capital or to the various administrative centers. The indigenous custom of assigning state lands in each conquered chiefdom is confirmed in a report sent to the Consejo de Indias by *Licenciado* Joan de Obando on January 2, 1568, which indicates that the Incas held lands in each province, which were worked by the natives of the region and were considered tribute. All the products of the harvest on such lands were kept in the state storehouses (Archives British Museum, Spanish Documents, No. 33983). The ancient custom by which each chiefdom set aside part of its lands for the Inca, to be cultivated by the community, confirms this (RAHM A–92).

Another example is the land of the Guaynacapa in Macas, in the valley of the Chillón River, on which coca was cultivated for the Inca, with the young girls of the community responsible for harvesting the leaves (Espinoza, 1963:64, 67). A statement to the same effect was given by the natives of the *repartimiento* of the Chuchaychos, who said that they took to Huanuco Pampa the maize produced on the land they cultivated in "this valley on the lands of the Inca" (Ortiz de Zúñiga, 1967, vol. 1:25).

More data concerning the lands of the Inca scattered throughout the small chiefdoms are given in detail in the *Visitas* carried out in 1549 and 1553 to the *señorío* of Canta. In each of the principal villages the natives were questioned regarding state lands (Rostworowski, 1978a, appendix 2).

In the Canta *ayllu*, they responded that there were nineteen small fields of potatoes and *caui* (*Oca oxalis*), and another of maize. The inhabitants of Causso claimed not to have state lands because theirs was a very high region, in which they only cultivated *maca* (*Lepidium meyenii*). In Carcas, they said that ten small fields belonged to the Inca. In Racas, the state possessed two fields of potatoes and *caui* and two of maize. In Yaso, they cultivated "a quarter of a field of maize" (Rostworowski, 1978a:243). In Locha, the Inca possessed four fields of maize; in Pinche, the lands belonging to the ruler corresponded to the Andean measure of one *mati* of maize and another of potatoes. In Ayas they worked only one field of maize for the Inca; in Urco, the field measured half a *fanega* of maize; in Lachaque, also only half a *fanega*; in Copa the answer was negative; in Isquibamba, lands corresponding to half a *fanega* are mentioned. Concerning Quiso and Cararura Ayllo, there are no references; in Carua half a *fanega* of "sowing" of maize and another half a *fanega* of potatoes were worked; and in Bisca the Inca possessed three parcels of "sowing" of one and a half *fanegas* (about 1.60 bushels) of potatoes and another two of maize.

The preceding is an illustration of the land ownership of the Inca in a small chiefdom and the existence in each *ayllu* of state lands. As the Inca state expanded, so did its needs, and eventually it had to face the need for greater agricultural production, and consequently for more lands.

A first measure was to increase the lands assigned to the Inca. An evolution of this process is illustrated in the *Relación de Chincha* of Castro and Ortega Morejón (1974), where General Capac Yupanqui is named as the first Cusqueño to appear in the *señorío* in question. As a result of his visit, reciprocity was established between Cusco and Chincha. Years later, Tupac Yupanqui arrived with his army; among his impositions was the requirement of state lands. Later, Huayna Capac did the same, drawing new boundaries that increased the landholdings of the ruler.

The Inca presence in a "province" consisted of state administrators informing the *guaranga* and their respective *pachaca*, which lands the local people were to cultivate for the Inca (Castro and Ortega Morejón, 1974: 101). The fruits of the harvests were then delivered, to Cusco, Jauja, or Pachacamac, for example, according to the instructions of the administrators (ibid.).

Similar information is found for the valley of the Chillón River on the central coast, in Quivi. The first ruler to appear in the region was Tupac Yupanqui, who took ownership of the coca fields and ordered that they be cultivated by *mitmaq*. During the regime of Huayna Capac the lands belonging to the Inca were increased, as was the labor force assigned to them. In this case, because of a scarcity of local labor, *mitmaq* replaced the local people. In Quivi, as we have seen, the original population was decimated after its inhabitants conspired to damage the health of the Inca through the sorcery of a *huaca,* and its lands were granted to neighboring people loyal to the ruler as *mitmaq* (Rostworowski, 1988b).

The situation in Cochabamba was similar to those already cited. When Tupac Yupanqui conquered the region, he claimed "certain fields" and proceeded to a first assignment of *mitmaq* to guard the borders. When Huayna Capac came to power, he ordered the massive transfer of approximately 14,000 *mitmaq* to intensify agricultural production on state lands. Such was the solution devised by the Incas to increase agricultural production and thus obtain greater income. The central government was under constant pressure to increase subsistence production to maintain the functions of its vast state (Wachtel, 1980–81).

The preceding data indicate that the state lands could be worked in various ways. When it was a question of small parcels located in each *ayllu* of a *señorío*, the commoners could take care of them. As their size increased and they were transformed for large-scale production, local labor typically became inadequate and had to be supplemented by the massive importation of *mitmaq* as agricultural labor. On the private estates of the rulers, such forms of labor were used, along with greater or lesser numbers of *yana*. It appears likely that the coastal model of land tenure differed from that of the highlands, and this should be the subject of more archival research.

There are references to the effect that in certain coastal valleys, such as that of Piura, all the land belonged to the ethnic lord, who in turn distributed it to the commoners "in the form of a lease." In compensation, the peasants were obligated to give part of the harvest to their lord (Relaciones Geográficas de Indias, 1885, vol. 2:240). Something similar occurs in the valleys of Chincha and Huarmey (Rostworowski, 1977:39–40). There is evidence for this system of "leasing" in the terms listed in the *Lexicón* of Fray Domingo de Santo Tomás (1951):

> *cacay:* to collect tribute
> *cacani, gui* or *cacacuni gui:* to pay tribute
> *cacac:* he who contributes

On the other hand, the dictionary of Gonález Holguín (1952) does not contain a single word related to tribute or tax, which supports the hypothesis that the coastal system of land tenure was different from that of Cusco.

The Private Lands of the Incas

Let us now look at the lands of the royal *ayllus* and *panaca* located in the vicinity of the capital. Pachacutec Inca Yupanqui, after his victory over the Chancas, ordered the lands around Cusco evacuated so that a new distribution of land could be effected, certainly for the purpose of rewarding those who had supported him in the war.

The chronicles, and above all, the archival documents as well as the documents of the Real Hacienda del Cusco (AGN, Lima), and the Parish Books mention the lands under the control of the various *ayllus* of the Cusco nobles. These lands can be identified and reconstructed. Their distribution, however, left the rulers limited to the lands in their own *panaca*, without estates of their own. It is likely that private property was established only under the last rulers, owing to the previous limited expansion of the chiefdom of Cusco.

These estates comprised arable lands and also pasture land where the Inca's flocks grazed. An early reference to such royal estates is repeated in various documents, and confirmed in one document referring to the *Repartimiento* of Doña Beatriz Coya, daughter of Sayri Tupac (Rostworowski, 1962, 1970).

In these testimonies there are references to the properties of Viracocha

Inca in Caquia and in Jaquijaguana. Pachacutec took for himself Tambo (Ollantay Tambo) and Pisac. Tupac Yupanqui took Chinchero, Guailla-bamba, and Urcos. Huayna Capac took the fertile valley of Yucay and the valley of Quispeguanca. Finally, Huascar took for himself Calca and Muyna.

In the document concerning the *repartimiento* of the Coya Beatriz, we are told that the estate of Huayna Capac was worked by local people as well as *mitmaq* and *yana* (Rostworowski, 1970:230). As for the estate of Tupac Yupanqui, there are still some *ayllus* called Yanacona in Chinchero. As we have seen, the use of *yana* labor offered the ruler the advantage that he was not then bound by ties of reciprocity.

It is surprising that the queens of the Incas also had access to private property. The testimonies refer to the lands that belonged to Mama Ana-huarque, "legal wife of Inca Yupanqui, Lord of this Kingdom" (Rostwo-rowski, 1962). It is especially interesting that the property of the queen was inherited by her nephews and not by the *panaca* of her husband. We know very little about the system of inheritance in the Andean world, a subject about which there is much to investigate.

To conclude, we can say that the distribution of the state lands and its tenure in general followed the same model as the lands belonging to the ethnic lords. The difference is that their distribution took place at the level of the Inca state as a whole. As for the private lands in the vicinity of Cusco, on the death of the ruler they became property of the royal mummy, which in reality meant they stayed in the hands of the corresponding *panaca*.

Lands of the *Huacas*

It was an established custom from ancient times in the Andean world that each *huaca*, however small, had at least a small piece of land whose usufruct provided the offerings and, above all, the preparation of beverages for the participants in the celebrations of its rites and festivals. The documents concerning the abolishment of idolatry provide considerable information on this subject. We find in the testimonies an entire system of land tenure applied to the lesser idols, similar but amplified for the important *huacas*, with the difference that the latter had more widespread estates, including lands situated in different valleys, as in the case of Pachacamac.

In a letter by Hernando Pizarro to the Real Audiencia of Santo Domingo (Fernández de Oviedo, 1945, vol. 12), he says that the "*mezquita*" (mosque) of Pachacamac received "tribute" from the entire coast, and was one of the two most important temples of the Inca realm, along with the sanctuary of the Sun in Lake Titicaca. The great religious influence of Pachacamac per-mitted the center's survival over time, and its famous oracle must have contributed to its fame. In some chronicles and native testimonies there are references to the "sons" or "women" of the *huaca* residing in various places. Thus, according to Dávila Briceño, the wife of Pachacamac lived in Mama (Relaciones Geográficas de Indias, 1881, vol. 1), while Avila (1966:59) mentions a "son" belonging to the god living in the ravine of Lurín. Santillán tells of several "sons, one of which lived in Chincha, another in Mala, and a third in Andahuaylas" (Rostworowski, 1977; Santillán, 1927:3).

In the old Libro de Cabildo (town records) of the Villa de Cañete the municipal pastures listed include some fields, located in Cuyba, belonging to Pachacamac (Angulo, 1921:42). There is still an irrigation channel called Pachacamilla on the Siuba estate (Rostworowski, 1978–80).

These data concerning lands granted to the *huacas* explain why the designation by the Incas of lands for the Sun would have caused no surprise, since this was an ancient Andean custom. The same model used for the lands of the lords and, later, for the state was repeated for the cults. Naturally, the fields in question could be larger or smaller according to the circumstances, but the principle was the same.

In general, the lands of the *huacas* were worked by the local people. The lands of some principal gods, however, including those of the Sun, could possess *mitmaq* and *yana* to cultivate their fields, should they be extensive. The Cusco government might reward a *huaca* with new lands and labor, as recognition for services rendered, or for an oracle accurately given. An example is the *huaca* of Copacabana, which enjoyed many servants of *mitmaq* status. An example illustrating the universality of the solar lands is the small chiefdom of Guancayo, in the middle valley of the Chillón River, where an orchard and coca fields were dedicated to the Sun and green leaves were burned as an offering to the god (Espinoza, 1963:63).

Lands of the *Ayllus*

Each *ayllu* possessed its own agricultural lands, pastures, and waters. The chroniclers tell us that every male head of household had a *tupu* of land, and that with each new child his parcel was increased. The *tupu* was a relative measurement of area, however, since the quality of the land and its required fallow time were taken into account. In other words, it was a relative measurement that varied in actual area but was sufficient to feed a married couple (Rostworowski, 1960, 1981d).

The members of the *ayllus* knew the boundaries of their lands. Their landmarks were generally hilltops, rivers, ravines, and occasionally irrigation canals; these landmarks are mentioned in the archival documents.

Land as Remuneration for Services Rendered

In this chapter on land tenure, I cannot but mention a case discovered on the coast in which land could replace money as payment for service rendered. When the chief of Mala needed manpower to carry out special projects, such as cleaning the hydraulic canals or draining a fishpond, he requested the cooperation of the neighboring chief of Coayllo, in the valley of Asia, in exchange for which he made available to him certain lands on a temporary basis (BN, A–199). This kind of occasional loan is very significant and should not be confused with the "archipelagos" or enclaves. Probably other places also used land as compensation for favors, a hypothesis supported by the example of Mala.

Another such example is a conflict that arose between the highland lord of the Guambos and the coastal lord of Jayanca. It appears that the highland chief demanded that the coastal lord pay "a ransom" for the water that ran down from the high valleys and irrigated the dry coastal lands (Espinoza, 1975:271). More information concerning water rights and "payment" for water resources can be found in a 1566 document from Túcume on the north coast. This document relates the complaints expressed by two principal lords before the *Oidor* (judge of the *Audiencia*) Gregorio González de Cuenca regarding excessive "tribute" that they were obliged to pay a third lord for the water from a secondary canal that irrigated their lands (AGI – Justicia 458, folio 2013r).

It appears that the chief of the coastal macroethnic group demanded of his two principal subordinates some form of payment for the use of the water, and that his imposition was a way of recovering the "payment," as expressed in Spanish terminology. Some light is shed on this problem in the proceedings just mentioned regarding the payment by the lord of Mala to the chief of Coayllo for his help with labor services. If our hypothesis is correct, land might be used in some cases as a form of payment or temporary loan to cover a debt that had been incurred. It is not unreasonable to assume that, in the same way, the "tribute" of the coastal lord of Jayanca involved his temporarily loaning lands in the coastal zone for cultivation by highland people.

Gölte (1972), in an interesting view of labor in the Andean world based on an analysis of sixteenth-century Quechua, finds that the word *arimsa* expresses "a relationship of mutual service, in which one party provides the land and the other the labor." In this context, however, it also indicates that the product was shared by the two parties. This second sense of the word alludes to the fact that, as we have already noted, all land belonged to the ethnic lord and that he distributed it among the commoners.

Discontinuous Territoriality

The concept of territoriality in the Andean world had particularities that cannot be entirely explained at this time, but they manifest themselves in a variety of documents.

The least studied notions, and those most difficult to understand, are related to space and territory. According to Godelier (1978:17), "territory" refers to that part of nature and space that a society claims as the place where its members find the conditions and material means necessary for their subsistence on a permanent basis. The forms of property within a territory are an essential part of what we call the economic structure of a society and constitute the "legal," or at least "legitimate," conditions for access to the resources and means of production.

In some documents we find data concerning the discontinuous land holdings of the *ayllus* and the *pachaca*, with the fields of some *ayllus* interdispersed with those of others within a single microclimate, without any explanation of the situation.

We have the concrete case of the chiefdom of Acarí at the time of the *Visita* of 1593 (Rostworowski, 1982; Visita de Acarí, 1977). We learn from the accounts that the individual parcels of its inhabitants were scattered throughout the valley of Acarí, as well as the neighboring valley of Yauca. This dispersion of lands, however, characterized only that of the original *ayllus*, which differed from the agglomerated blocks of fields of the *mitmaq*.

It can be observed that in Acarí the lands of upper and lower moieties were interdispersed among one another, and that a similar situation was to be found in the 1594 *Visita* to the valley of Ica (Guillén y Guillén, 1963). Gabriel Martínez (1981) reached a similar conclusion in his analysis of the moieties mentioned in the *Visita* de Chucuito (1964).

The most extraordinary case of territorial discontinuity is contained in the report of a *Visita* to Cajamarca, which describes the fields of *pachaca* and *guaranga* scattered in places belonging to other *ayllus*, in apparent disorder, without any obvious rule or motive (Rostworowski and Remy, 1992).

Camino (1980:28), in his study of Andean subsistence strategies at Cuyo-Cuyo, finds that traditional agriculturalists are especially concerned with minimizing risks and therefore try to obtain security through food storage. In addition to use of vertical strategies, risks could be minimized by means of horizontal diversification, by giving peasant families access to different kinds of soils and crops in the annual distribution of lands. The use of these strategies in pre-Hispanic times may explain the prevailing territorial discontinuity in the region.

All these data show the need for more research regarding different models of land tenure in the Andean world. An examination of the archival documents for different Andean regions would provide a more precise understanding of the problem.

Before leaving this topic we might compare Andean agricultural development with that of Europe, where a knowledge of iron and steel permitted substantial improvements in toolmaking and a consequent specialization in agricultural production. In pre-Hispanic Peru, however, tools remained rudimentary. In the highlands, soil was broken with the *chaqui taclla*, or foot plow, while on the coast a shovel called a *llampa* (the origin of the modern Peruvian term *lampa*, or shovel) was employed for this purpose.

There are also important environmental differences between Europe and Peru, as well as similarities. Thus, we can contrast labor and productivity on the fertile, level soils of France with that of the mountainous, steeply graded lands cut by multiple ravines, the cold *punas*, and the coastal deserts of the Andean region.

Andean man, with his primitive tools, needed great ingenuity to overcome such environmental difficulties, and he showed himself to be inventive enough. The validity of this statement is demonstrated by present-day efforts to revive ancient pre-Hispanic technology and apply it to modern agriculture.

In the craggy ravines they built irrigation terraces with elaborate systems of canals that not only controlled soil erosion but also increased and improved cultivable areas. There still exist miles of unused terraces, mute witness to the efforts of Andeans to increase their tillable land (Araujo, 1986a, 1986b).

At high altitudes around Lake Titicaca (3,803 m), the natives conceived the innovation of raised fields, called *waru-waru*, that cover a total of 82,056 hectares (Erikson, 1987). The variety of these raised fields is impressive, considering their early origin. It is estimated that the system was begun about 1000 B.C. and permitted an economy based on a combination of camelid pastoralisms and the cultivation of tubers (*Solanum* sp.) and diverse chenopodium. The *waru-waru* consist of long rows of ridges, which provide protection to a variety of high-altitude cultigens planted between them.

An equally impressive system is that of the *qocha* (Flores Ochoa and Paz Flores, 1983; Rozas, 1986) also used in the *puna* at 3,883 meters, which are found covering a surface of some 256 square kilometers. These are rectangular depressions or lagoons used to store rainwater and function as sunken fields (Rozas, 1986:113). These artificial pools or ponds vary in size from small lagoons to ones that reach 3,800 square meters. They possess drainage canals to manage the flow of water. These lagoons continue to be used by the peasants, who cultivate most of their food produce in them. Their preservation serves several purposes, including humidification of the soil, as well as providing water for animals and for domestic use. There exists an entire appropriate technology for the use of the lagoons, concerning which we defer to the authors just cited.

On the coast, a variety of hydraulic systems permitted the cultivation of the river valley deltas and parts of the adjoining deserts. To make these technical improvements the natives drew on their profound knowledge of hydraulics, obtained through observation and the application of solutions to problems as they occurred. Regarding the coastal hydraulic system, I should mention the utilization of a system of "*hoyas*," or sunken fields, that expanded the available arable land in desert zones through use of water that could be released from subsoil levels (Soldi, 1982). With this knowledge they were able to achieve greater levels of food production than is obtained today, in spite of the absence of sophisticated tools. The cultivated areas were more extensive, as even lands close to precipices were exploited, according to Avila's informants; more work and exceptional dedication compensated for their primitive tools.

The chroniclers did not find hungry or undernourished populations, probably because at that time agriculture was supported by the entire labor force. For this reason, we are today reevaluating pre-Hispanic Andean technology, from which the present and future generations have much to learn (Araujo, 1986a, 1986b).

LIVESTOCK

Camelids played an important role in the development of the Andean cultures, especially in the highlands, where only plants adapted to the high altitudes could be cultivated and where food resources were limited. The two domesticated species, the llama (*Lama glama*) and the alpaca (*Lama paco*), were called *ovejas de la tierra* (sheep of the land) by the Spaniards. Two additional wild species were the vicuña (*Lama vicugna*) and the guanaco (*Lama guanicoe*). Vicuñas were highly regarded for their silken wool, for which they were hunted, sheared, and then set free, so as not to reduce their numbers. The guanaco, on the other hand, was hunted for its meat.

No other animal in the Andean world was as useful as the llama. Its uses were multiple. Its wool was used for the common garments called *abasca*. Along with cotton from the coast, these were the fibers used for the clothes of the common people, while the wool of the vicuña and alpaca was used to make the finer and more luxurious textiles known as *cumbi*.

The meat of the llama was easily preserved, dried in the sun and dehydrated, in which form it could be kept in the storehouses. It could also be consumed fresh, for which there is archaeological evidence. There was a custom of bleeding the animals from a vein in the jaw and preparing a special pottage with the blood. It is likely that this custom came from Collao, since in Bertonio's (1956) Aymara dictionary we find the term *suu villa* given to blood recently taken from the animal, to be used for food preparation (Rostworowski, 1970, 1977).

The hides from the necks of the camelids were used to make Andean footwear, and specialized craftsmen used them to make the sandals of the Inca (Rostworowski, 1977:135). The rest of the hide was used in making cord and fasteners of various kinds. The dung, or dried excrement, was a good combustible, especially useful in the highlands where trees and firewood were scarce.

The llamas were also valued as pack animals, one of the reasons for the extensive state herds essential to the economy of the Inca state. Finally, camelids were also employed for religious purposes, as offerings to the *huacas* and also in auguries. Guaman Poma (1936:88) illustrates and describes the method of sacrificing the animals, making a cut to the side of the heart, which, still palpitating, was extracted by the sacrificer with his hand. Perhaps, had camelids existed in Mexico, human sacrifices would not have been so numerous there.

Documents concerning the eradication of idolatries contain abundant information regarding such sacrifices. The chroniclers refer to the ceremony of the *callpa*, which was performed to tell the future. Shortly before he died, Huayna Capac instructed the priest to perform this kind of augury to determine which of his two sons, Ninancuyuchi or Huascar, would be the more successful.

Avila's informants, as we have seen, told of a ceremony in honor of Pariacaca and of the grim omens seen by one of the priests, of Llacua origin, who predicted the end of the Andean god.

The Camelid Herds

Acosta (1940, book 4, chap. 41) mentions the division of the herds of camelids by their colors. There were white, black, brown, and *moromoro*, as they called those of several colors. In addition, the chronicler says that the colors were taken into account for their great sacrifices, in accordance with their traditions and beliefs.

Garcilaso de la Vega (1943, vol. 1, book V, chap. 10) adds that when a calf was born of a different color from the rest of the herd, once grown, it was sent to the appropriate herd. This division by colors facilitated the count of the *quipu*, whose cords were of the same color as that of the animals being counted (Flores Ochoa, 1981; Palacios Ríos, 1981).

The possession of herds of camelids and of the pastureland necessary to feed them followed the pattern discussed already for land tenure. Each *ayllu* in the mountains held pasturelands for its animals, which also included the personal animals of the commoners. In the same way, there were herds belonging to the local chiefs, the great lords of the macroethnic groups, the *huacas*, and those of the Inca, whose animals were kept on special pastures called *moya*.

In Sucyahuillca, situated on the heights of the village of San Damián, in the present Department of Lima, some herds belonging to Pachacamac were grazed in preparation for sacrifice. The herdspeople of such flocks were *yana* from the *ayllu* Yasapa, belonging to the highland Yauyos group (Avila, 1966:141). Great expanses of the *puna* were dedicated to the herds of the Sun, which were usually white, as well as to animals belonging to the state.

The 1567 *Visita* of Garci Diez de San Miguel (1964) to the "province" of Chucuito is a document containing excellent data concerning the wealth in pre-Hispanic times of a region that is today completely impoverished as a result of uncontrolled grazing. A commoner could possess 1,000 camelids (ibid.:43); so if we consider the benefits obtained from each llama, economic well-being must actually have been the rule for the inhabitants of the highlands. In turn, a principal lord such as Don Juan Alanoca possessed 50,000 animals.

In the 1567 *Visita*, the number of head of "cattle of the land" was noted for some parcels. For example, in Juli, in spite of a decrease in the size of the herds resulting from the Conquest and civil wars among the Spaniards, they still calculated 16,846 head, female and male. In Pomata, there were 36,000 camelids and in Zepita, 2,347 (ibid.: 122–23), much lower figures than in pre-Hispanic times, when the pastures were filled to capacity.

Murra (1964:423) notes that during the second half of the sixteenth century, cattle were easily exchanged for money or for other goods, in both the Andean economy and the European. The Spaniards were amazed to find a well-fed and well-clothed population, with external signs of wealth, in an apparently inhospitable region.

The *señorios* of the Collao zone and the lacustrine regions were not the only ones that emphasized raising camelids. Throughout the highlands, from the southern to the northern limits of the Inca state, there were great herds. Between 1533 and 1534, the Huanca lord of Hatunsaya provided more than 50,000 head of cattle to the Spaniards for the transport of arms and supplies for the armies, animals that were never returned to their owners (Espinoza, 1972). During the civil wars among the Spaniards, both sides used camelids to carry military stores and munitions, which also contributed to their decrease in numbers. The resource was so abundant that it appeared to be inexhaustible, and was therefore wasted without a thought to the future and the impoverishment of the region.

The Presence of Camelids on the Coast

Thanks to archival documentation and archaeological work, today we are able to confirm that herds of camelids have existed in the coastal environment since ancient times. According to Bonavia (1982:392–93), there is archaeological evidence of camelids – perhaps vicuñas – on the coast, in the area of Paracas, at least as early as 4000 B.C., in the form of skins of wild animals brought from the highlands. There is no reason to believe, however, that camelids were obtained exclusively from the mountains. Until a few years ago, guanacos were hunted in Atiquipa, in the *lomas* region, where that animal flourished in the seasonally humid environment characteristic of that part of the Peruvian coast.

This *lomas* region – in which it never rains but which is seasonally covered by a mist or fog that is hospitable to a variety of flora and fauna – was without doubt a meeting place for inhabitants of coast and sierra. The seasonal pastures of the *lomas* region were exploited by man for hunting and gathering from prehistoric times. This should be considered when evaluating the resource potential of the coastal strip of ancient Peru. Sadly, during modern times, the *lomas* have experienced a prolonged period of aridity resulting from the slight climatic fluctuations that can interrupt its delicate ecological balance, as well as by the severe damage caused by overgrazing during the Colonial Period.

Archaeology not only confirms the presence of camelids on the coast in prehistoric times, but shows that their numbers were much greater than had been commonly supposed. The presence of remains of these animals in Los Gavilanes, in Huarmey, was to be expected, since they were apparently already domesticated by the Final Preceramic Period. From the evidence, especially from the quantities of excrement discovered, they were probably used for transport, among other things (Bonavia, 1982:384, 395).

Shimada and Shimada (1985) confirm the presence of camelids on the north coast since the Early Horizon and – by the accumulation of excrement and bones – that herds of camelids were raised on the coast beginning in the Middle Horizon. The discovery of bones with signs of butchering appears to indicate that we are not dealing with *charqui*, or dehydrated meat, brought from the highlands.

On the north coast, the llamas served as transport and were a principal source of protein in the diet of the inhabitants. Burials of animals sacrificed to the *huacas* and the dead have also been found. Herding in the *lomas* was practiced not only by highland groups, as is the case today, but by the coastal people themselves, who also possessed camelid herds. Given the scarcity of pastureland in the lowlands, it is natural that the llamas would be sent to graze in the *lomas* during the green season.

During the dry season in the *lomas*, the camelids fed on the pods of the *algorrobos* (*Prosopis chilensis*). The same seasonal fluctuations in feeding habits is found during the Colonial Period, when the imported species spent one season, of relative greenery, in the *lomas* and meadowlands, and the other in the thorny woods of the coast. The excessive numbers of cattle, horses, mules, goats, and other species on seasonal pasturelands are well documented in the archives, and were responsible for the rapid decline of the land. The data concerning herds of camelids in the archival documents and in the chronicles are scattered but testify to their existence. Cieza de León (1941) could say in 1547 that in San Miguel de Piura "there used to be great numbers of cattle called Peruvian sheep; at this time there are very few." If the chronicler could make such an assertion for the region of Piura, it would seem likely that there were large herds in the colder zones.

The 1540 *Visita* to Jayanca provides similar data. In Lambayeque, the torrential rains of 1578 destroyed a number of settlements. Llamas and horses are mentioned among the losses. In the 1593 *Visita* to the valley of Acarí as well as that of Atico in 1549, the presence of camelids is mentioned (Rostworowski, 1981a).

To this information can be added that of the *"Aviso"* (Rostworowski, 1970:169), whose account provides data concerning the *señorío* of Chincha, and among other subjects mentions a prohibition against eating llamas, excepting only the lords of *guarangas*. Unlike on the north coast, in Chincha camelids continued to be kept for transport, no doubt because of the intense exchange carried out by this chiefdom with the highlands of Collao and Cusco. The "traders" gave first priority to exchange and its transportation requirements, and to this end they maintained and cared for their herds.

It appears likely that on the coast the possession of herds of "sheep of the land" was a privilege of the lords and the "traders," and not within the reach of commoners. During the period of Inca rule, herding, carefully administered by the state with the aid of *quipu*, provided the government with abundant resources.

THE STATE STOREHOUSES

A large labor force that worked the state fields and extensive pasturelands with large herds of camelids constituted inexhaustible sources of wealth that were translated by the Incas into power. A substantial surplus in agropecu-arial production not only benefited state-level redistribution and satisfied the demands of reciprocity; it also conferred on the Inca government an accumulation of goods that symbolized its power. In addition, these goods gave the Sapa Inca an incontestable superiority over the lords of the macroethnic groups who had become increasingly impoverished as the Incas flourished. For these reason, one objective of Inca administration was to keep the state storehouses filled with goods.

That there were great numbers of state storehouses is confirmed in the chronicles. Cobo (1956, vol. 2, chap. 30) describes them in greatest detail. The maintenance of the storehouses followed the same principle as for planting and harvesting, that is, those charged with their care were sup-ported by the estate for which they were responsible, as were the porters and herdsmen who transported the accumulated wealth from one place to another.

To keep accounts and care for these products, majordomos, accountants, and administrators were required. The chronicler says that the storehouses were in the principal towns of each "province," in the official residences of the principal administrators, and in the city of Cusco. The storehouses of the Inca were located close to those of the Sun, which were fewer in num-ber.

All kinds of products were stored, including arms, fine and rustic cloth-ing, and the most varied kinds of foods. We know from archival documents that coca leaves were stored in baskets of a specified size. The same was true for dehydrated meat, partridges, and doves, which were kept in small boxes of straw or wood, as were dried fruit and dehydrated shrimp (Rostworowski, 1981c). After the fall of the Inca, despite the turmoil of the Conquest and civil wars among the Spaniards, the natives continued to fill the storehouses assuming that with the return of peace they would be held accountable for the goods produced in the intervening period.

So it was that La Gasca, pursuing Gonzalo Pizarro with his army, could remain in Jauja for six months, feeding his troops with produce from the storehouses that, according to Cobo, contained more than 15,000 *fanegas.* The storehouses were generally built just outside the settlements, on the slopes of the hills, in high, cool, and well-ventilated places. They had the appearance of small towers, built in rows, separated to avoid the spread of fire, should one occur.

Archaeological excavations over many years by Craig Morris in Huanuco Pampa throw an interesting light on this Inca center, especially on the state storehouses. He distinguishes between the architecture of the storehouses and that of other structures by their topographical situation, the nature of their floors, and the lintels of their doors/windows. His observations with

Cobo's information to the effect that the storehouses were placed in rows following the contours of the hillsides.

The Incas employed various techniques for storing food produce and, according to Morris and Thompson (1985), the storehouses that have been studied can be distinguished according to the techniques used and the kinds of produce stored in them. Their study of storage in Huanuco Pampa reveals an extraordinary level of sophistication in terms of the utilization of climatic conditions and also provides quantitative data underscoring the enormous importance the Inca state gave to the storage of food products (Morris, 1981:328).

Morris identified more than 2,000 storehouses in the administrative center of Huanuco Pampa, of which he measured some 800 and excavated 112. The following is a brief summary of his findings. The structures were categorized as circular or rectangular. The circular structures generally had interior diameters of 2–6.3 meters and a single door facing uphill. The rectangular storehouses measured 3–5 meters wide by 3–10 meters long and generally had two doors/windows, one facing uphill and the other down. The circular structures were generally reserved for the storage of maize, and carbonized maize grains were found in six of these storehouses. Fragments of large jars were found on the stone-paved floors, indicating that the maize was stored in kernel form.

Morris found (1981:339) the remains of carbonized tubers in three rectangular storehouses. They were stored using a technique substantially different from that used for maize. Apparently the tubers were laid out over a layer of straw matting lightly sewn with fine thread, possibly to permit the circulation of air. Then they were tied up with thicker cord into bundles or bales.

Floors were found in many of the rectangular storehouses, suggesting concern with maintaining conditions suitable for the preservation of tubers. Loose stones were laid on the surface of the floor with spaces left between them. In addition, stone-lined conduits were found, with openings on either side of the structure, some facing uphill and others down, thus creating a system of ventilation that could be controlled using stones to close the openings. In general, it appears that the rectangular storehouses, with their windows/doors and conduit openings, were designed to take advantage of the prevailing winds for ventilation. Morris also analyzes the advantages of the high altitude, which protected the maize and tubers from fungus and insects. The use of covered jars to store the maize protected the contents from rodents.

Finally, the author indicates that Huanuco Pampa had been built ex novo, entirely by the Incas, and that the entire storage system was typically

Inca. Archaeology has revealed examples of other food preservation techniques in pre-Hispanic Peru, from other times and places, such as the structures in Cajamarquilla, in the valley of the Rimac River; those at Tres Palos in the lower valley of Lima, excavated by Dr. Josefina Ramos de Cox and the Seminario de Arqueología of the Universidad Católica; and the storehouses at the Sanctuary of Pachacamac (Jiménez Borja, 1970).

A separate mention is due the *hoyos*, or pits, found by Bonavia (1982) in the desert near Huarmey, on the coast. These pebble-lined pits were used to preserve food products, especially maize, buried in the sand. Ethnographic questioning revealed that the older inhabitants remembered the practice of keeping maize in the ground as protection against insects.

Further confirmation of the use of this system is found in a document referring to the terrible havoc wreaked by the torrential rains of 1578, caused by the appearance that year of El Niño. The Lambayeque zone was the hardest hit, and among the many calamities that befell the inhabitants of the northern valleys, according to the natives, was the rotting of the maize they had stored in the sand, as well as the grain stored in jars in their homes (BN, A-534, folios 309v, 313v, 318r, 321r).

6

Economic Models

When we speak of economic models in pre-Hispanic Peru, we must keep in mind that we are dealing with economies that neither used money nor were organized on a market basis. The Inca economic model had been termed redistributive, owing to the many functions performed by the government itself. This means that a large part of the production of the countryside was controlled by the state, which in turn distributed this wealth according to its own interests.

Valensi (1974) provides a definition of the principle of redistribution that assumes a model of institutional centralism. In societies dominated by redistribution, the production and distribution of goods are organized around a center – whether a chief, a lord, a temple or a despot – that collects the goods, stores and redistributes them to reward its supporters, ensures the maintenance and defense of public services, and preserves the social and political order, as during the celebration of public festivals. Reciprocity intervenes in the production, labor services, and periodic distribution of lands, as well as in the apportionment of goods produced, in the practice of gift-giving, and so on.

Polanyi admits that redistribution can play a role in quite diverse societies, including homogeneous as well as stratified ones. Reciprocity and redistribution can be combined in the same society – the former corresponding to the horizontal form of exchange, the latter to the vertical form between local units and the central authority. The formation of the Inca state was accompanied by increased production and the dynamic economic growth of the region.

For many years Inca organization was admired by Europeans and praised as a kind of utopia. It was believed that the storage of goods of all kinds served humanitarian ends, such as rescuing the population in case of natural disaster. Such an interpretation demonstrates a lack of understanding of the economic mechanisms of the Inca state.

Most of the redistributed goods were consumed by the system of reciprocity, by which the state was under constant obligation to renew great "gifts" to the various ethnic lords, military chiefs, the *huacas*, and so on. To meet these obligations, a system of state storehouses was built, as discussed in the Chapter 5. The power of the state, in turn, depended on the success with which the government managed these enormous quantities of accumulated goods. Stored goods represented power in the Inca realm.

THE HIGHLAND ECONOMIC MODEL

The Southern Highlands

The southern economy of the state has been studied, especially by John Murra (1964, 1967, 1972), whose work has been followed by many researchers. To obtain products from diverse ecological settings, the natives favored a system of enclaves, called by Murra "vertical archipelagos," whose highland nuclei controlled various zones situated in different microclimates, some quite distant from one another, by means of multiethnic colonies.

We use the word "distant" with reference to microclimates located at a distance of more than one day's journey by foot. The enclaves of the highland nuclei are, to date, the classic Andean models for securing products unavailable in the nuclei themselves. These enclaves are on the coast and in the jungle region at distances of several weeks' journey by foot. This point is important, since it represents the difference between the models of the southern highlands and the central region.

Murra has investigated in great detail the Lupaca macroethnic group, and it has been confirmed that the same model describes the other *señoríos* of the Collao plateau, such as the Pacajes, the Hatun Collas, and the Azángaros, which also enjoyed enclaves in climatic zones different from that of their own habitat.

At issue concerning the beginnings of these enclaves is whether they originated as the result of conquest. Valuable data in a document in the Archivo Arzobispal de Lima describe how the highland Yauyos threw the Calango coastal people from lands they possessed in Callaguaya and settled members of various highland *ayllus* in their place (Rostworowski, 1977:31–32).

We need more research on the coastal groups of the southern zone to understand how they were dominated by highlanders. Possibly this was because there was no hegemonic power on the coast that could defend itself against the advance of the highlanders. The region between Camaná and Tarapacá, called Colesuyu, differed from the four classical regions that formed the Inca state, and must have defined a geographical space rather than an actual political entity. Its coastal population was composed of agriculturalists and fishermen who were divided among a large number of chiefdoms (Rostworowski, 1988c).

While the 1567 *Visitas* by Garci Diez de San Miguel (1964) and Ortiz de Zuñiga to Huánuco (1967, 1972) appear to describe classic examples of highland enclaves, there are references in both documents to "*recates*" in cattle, wool, and clothing. Such repeated references appear to indicate that at some time during the year a kind of exchange took place.

The Central Highlands

The situation in the Maritime Cordillera of the central region of ancient Peru was very different from that of the altiplano and the highlands in general. The special topographical conditions characteristic of that region caused the natives to adopt their own economic model. It is important to demonstrate how a given model can vary in response to different local conditions.

This particular application of the pattern of "verticality" shows that this system was not rigid but could change according to circumstances. Evidence of this is found in the 1549 and 1553 *Visitas* to Canta. Both are early accounts from before the Toledo reforms, and give the impression of a zone with very special circumstances.

The region of Canta is characterized by steep terrain and therefore widely varying climates over relatively short distances, permitting the exploitation of a variety of natural products. I shall explain briefly its quite original form of economic organization and how it dealt with the problems and opportunities of verticality. The chiefdom of Canta comprised eight *ayllus*. In order to cultivate fields situated at different levels in different ecological zones, at distances from one another of one or two days by foot, the inhabitants devised a system of rotational, seasonal, communal labor involving the members of the eight *ayllus*. When they completed a communal labor task, they would move from that location to a different spot to carry out another set of agricultural tasks. This limited agricultural transhumance led to their possessing, in addition to their permanent towns, a number of communal villages inhabited on a seasonal basis while they performed their labor in that zone, for example, when they went to the *puna* to plant and harvest a high-altitude plant called maca (*Lepidium meyenii*) or to shear their camelid herds. During another season they would go down to their coca and maize fields in the warm region of the *chaupi yunga*. They also used this rotational system to perform nonagricultural labor such as the production of subsistence products for the community, including textiles, pottery, *ojotas* (Andean footwear), and *charqui.*

Because of the short distances among the various microclimates and natural resources, the natives of Canta remained outside the system of multiethnic enclaves and *mitmaq* that were introduced elsewhere with Inca domination (Rostworowski, 1978a).

THE COASTAL ECONOMIC MODEL

Specialization of Labor

Given that the organization of the highland economy bore a necessary relationship with the environment of the Andean valleys and the highland plateau, it is logical that the different geography of the coast would favor a different kind of economic model. It is important to keep in mind that the coastal region, in spite of its vast deserts, was a region rich in renewable natural resources. Its greatest source of well-being was the sea, a sea that was extraordinarily rich in fish resources (Rostworowski, 1981b).

Unlike in other areas of the world, in the beginnings of civilization in ancient Peru rapid population increase and the construction of ceremonial centers did not depend on agriculture (Moseley, 1975). These early cultural advances resulted from the exploitation of the resources of the sea and thus indicate the earlier development of the coastal region.

From early times both fishing and agriculture were established on the coast. Separate groups were formed, each with its own chiefs, and products were exchanged between them. The fishermen, however, limited to their beaches and coves, remained subordinate to the lords of the macroethnic groups of coastal agriculturalists.

The earliest information concerning the existence of these divisions within a chiefdom is provided in the *Relación de Chincha*, which I have called the *"Aviso"* (Rostworowski, 1970a, 1977a, 1989). According to the *"Aviso,"* a population of 30,000 tributaries was composed of 10,000 fishermen, 12,000 agriculturalists, and 6,000 traders. These figures indicated a greater division of labor than what had been known for the Andean world.

The surplus fish that was not consumed locally was dried, a process that permitted its preservation. This surplus facilitated the development of trade, not only to acquire subsistence goods within a single valley but to exchange dried fish for highland products.

With the evolution of an increasingly wealthy society, the inhabitants found themselves with leisure time for other than subsistence pursuits. Their

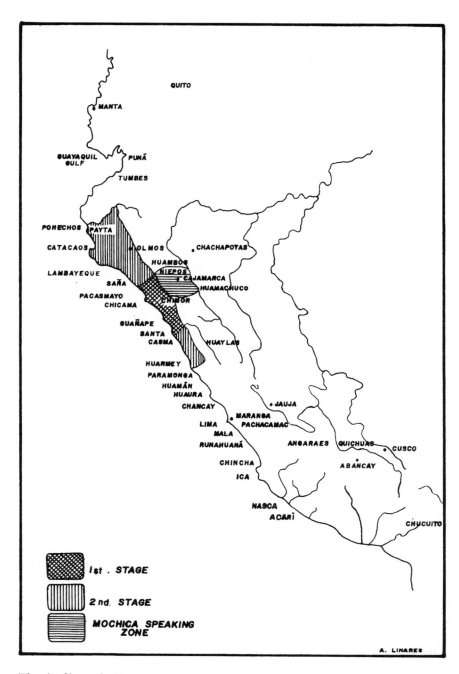

The chiefdom of Chimor.

well-being improved, while the pomp and magnificence of the lords and priests flourished, along with artistic expression. One consequence was the formation of new labor groups of artisans dedicated to metallurgy, textiles, ceramics, and other crafts. The exclusive dedication of each labor group to a single craft is characteristic of coastal society.

Diversification and specialization also took place in other occupations, such as saltmaking, dyemaking, carpentry, food preparation. Perhaps the most prestigious craftspeople were the silversmiths. The Incas took full advantage of the artisans of the principal coastal valleys, sending them to Cusco to work for the state. In fact, Huayna Capac brought a group of silversmiths from Huancavilca and installed them in Cusco, in Zurite, on lands belonging to the Tumipampa *panaca* (AGN – Títulos de Propiedad, cuad. 431, years 1595–1710). This information should be taken into account in studying silverworking in pre-Hispanic Cusco; although aesthetically it followed highland models, the technology was often of coastal origin.

Before we learned of the *"Aviso"* document, little was known about specialized occupational groups, and even their existence was questioned. We now have additional evidence in the granting of an *encomienda* to Hernando Pizarro in 1534, which mentions a commitment on the part of the *encomendero* to permit the Chincha traders and silverworkers to practice their occupations freely (Rostworowski, 1977a; AGI – Justicia 1075).

A detailed archival investigation revealed the high degree of labor specialization on the coast. Each occupation, each task was carried out by specified individuals, with no one able to change his work for another, a custom that subsequently received the full support of the Colonial administration. In the *Ordenanzas* dictated by the *Oidor* González de Cuenca in Jayanca in 1566, we find:

> The Indian officials work as weavers of fine textiles, sandalmakers, makers of horse collars, silverworkers, and carpenters, and other occupations are performed to be able to sell in the market and elsewhere, and they do not leave their occupations, and the alcaldes of the Indians compel them to continue to practice them, for the well-being and benefit of the community of the *repartimiento* to which they belong, and the Indian official who rejects his occupation is punished with fifty public lashes in the market. (AGI – Patronato 189, Part 11; Rostworowski, 1977)

The importance of craft activity is confirmed in the same *Ordenanzas*, which prohibit the local lords from forcing the craftspeople to perform the peasant *mita* or work in the homes of their *encomenderos*.

According to the system of specialization, many tasks that are not considered craft activities were counted as such, and the performance of any other labor was prohibited. An example illustrating this coastal custom was that of the *chicheros*, or brewers, a specialty reserved for men. In the highlands the women prepared such beverages for the family at home. When great quantities were required for religious rituals or for the ceremonies of the Inca, the *mamacona* were responsible for preparing it. On the coast, however, as we have seen, this was an exclusively male occupation.

Coastal Exchange

In archaic societies, according to Polanyi (Polyani, Arenberg, and Pearson, 1957), the redistributive model predominates, even though in some places the custom of exchange existed. This practice followed by the coastal chiefdoms constituted an important difference from that of the highland *señoríos*.

Reciprocity as an integrative practice was stronger on the coast, where it was employed together with redistribution and trade, which was based on established equivalencies, and could provide products that were not produced locally. An empirical study of the so-called primitive economy takes into consideration all three economic models: reciprocity, redistribution, and trade.

To understand exchange in the coastal societies of ancient Peru, we have to clarify that it took place on two very different levels. The first occurred among commoners, for the purpose of securing subsistence goods necessary for daily existence. Possibly equivalencies were established and accepted by all parties. The second level of exchange took place among the upper social classes.

We have information regarding two different locations that offers us a perspective of the situation on the coast. In Chincha, as already noted, long-distance exchange was carried out by "traders" recognized as such. We have only limited data concerning lords in the north who managed trade in both sumptuary and subsistence goods. Let us examine these two situations.

Local Exchange

The specialization of labor on the coast required establishing local trade among the inhabitants by which they could obtain subsistence goods and others that they did not produce individually. I have referred to the specialization of all labor, which brought constant, intensive exchange. An example can be found in the 1574 *Visita* by Juan de Hoces to the Trujillo region. The *Visitador* perceived a need to regulate the equivalencies between the maize provided by the agriculturalists and the beverages prepared by the brewers. He also fixed the values of beads, wool, and other objects that were traded (Rostworowski, 1977a:243).

The brewers were free of any other labor obligation and could not be forced to participate in the *mitas* of the *encomendero*, local *cacique*, or principals. They were obligated only to help repair the principal drainage canal of the valley, a fact that shows, in turn, the importance attached to any emergency work on a coastal valley's hydraulic system. Although the measures in question date to colonial times, they clearly reflect the pre-Hispanic customs of the coast.

Archaic societies tend to reject the idea of profit from transactions that involve foodstuffs; these are limited to maintaining equivalencies. Trade at the local level in a coastal valley did not involve profit but was a necessary accommodation to the specialized labor system that characterized coastal society.

The Chincha Traders

Although the Chincha traders have already been mentioned in discussions of social classes and the social hierarchy of the Inca state, we have not yet discussed their voyages and what these represented in the Andean context. The Chincha headed north in rafts, whose numbers are mentioned by Atahualpa himself in a dialogue with Pizarro. The Spaniard inquired about the reason for the presence of the lord of Chincha, who, we will recall, was the only lord in the Inca's entourage carried in a litter at that fateful meeting in Cajamarca. The use of a litter was an outstanding honor, when so many other nobles participated in the journey on foot. Atahualpa responded that the Chincha lord was his friend and the greatest lord of the lowlands, who possessed "100,000 rafts in the sea" (Pedro Pizarro, 1944:186). Of course, this number should not be taken literally. Probably some of these rafts were of logs while others were made from great bundles of reeds tied together. These were steered with wooden boards fixed between the bundles, which were manipulated up and down as rudder and keel (Rostworowski, 1981a).

It is necessary to determine what Chincha trade comprised. The *"Aviso"* document declares that the "traders" were "very daring, intelligent, of good breeding" and the only ones in the Inca realm who used "money," since they bought and sold with copper. This would mean that the basis of their transactions consisted of exchanging that metal for other goods. They obtained the copper from the highlands on their land route covered by herds of camelids and numerous porters, probably included among the 6,000 "traders." In what form was the copper transported? It appears likely, although not confirmed archaeologically, that the Chincha manufactured and used "ax-money" similar to that found in Ecuador, where these objects were used for exchange (Holm, 1966–67).

Such ax-money can be distinguished from utilitarian axes by the absence of a sharpened edge and their extreme thinness. Holm's study of these axes led him to conclude that their weight is related to a quinquennial system of measurement, based on the ratio of their lengths and widths. This latter conclusion is especially interesting when we consider that the *"Aviso"* document makes reference to a decimal system used in alloying and in determining the value of metals.

These ax-monies, also called *"naipes"* (playing cards) by treasure hunters who abandon them as worthless because of their highly eroded condition, have been recovered in excavations dating to the Middle Sicán Period (Shimada and Shimada, 1985:384). In the excavations of the Huaca del Pueblo, also in Batán Grande, Shimada found the smelting furnaces and all the necessary equipment for smelting copper. Apart from these finds, ax-monies, of uniform size were found in tombs, carefully wrapped and tied in small bundles, and others of diverse sizes were found separately. Shimada mentions several of these packets, each containing five hundred ax-monies. Radiocarbon analysis of the perishable material in which they were wrapped provided dates of A.D. 900–1050.

The ax-monies found in tombs appear to be offerings to ensure the well-being of the deceased in the next life. Ax-money was not for everyday use, but served as symbolic value for certain kinds of exchange. Holm (1966–67) believes these "monies" were brought to the Ecuadorian coast from elsewhere, since there are no copper mines in that region. In another work he indicates the presence of ax-monies in pre-Hispanic Mexico, which leads us to believe that we are dealing with an exchange object and a type of primitive money that circulated and was of some value (Holm, 1975).

As for the production of bronze, in pre-Hispanic times the alloying of copper and tin predominated in the south, whereas on the north coast copper alloyed with arsenic was used. Possibly these differences, reflecting long local traditions, were based on religious, as well as technological, concepts (Lechtman, 1979).

While Shimada's discoveries do not answer all our questions regarding the trade in copper carried out by the Chincha, they do indicate its great antiquity and possible changes over time. They also tend to confirm Holm's conclusions concerning the existence of long-distance trade from Chincha to the Ecuadorian ports and farther north.

On the return voyage south, the "traders" would bring beads and *mullu* (*Spondylus* shell), highly valued, as we have seen, for their red color and religious significance. *Mullu* was important in the rituals of the *huacas* as offerings to ask for rain, and was also used in making figurines, necklaces, and other ornaments. Ancient *Spondylus* shell workshops have been found in Tumbes and at various locations along the Ecuadorian coast (Marcos and Norton, 1981). The archaeological data indicate the presence of two types of shell, *Spondylus* and strombus, both originating in warm seas, as early as the Early Horizon (Paulsen, 1974).

A Chincha raft may have been captured off the Ecuadorian coast by the pilot Bartolomé Ruiz during Pizarro's second voyage, while he was exploring the coast (Sámano-Xérez, 1937:65–66). The description in this account indicates a raft of very large dimensions, capable of carrying twenty men in addition to a large cargo of fine wool and cotton cloth, gold and silver objects, jewelry, ceramic vessels, *Spondylus* shell, and other items. From this it appears that Guayaquil or Puerto Viejo may have been what Polanyi (Polanyi, Arenberg, and Pearson, 1957) and Chapman (1957) called a port of trade, and was the destination of the Chincha rafts (for northern traffic, see León Borja, 1977). According to Chapman (1957), such long-range trade used not markets but "ports" where exchange took place. She distinguishes between markets and ports, which disappeared immediately under the impact of European conquest.

The motivating force behind this exchange was not economic gain but a need for specific goods on the part of the elite and the gods. Most long-distance trade, then, consisted of securing objects whose value was apparent only to the interested party. For this reason, Chincha trade did not last beyond the Conquest, since the objects exchanged had no value in the eyes of the Spanish. These preindustrial, nonmarket economies did not involve trading of large amounts of imports and exports. Long-distance exchange was difficult and dangerous, mostly because of the limited shipping technology available and the risks of the voyages themselves.

Chincha expeditions must have been sporadic and carefully scheduled to accommodate natural phenomena such as sea currents, prevailing winds, and the annual seasons, both for departures and for return travel. According to Sabloff and Lamberg-Karlovsky (1975), this ancient long-distance trade was fundamentally different from modern commerce: It was not based on costs, and imported goods were sought because they were not available in the place of origin. In addition, it was characterized by being limited to relatively few trade items.

Why did the Chincha become seafarers, and how did they learn the skills of navigation? Our present knowledge does not permit a satisfactory answer. Perhaps they came into contact with navigators from distant places, who taught them their maritime skills. Two legends, that of Naymlap for Lambayeque and that of Taicanamo for Chimor, refer to men who arrived in these valleys in fleets of balsa rafts, settled, and started new eras. Possibly something similar occurred in Chincha. The information provided by Albornoz (1967) concerning the worship of a star called Cundri by the "traders" leads us to believe that perhaps it served for navigation.

Further archaeological fieldwork is needed in Chincha, as well as documentary information on the sporadic exchange along the Pacific Coast, ethnographic studies on the coasts of Peru and Ecuador, and a systemic investigation of maritime practices among the fishermen of the region – all of which would contribute to our understanding of the Andean coastal world, which has been to some extent overlooked by scholars.

The Northern "Traders"

We have relatively little information concerning the northern "traders," and not enough to give us an idea of their sea routes. We do not know how they called themselves in the Mochica language, other than the term "*caefoer*," or "*cafaereio*," which means trade or payment for some item. The "traders" themselves refer to pre-Conquest trade carried out "the Indian way" (Rostworowski, 1981–82, 1989). As we have already noted, the trading nobles requested permission of Dr. Cuenca to carry out their trade and travel freely through the villages without harm. We also indicated that their trade goods consisted of wool, cotton, silver and shell beads, beans, dried fish, and "other things."

Among the trade goods mentioned are not only luxury items but also food produce, which contradicts the idea of exclusively sumptuary trade. Quite possibly these northern lords maintained sporadic trade with Guayaquil in pre-Hispanic times. At least the fishermen went north to acquire the logs they needed to build their rafts, a practice they continued until the demarcation of the national borders in the nineteenth century.

Trade during Pilgrimages

One of the distinctive characteristics of the Andean peoples is their love of religious pilgrimages to prestigious shrines or recognized oracles. Avila's informants (1966, chap. 9; Salomon and Urioste, 1991) tell of the participation of coastal people in the pilgrimage tradition, including their travel to the important *huaca* of Pariacaca to participate in its festivals. This shrine in the highlands of the Central Maritime Cordillera was visited by people from several coastal regions.

It is assumed that the inhabitants of the highland valleys participated in the celebrations honoring Pachacamac, the coastal god par excellence and lord of earthquakes. In addition, his oracles enjoyed great fame. No doubt in the tradition of reciprocity, highlanders came to join with coastal people in the celebration of the god's festivals. Cieza de León (*La Crónica*, 1941, chap. 71) mentions the great annual pilgrimages that were realized in the name of Pachacamac. People came from distant places and stayed in great temporary lodges prepared for the occasion.

It seems likely that the important *huacas*, through their religious influence, played major roles in exchange and economic development in pre-Hispanic times. In addition, Pachacamac, for reason of his great prestige, possessed sanctuaries related to his cult in a variety of places. In some chronicles there are native accounts concerning the "sons" and "wives" of the idol, as they were called (Rostworowski, 1977). Among the "wives" stands out the *huaca* of Mama (now Ricardo Palma in Chosica) and the island of Urpay Huachac in Chincha, the goddess considered the mother of fishes. There were temples and lands belonging to the god Pachacamac in Mala, Guarco (Cañete), Chincha, and Andahuaylas. Santillán (1927) tells of several of the idol's "sons," one of whom inhabited Chincha and was perhaps related to the oracle established in that valley. Possibly these "sons" and "wives" represented kinds of enclaves or religious archipelagos, benefiting not only the priests of the temples but their followers too.

Another example of a ceremonial center visited annually by pilgrims of various social strata was the place of Noquip, near Chérrepe, in the north, surrounded by marshes and sacred hills. Throughout most of the year it was inhabited by a few agriculturalists and fishermen, but during the celebration of its festivals it became filled with visitors, commoners as well as the higher nobility. All together they celebrated its ancient rites with song and dance. The Spanish administration, ever fearful of idolatrous practices, ordered the abandonment of Noquip, and its inhabitants were dispersed according to their occupations, the agriculturalists to the town of Guadalupe and the fishermen to Chérrepe (Ramirez-Horton, 1978).

A third ceremonial center is described by Felipe Medina, eradicator of idolatries, in 1560. It was a very ancient *huaca* called Choque Ispana, located at the edge of the sea near Salinas de Huacho. From Medina's description it is evident that the center must have originated in the Chavín period. Both highlanders and lowland people came to this sanctuary. Of the four entrances to the temple, two were reserved for *costeños* – one for men and the other for women – while the two remaining entrances were similarly designated for highland men and women.

The mention of highland personages indicates that the participation of highlanders in these pilgrimages was an established custom (Millones, 1986: 229–40). These references and the custom today of celebrating festivals in honor of the Virgin or one of the saints in various locations during a particular time of year support the hypothesis that such festivities and pilgrimages represent the superposition of pre-Hispanic customs and cults, traditions maintained even in present-day Peru. Such celebrations are characterized by their seasonality, almost always taking place in isolated, unpopulated locations and attracting the faithful from distant places.

If these pilgrimages had their origin in ancient tradition, it is natural that trade between highlanders and coastal people would take place during them, stimulated by the presence of peoples from diverse microenvironments. This subject deserves more attention, as does the geography of the present-day sanctuaries and their reciprocal relations (Poole, 1982; Sallnow, 1974).

The cults of *huacas* located both in the sierra and on the coast must have promoted complementarity between the two zones and an important exchange of goods. These pilgrimages took place during fixed times of the year, when entire populations were mobilized for religious ends and also to carry out trade.

The Importance of the Hydraulic System

Access to water and therefore to irrigation was as important in the Andean world as access to land was. Myths and legends tell of the beginnings of the hydraulic canals in a magic time, when the animals could speak (Avila, 1966; Salomon and Urioste, 1991). The springs came forth as a result of rivalries among celebrated *huacas*, who challenged each other to test their powers, urinating in those places which became the springs (AAL – Idolatries). The sea, the lakes, the springs were venerated as the places of origin of numerous ethnic groups. The lagoons were considered to be manifestations of the sea and the origin of water in general (Sherbondy, 1982a and b).

In order to practice intensive irrigation agriculture, which was known throughout the Andes, it was necessary to have knowledge of hydraulics. Tubers could be planted on unwatered land, but maize needed irrigation, and perhaps its introduction on previously nonarable lands brought about the development of hydraulic systems (Mitchell, 1981). Not only were complex and sophisticated hydraulic techniques practiced during various stages in Andean development in order to improve agricultural production, but the sanctuaries, like that of Pachacamac, used canals to bring water over long distances to the temples (Hacienda Las Palmas, information provided orally by Tello, 1946). The two small rivers that run through Cusco, the Tulumayo and the Huantanay, were channelized with stone-lined beds.

Archaeology has recognized the systems and models employed in Andean hydraulics, especially those on the coast, where irrigation was always an unavoidable necessity. Analysis of the hydric conditions in each coastal valley offers interesting information about the development of the centers of power, which could fluctuate through time in terms of coast-highland relations. The diverse circumstances in which the hydraulic models evolved in each coastal valley are an expression of its past and its relations with its immediate highland neighbors.

The information obtained for a given river valley cannot be applied to other valleys, unless confirmed by documentation. Experience, in fact, demonstrates the existence of differing circumstances, fluctuations, and changes in coast-highland relations through time, not only among geographically distant centers but among centers within the same valley. To illustrate this point, it is enough to compare the strong control exercised by the altiplano highlanders over the southern coast during the Late Intermediate Period with what was happening in Chimor during the same period. In the south power centers in the sierra dominated and projected their power toward the coast, while on the north coast a strong state dominated part of the llanos or plains in addition to establishing *señoríos* of probable coastal origin in part of the sierra of Cajamarca, adjoining the coast (Rostworowski, 1985; Rostworowski and Remy, 1992).

The centers of power changed over time, and with them control over the irrigation systems of a valley, since the center that controlled the canals controlled the land. The following examples of developments on the central and south-central coast explain this further.

In the valley of the Chillón River during the Late Intermediate Period, the macroethnic chiefdom of Collec, or Collique, defended itself from various possible attacks by the highlanders of Canta by means of a series of fortresses in the valley. The seat of the local lord was itself a palace-fortress, with high walls surrounding a substantial piece of cultivated land, irrigated by two springs. This defensive system permitted the lord of Collec to resist any highland attack (AGI – Justicia 413). This example illustrates a center of coastal power defended from any attack from the highlands and with sufficient water for its crops in case of a prolonged siege.

In the document just cited, the aggressive intentions of the chief of Canta regarding the valley lowlands were based on the fact that the water needed to irrigate the coastal fields originated in the Canta highlands. I maintain that this case illustrates the highland way of thinking and dealing with the people of the coast. Even so, in times of great droughts lowland people and highlanders alike would unite to obtain water by opening mountain lagoons at high altitudes (AGI – Justicia 413; Rostworowski, 1988b).

During the same period, the absence of defenses in the middle valleys of

Lurín and the Rimac River, united at that time under the hegemony of the religious center of Pachacamac, suggests they were dominated and oppressed by the Huarochirí macroethnic group. It is possible that the highlanders were content with exercising power from a distance out of respect for, and fear of, the coastal god – especially from a fear, frequently mentioned in the archival documents, of the coastal climate, in which, they said, they would become ill and die.

Contrasting with this situation on the central coast is that of the Guarco, in present-day Cañete, who were able to maintain their freedom from highland oppression through military prowess. Their valley was defended by high walls and fortresses, and further protection was afforded by the river, which ran along the edge of the valley instead of down the middle. In Ica, the macroethnic group dominated the highland water source for the canal system (data from the 1594 *Visita*; Guillén y Guillén, 1963). The Iqueño lords did not offer resistance to the Inca troops, thus avoiding Inca reprisals.

During all periods, water rights were very important on the coast. In the chapter on land tenure we saw the case of the highland chief of the Guambos who demanded payment from the coastal lord for the use of water originating in his high ravines. We also saw a coastal chief claim compensation from his subordinates for the use of secondary canals. This submissive attitude on the part of the lowland dwellers may be primarily an Inca-period phenomenon; during earlier times the coastal dwellers must have been careful to protect their water intakes to ensure their water rights.

A principal function of the coastal ethnic lords was undoubtedly the control and administration of their water resources and intakes. This was carried out on two levels. The first comprised their relationships with their highland neighbors, involving the protection of their water sources. The second consisted of their control over the distribution of water within their own valleys. Both involved complicated sets of priorities and conflicts with and among their subjects.

In another work (Rostworowski, 1985) I indicate the presence of a coastal ethnic group in the communities of Celendín, Contumazá, Chota, Hualgayoc, and San Miguel, in the region of Cajamarca, long before the arrival of the Incas. The coastal origin of these inhabitants can be recognized linguistically, since many of their surnames contain the consonant sound "f" used exclusively in the Mochica language. These references are found in the *Visita* to Cajamarca carried out during the Toledo regime in two stages, the first in 1571–72, before the native reductions, and the second, which is the less valuable ethnohistorically, in 1578 (Rostworowski and Remy, 1992).

The population to which I refer was not placed there by the Incas, but had resided in the zone since long before the Late Horizon. The *mitmaq* transferred there by the Inca rulers are specifically mentioned in the document as forming a special *guaranga* comprising Quechua, Cañari, Guayacondor, and Colla groups.

Possibly the coastal presence in the highlands sprang mainly from the need to control the water intakes, and thereby the entire coastal hydraulic system. This was perhaps a kind of preventive conquest during the coastal apogee to ensure access to water for their canal system (Rostworowski, 1985; Rostworowski and Remy, 1992).

Schaedel (1985a and b) suggests that the *costeño* group established in the sierra constituted a *señorío* apart from the coastal chiefdoms. Given the political pattern observed in Chimor, of small local lords such as Changuco and Guamán under the hegemony of greater lords, this assumption may be valid (Rostworowski, 1976). In any case, we are facing a situation completely different from the one that existed during the period of Inca domination, when the coastal people no longer controlled their water resources and intakes. According to my hypothesis – which only archaeology can confirm or refute – at some indeterminate historical moment, perhaps during the Middle Intermediate Period, there was a coastal advance along the length of the coast toward the cisandine sierra, followed by a retreat toward the coast in the face of a surge of new centers of power in the highlands. The same events appear in Avila's Quechua text (1966; Taylor 1980), which relates the expulsion of the coastal people from their towns in the cisandine sierra of the Pacific watershed by the new conquerors, worshipers of the god Pariacaca. The invaders occupied the villages, homes, and fields of the coastal people, who were forced to flee toward the coast.

The god Guari, a *huaca* whose *pacarina* was the sea, taught men to construct terraces and irrigation canals and was worshiped throughout the north central highlands (Rostworowski, 1983). It is significant that a divinity of coastal origin was considered responsible for these technological advances.

When the coastal inhabitants did not dominate the highlands adjoining their valleys, they would maintain strategic fortifications to defend the valley entrances, of which the castle of Tomaval in Virú is an example (Willey, 1953). According to John Topic and Teresa Lange (1978), during the Late Intermediate Period three fortresses were built in Chimu, two in the valley of Moche and a third in the valley of Chao. The structures showed little evidence of having been occupied for any length of time. The two former fortresses controlled access to the entire length of the valley, while two smaller forts on either side of the river at its narrowest point defended the entrance to the valley by the mountain route. Possibly these structures were built in the face of an imminent threat of an Inca invasion, but the Inca strategy of cutting off the water that flowed from the mountains to irrigate the coastal fields apparently took the inhabitants by surprise (Rostworowski, 1953).

Ortloff (1981) concludes that the existence of the coastal states presupposed two conditions: first, an accomplished knowledge of techniques of administration and control of water resources and intakes and, second, the ability to mobilize and coordinate labor forces capable of maintaining the existing irrigation systems and building new ones. To these I would add two other requirements: first, control of their water sources and intakes and, second, freedom from highland domination. Without these conditions it was impossible for coastal dwellers to ensure control over their water resources and, with it, their autonomy.

Irrigation water from the rivers that flowed down from the sierra was always subject to changing power relationships in the highlands. The largest hydraulic complex on the coast was that of Lambayeque, which covered five river basins (Kosok, 1965). At the apogee of the Chimu, during the Late Intermediate Period, a canal called La Cumbe was built to bring water to the city of Chanchán over a distance of 84 kilometers (Farrington, 1974; Keatinge, 1975; Kus, 1974; Moseley, 1974). Its construction demanded a sophisticated knowledge of hydraulics because the embankments had to conduct the water to a certain level. La Cumbe is often considered the most prodigious hydraulic project in pre-Columbian America.

The advanced technology applied in the coastal irrigation systems demonstrates the availability of a considerable labor force, which functioned under the direction of technicians with great empirical knowledge. The need for complex hydraulic skills probably led to the appearance of specialists in this field.

The irrigation works carried out by the northerners are comparable only to those constructed in Nasca, where an extensive network of underground canals was built. Parts of these canals were lined with stone slabs, while others have roofs with beams of *guarango* wood (*Prosopis* sp.). Access to the canals was through vertical wells, which were necessary for their maintenance. The system continues to function and provide water for cultivation to the present day. The difference between the northern hydraulic system and that of Nasca lies in the techniques used by the latter: filtration galleries, underground tunnels or open trenches that brought water from the subsoil to the surface. A much smaller labor force was required for the construction of this system as compared with the northern variety (Gölte, 1980b; González García, 1978).

Undoubtedly these ancient inhabitants of the coast, over centuries of great effort, achieved levels of technical sophistication surpassed only by modern technology.

Final Reflections

This history of the Inca realm relates the rise of a small chiefdom, lost in the immensity of the Andean cordillera, to become a great state. It is the mythical narration of its beginnings and of the legendary war against many dangerous enemies. It is the epic of an illiterate people that knew how to benefit from the experiences of remote cultures that long preceded it, knowledge acquired by the inhabitants of the Andes over millennia.

The Incas assumed that past and transformed it to achieve hegemony throughout the western region of South America. The natives created organizational structures that amazed the European world, where the Inca civilization was seen as a kind of utopian state where hunger, need, and misery had been abolished.

The originality of the Andean cultures is the result of their isolation and of the ingenuity of the inhabitants in overcoming enormous environmental obstacles. This state, however, succumbed to a group of foreigners arrived on its coasts, as a result of internal weaknesses related to the same factors originally responsible for its expansion.

As the Inca state expanded, there were significant changes in the objectives and methods of its conquests. In the beginning, battles were fought for the purpose of seizing the spoils of the defeated peoples to enrich the victorious lord. These wars took place more or less close to Cusco, and the enemies remained the same over several generations of rulers. This desire for plunder motivated the armies of all the participants. After the conflicts between Chancas and Incas, from which the latter emerged victorious, the goals of the Inca wars changed, and the principal objective became control of foreign labor by means of territorial expansion.

The system of reciprocity usually made it possible to avoid actual military conflict, but this practice brought with it unforeseen consequences. The need to accumulate enormous quantities of agricultural and manufactured products to satisfy the constant demands of reciprocity forced the Inca rulers to accelerate agricultural production with new methods and technologies and to undertake the massive exploitation of *mitmaq* and *yana*, who labored on the state lands and whose production served to fill the government storehouses.

The state saw itself pressured to give continuous gifts to diverse categories of lords and innumerable military chiefs. We saw earlier the desertion of an Inca general and various noblemen because they were not rewarded according to the rules of reciprocity.

As the state expanded, the large administrative class belonging to the Cusco nobility grew as well. They too required constant and uncompromising satisfaction. Similarly, the members of the *panaca* expected continual gifts in exchange for their loyalty to the reigning Inca, even though they had their own estates on the best lands in the Cusco region. To these demands must be added the costs of maintaining the armies in the field on a permanent basis and the demands of the priests of the powerful sanctuaries and *huacas*, who had to be appeased with favors to keep their protection and neutralize their potential discontent, which would be unfavorable for the Inca.

Such tremendous requirements for state products demanded inflexible and uninterrupted compensation. For the Inca economy, reciprocity was like a bottomless vortex requiring new conquests and territorial annexations, which in turn led to increasing demands and "requests" for "favors." The Sapa Inca was constantly compelled to find new sources of riches to meet these uncontrollable demands, and was ultimately forced to search for the solution in new conquests.

The same institutions that in the beginning permitted the growth of the Inca state were the ones that made it fragile and vulnerable in many respects. In addition, the absence of an adequate law of succession left the field open to the "most able" of the pretenders. While this custom had permitted the succession of three personages of great ability in Pachacutec, Tupac Yupanqui, and Huayna Capac, this same custom encouraged civil war, which, given the magnitude of the state, reached almost continental proportions and facilitated the Spanish Conquest.

Moreover, the presence and treatment of the deceased rulers as if they were still alive, which in the beginning was a source of support and continuity for the government of Pachacutec, with time became a menace as the increasing numbers of mummies, including the rulers' women and servants, led to further alliances, privileges, and intrigues. Finally, these too gave rise to increasingly powerful and threatening political factions that had to be constantly satisfied with many gifts.

Thus, the institutions that had permitted the creation of the Inca state turned against their agents and pushed them toward a disastrous unlimited expansion. The situation became worse during the short rule of Huascar, who tried to solve his problems by threatening to seize all the possessions of his ancestors. Paradoxically, the living genealogy represented by the mummies of the deceased rulers, whose purpose was to testify to the past of an illiterate people and communicate a kind of glorious halo to the Inca state, with the passage of time led to an accumulation of wealth and power that encouraged the royal descendants to conspire against the ruler of the state. This was, in fact, the direct cause of the downfall of Huascar, whose confrontation with the *panaca* led them to conspire against him in favor of Atahualpa.

The spectacular collapse of the Inca state was produced by a series of factors that fall into two categories: the visible causes and the underlying causes. The visible causes are well known, and include the fratricidal war between Huascar and Atahualpa and the consequent divided power of the state, the surprise factor in the Spanish ambush at Cajamarca, and superior European military technology, including the harquebus, small cannon, the steel sword, and the horse.

All these were factors in the outcome of events, but they were not the only ones that determined the victory of the Spaniards. There were others that played a decisive role in the natives' defeat: the absence of national unity, the lack of cohesion among the various ethnic groups, the increasing uneasiness of the great "provincial" lords with the policies of the Inca rulers, aggravated in turn by the raising of large armies for extended periods and the rapidly increasing numbers of *mitmaq* and *yana*.

We can examine in detail these important conclusions in order to understand better the events in question. The Inca state was not considered by the natives as belonging within their concept of nationality. We do not know if the word "Tahuantinsuyu" ("the four regions united among themselves"), which contains the idea of integration, was used or even known before the Spanish Conquest. It appears for the first time in the documentary record at the end of the sixteenth century (Avila, 1966, chap. 17; Guaman Poma, 1980:160). Perhaps it was a term applied after the Conquest in order to explain the special divisions that had existed since much earlier times, but without expressing a kind of will to unity.

The Inca rulers did not try to abolish the great macroethnic groups, since their socioeconomic structures depended on them. The individual ethnic characteristics of these groups were therefore not suppressed. For the Inca it was sufficient to receive recognition of his absolute power, which would give him access to the labor force necessary to carry out state works and authority to designate state and cult lands. Apart from these demands, each macroethnic group preserved its regional traditions, free from any effort by the Inca state to eliminate its individual character.

The only centralizing measure ordered by the Inca was the imposition of a single language throughout his territories. Its purpose, naturally, was to facilitate trade and administration in the face of a multiplicity of languages and local dialects, but we cannot say if there was also an intention to promote some idea of cohesion. Spanish references to a "general language of the Inca" show that the languages of the Andean world did not enjoy proper names but were referred to as "the language of the people" (*el habla de la gente*).

If the concept of identity at the state level appears doubtful, let us see if it can be found at the level of the local lords. Here, also, the task is difficult. The chroniclers name "provinces" and "*repartimientos*" with great imprecision. For example, they refer to the Conchucos, the Cajamarcas, the Lucanas, and others without going into detail. They do not mention their ethnic components or their territories. Pizarro, in his haste to please his many Conquistadores, created large numbers of *encomiendas* and proceeded, without a second thought, to make arbitrary divisions of the ancient indigenous macroethnic groups.

Another measure that dismantled the ancient Andean structures was the system of reductions ordered by Toledo, under which the natives were forced to abandon their communities and settle in new villages organized according to the Spanish model. The granting of large numbers of *encomiendas* and the forced resettlements under the policy of reductions frequently caused the viceregal provinces not to correspond to the great Andean chiefdoms of pre-Hispanic times. All these events make more difficult the reconstruction of the earlier political boundaries. The Andean ethnic groups were mutilated and cut apart, greatly hindering efforts to investigate their past.

What were the elements that permitted the peoples of the Inca state to identify with their respective macroethnic groups? When we analyze the situation, we find that lords of ancient lineages had a cohesive effect on the members of their groups, creating among them the necessary elements to integrate at the chiefdom level. The principal elements were a mythical common origin, a common language or local dialect, a common dress, and economic and political unity.

Let us look again at each of these elements. The myths and legends reminded each group of its place of origin. The Incas were said to have appeared from a cave; the Chancas, from the lagoons of Choclococha and Urcococha. Other *ayllus* were said to have come from a particular hilltop, emerged from the sea, or the like.

The regional *huacas* and their mummified ancestors grouped their descendants and followers around them. They, in turn, made sacrifices and offerings to them and asked for their protection and aid. When the *mitmaq* left for distant lands, they carried their idols with them. The humble people turned to their own *huacas* when in need and not to the Sun of the Incas or to Huanacauri, who probably filled them with dread.

Despite the obligation to speak the "common language," the people preserved the use of their own languages and local dialects. In the *Relaciones Geográficas de Indias* (1881), there are several references to the languages spoken in each place, which were termed *hahua simi*, or languages other than the common language of Quechua (Cerron Palomino, 1985; Torero, 1984).

Regional dress was another means of group identification, and of confirming that groups distinguished themselves from one another and were recognized as such. Cieza de León is the chronicler who provides the most details regarding traditions of headwear in the Inca state. In *La Crónica del Perú* (1941), he recounts that in Tumbes and San Miguel they wore around the head a round wool fabric adorned with gold or silver beads. In Cajamarca they wore bands on their heads with cords like thin ribbons (chap. 76). The Chancas, on the other hand, wore their hair long, tightly braided, with wool cords tied beneath the chin. The Colla men wore wool caps called *chuco*, and the women wore *capirotes*, or hoods adorned with half moons made of silver. These details regarding ethnic dress are too numerous to repeat here in full. It is possible that among the Mochica each occupation or specialization had its own headwear, which also indicated the social status of the individual.

In the preceding chapter, we dealt with highland and coastal economic models. We saw how the chiefdoms created their own local economies that included reciprocity, redistribution, and a labor force serving the ethnic lord and others, with local differences such as those of the Chincha people and their long-distance trade.

These reflections on Andean identity demonstrate that the inhabitants of the Inca state were not shaped into a single national identity. Rather, the Incas limited themselves to the recognition and exploitation of the human and territorial resources under the control of the ethnic lords.

This examination of Andean society at the close of the fifteenth century reveals a hierarchical society, which before Inca domination was composed of macroethnic groups governed by their chiefs, who in turn had under their authority a series of lesser lords. While in this respect social structure remained unaffected by Inca rule, for the great lords the advent of the Incas meant a loss of power and a good part of their wealth.

Among the productive elements in the Andean world, the most important was control over labor, to be employed for the benefit of the lords themselves. With the formation of the state, this labor force came under the control of the central government. A second productive element was the possession of lands. Under the Incas, the best lands of a *señorío* were confiscated and came into the possession of the state, and with them the products from the lands that went to fill the state storehouses.

In addition to this considerable decrease in resources, the ethnic lords were threatened with the loss of their power and their replacement by individuals loyal to the Incas. We can perceive that these measures promoted the impoverishment of the ethnic lords during the period of Inca hegemony, and that their wealth passed into the hands of the Inca elite. By way of compensation, the Inca, according to the traditions of reciprocity, rewarded the lords with gifts and favors, but these could not hide their diminished condition. While this was the situation of the privileged classes, the popular classes were equally discontented. For the common people, Inca hegemony meant passing from the authority of the local high lords to the absolute power of the Inca.

For the commoner, this change had several negative aspects. For many common people, it meant being sent as *mitmaq* to foreign lands, and while they marched into exile accompanied by their own subordinate chiefs, they were controlled by the Inca administrative officials. Others lost the status of commoner and became *yana*, which meant breaking all ties with their places of origin.

Further, the need for more troops to carry on the wars in the north led to long absences of men from their villages. The resulting scarcity of local labor would have fallen on those remaining at home, which must have contributed to a decrease in the production of the *ayllus*. The long absences and the dangers of war resulted in many of the warriors' not returning to their villages, which led to a decrease in the male population of the *ayllus*.

Widespread discontent must have reigned among the lords and the common people, a dissatisfaction that promoted and gave way to a desire to rid themselves of Inca domination. These sentiments explain the friendly reception given to Pizarro's forces by the natives. Only afterward, with the misery and suffering that battered the people under Spanish rule, was there a surge of nostalgia for the Inca past.

For these reasons, the great lords, together with their subjects, sided with the Spaniards and helped them with their armies and with supplies to achieve their conquest. From this perspective, it was not a handful of adventurers who brought down the Inca, but the natives themselves, unhappy with their situation and believing they had found favorable circumstances for recovering their freedom. That their calculations were wrong was the result of their unavoidable ignorance of future events. They were aware neither of the imperial designs of the Spanish Crown nor of its extensive conquests in Mexico and the Caribbean. The natives could not foresee these events or the massive arrival of larger numbers of invaders. They supported the Spaniards because they saw in them the means to throw off their Inca rulers during what appeared to be a favorable opportunity owing to the struggle for succession.

If new contingents of Europeans had not arrived, the natives would have destroyed the foreigners and recovered their autonomy. The fragility of the bases on which rested the power of the Inca state made it impossible for it to respond to the rebellion of the great Andean lords and the invading Europeans with their superior technology. The destiny of the Inca realm changed forever, as it abandoned its historic isolation to enter the concert of nations of the New and Old Worlds.

Glossary

Abasca   coarse woolen garment

Aclla   chosen woman

Aclla huasi   house of the chosen women

Allauca   the right (direction)

Altiplano (Sp.)   highland plateau of Lake Titicaca

Auca   enemy or soldier

Aucaypata   ancient name of the principal plaza of Cusco (Betanzos, Cieza, Molina)

Ayllu   a lineage group or kin-based community

Cacique (Sp.)   Indian chief or boss (ruler of a *cacicazgo*)

Callpa   the force or power of the soul or body; augur

Camayoc   official or majordomo, one in charge of haciendas or fields, craftsman

Capac   rich and powerful individual

Capaccocha   special sacrifice to the *huacas*, including human sacrifice

Capaccuna   list of kings (Betanzos)

Capullana   title of a female *curaca*

Ceque   imaginary lines that in Cusco radiated from the Temple of the Sun, along which were located *huacas* that were the responsibility of specific *ayllus*

Chaqui taclla   indigenous foot plow

Chasqui   messenger, term used in Cusco

Chaupi yunga   temperate lands, ecological level referred to in archival documents

Citua   according to Molina, a festival in the Inca calendar during which the evils of the city were expelled

228

Costeño (Sp.)   inhabitant of the coast

Coya   queen, very high ranking woman

Cumbi   fine woolen cloth or garment

Curaca   chief, principal lord of a village (whose domain is a *curacazgo*)

Encomienda (Sp.)   a royal grant of Indian labor to a Spanish settler (*encomendero*)

Guanca   stones, may refer to individuals turned into stones and sacralized

Guaranga   the number 1,000; in the Inca organizational system, 1,000 households

Hatun or atun   something larger or better

Hatun runa   adult males, commoners

Huaca or guaca   temple containing an idol, or the idol itself

Ichoc   the left (direction)

Llampa   hoe; Peruvianism: *lampa*

Mamacona   the "chosen women" who lived and worked in the *acllahuasi*

Mascapaycha   tassel, insignia or crown of the reigning Inca

Minka   system of reciprocal labor or fulfillment of obligations in agreed-upon forms

Mita or mi'ta   system of forced labor, often periodic or seasonal

Mitmaq or mitimae   persons sent by the state to a distant location to serve a specified function

Monte (Sp.)   tropical forest on the eastern slopes of the Andes

Mullu   *Spondylus* sp. (spiny oyster) shell

Nusta   daughter of the Inca, young woman of royal birth

Oidor (Sp.)   judge, under Spanish legal system

Oncoy   disease; *oncoy mita*: rainy season

Ordenanza (Sp.)   law, ordenance

Orejón (Sp.)   member of a high noble caste that served as a special guard of the Inca

Pacarina   place of origin (may be mythical)

Pachaca   the number 100; in the Inca organizational system, 100 households

Panaca   royal *ayllu* or lineage group

Parcialidad (Sp.)   piece of land

Piña   prisoners of war

Probanza (Sp.)   legal testimony

Puna (Sp.)   Andean highland savannas

Pururauca   stones that became mythical warriors

Quipu   strings and knots of various colors that were used to record objects and also historic events

Reducciones (Sp.)   new colonial settlements into which native populations were concentrated to facilitate Spanish control

Relación (Sp.)   report, narrative account

Repartimiento (Sp.)   forced labor, also known as the *mita*

Runa   person, male, man

Runa simi   the language of the people

Sapan Inca   from *sapa*: great; principal Inca, supreme ruler

Señorío (Sp.)   large organizational unit whose principal chief was a great lord

Sinchi   war chief

Suyu   region, division; *Hanan suyu*, upper division; *Hurin suyu*, lower division

Tampu   inn, Castilianized as *tambo*

Tupu   measure of area or length, also the verb "to measure"

Usnu or ushnu   small stone structure in the main plaza, which served as a throne for the Inca during certain ceremonies

Visita (Sp.)   royal inspection under the Spanish colonial system

Visitador (Sp.)   official appointed by the crown to carry out a *Visita*, inspector general

Yana   literally, servants; might serve as officials responsible directly to the Inca

Yunga or yunca   the coastal plains and also their inhabitants

Documents and Abbreviations Cited

Archivo Arzobispal, Lima, Peru (abbreviated AAL)

    Section: *Idolatrías,* legajo VI, expediente 18

Archivo Biblioteca Nacional, Lima, Peru (abbreviated BN)

    A–199, 1566
    A–534, 1578

Archivo Departamental del Cusco (abbreviated ACC)

    Legajo 8, cuaderno 22, 1713.

Archivo General de Indias, Seville (abbreviated AGI)

    Section: Justicia 398, 1552
             Justicia 413, 1558–67
             Justicia 458, 461, 456, 1556–57
             Justica 1075, 1534
    Escribanía de Cámara 501-A, folio 62
    Patronato: 140, Part 4, 1575
    Patronato: 189, Part 11, 1566

Archivo General de la Nación, Lima, Peru (abbreviated AGN)

    Section: Títulos de propiedad, cuaderno 431, 1595–1710.
    Section: Derecho indígena, cuaderno 53, 1595.
    Section: Derecho indígena, cuaderno 39, 1595.

Archivo Histórico Cusco (abbreviated AHC) Archivo Departamental, Cusco

Book 2, ind. 4, folios 154 and 155v.

Archivo Ministerio de Relaciones Exteriores, Lima, Peru (abbreviated AMRREE)

Document titled: Reclamo del título de cacique por D. José Leandro Masgo diciendo ser cacique y gobernador de la Guaranga de Cochaguanca, repartimiento de los Chupachos, del pueblo de S. Pablo de Pillao, fronteras de Panataguas de la jurisdicción de la ciudad de León de Huánuco, año 1620 s/n.

Archive of the British Museum, London

Spanish Documents, No. 33983

Biblioteca Nacional, Madrid

Ms. No. 3042

Real Academia de la Historia, Madrid (abbreviated RAHM)

A–92, sixteenth century

Bibliography

Acosta, Fray José de
    1940/1550 *Historia natural y moral de las Indias.* Fondo de Cultura Económica.
    Mexico.

Alberti, Giorgio, and Mayer, Enrique
    1974 *Reciprocidad e intercambio en los Andes peruanos.* Perú Problema 12.
    Instituto de Estudios Peruanos. Lima.

Albornoz, Cristóbal
    1967 La instrucción para descubrir las guacas del Pirú y sus camayos y hazien-
    das (late sixteenth century). See Duviols, *Journal de la Société des Amér-*
    icanistes.

Alcina Franch, José
    1976 *Arqueologia de Chinchero 1*: La Arquitectura. Misión Científica Española
    en Hispano América. Ministerio de Asuntos Exteriores, Madrid.

Alcina Franch, José, Rivera, Miguel, et al.
    1976 *La arqueología de Chinchero 2*: Cerámica y otros materiales. Misión
    Científica Española en Hispano América. Ministerio de Asuntos Exter-
    iores. Madrid.

Andenes y Camellones en el Perú Andino: Historia Presente y Futuro
    1986 Ministerio de la Presidencia – Consejo Nacional de Ciencias y Tecnol-
    ogía – CONCYTEC. Edition: Carlos de la Torre y Manuel Burga.
    Lima.

Angulo, Padre Domingo
    1921 Don Andrés Hurtado de Mendoza y la Fundación de la Villa de Cañete.
    Revista Histórica, vol. 7. Lima.

Annales
    1974a Economies, Societé Civilizations. No. 6 November – December. Li-
    brairie Armand et Colin. Paris.

1974b   Pour une Histoire Anthropologique: La notion de reciprocité. No. 6,
         November–December. Librairie Armand et Colin. Paris.
1978   Numero especial. Anthropologie Historique des Société Andines, 33,
         no. 5–6. Librairie Armand Colin. Paris.

Araujo, Hilda
1986a   Hacia una política nacional de rehabilitación de andenes, in *Andenería,
         conservación de suelos y desarrollo rural en los Andes Peruanos*. NCTL.
         Ministerio de Agricultura; Ministerio de Vivienda; Fundación Ebert.
         Edited by Javier Portocarrero.
1986b   Civilización Andina: acondicionamiento territorial y agricultura prehis-
         pánica. Una revalorización de su tecnologia, in *Andenes y Camellones en
         el Perú Andino*. Historia Presente y Futuro. Ministerio de la Presidencia,
         CONCYTEC; Ministerio de la Vivienda.

Arriaga, Fray Pablo José
1968/1621   *Extirpación de la idolatría del Perú*. Biblioteca de Autores Españoles.
            Ediciones. Atlas. Madrid.

Arteaga León, Arcadio
1976   *Mitos y leyendas andinos*. Lima.

Avila, Francisco de
1966/1598?   *Dioses y hombres de Huarochirí*. Translated by José María Arguedas.
             Instituto de Estudios Peruanos. Lima.
1980/1598?   See Taylor.

Bertonio, Ludovico
1956   Vocabulario de la lengua aymara. Facsimile edition. La Paz, Bolivia
         (1612).

Betanzos, Juan de
1968/1551   *Suma y narración de los Incas*. Biblioteca de Autores Españoles. Edi-
            ciones Atlas. Madrid.
1987/1551   *Suma y Narración de los Incas*. Transcripción, notas y prólogo de María
            del Carmen Martín Rubio. V Centenario del Descubrimiento de Amér-
            ica. Madrid.

Bonavia, Duccio
1974   *Ricchata Quellccani: Pinturas murales prehispánicas*. Fondo del Libro del
         Banco Industrial del Perú. Lima
1982   *Los Gavilanes*. Mar, desierto, oasis en la historia del hombre. Corpora-
         ción Financiera de desarrollo S.A. COFIDE. Instituto Arqueológico
         Alemán. Lima.

Borregan, Alonso
1948/1562?   *Crónica de la conquista del Perú*. Edited and prologue by Rafael Loredo.
             Publicaciones Escuela de Estudios Hispano-Americanos. Seville.

Bouchard, Jean-François
1983   *Contribution à l'étude de l'architecture Inca: etablissements de la valle du río Vilcanota-Urubamba.* Edition Maison des Sciences de l'homme. Paris.

Cabello de Valboa, Miguel
1951/1586 *Miscelánea antártica.* Instituto de Etnología, Universidad Nacional Mayor de San Marcos. Lima.

Caillavet, Chantal
1982   Ethnohistoire Equatorienne: Un testament indien inédit du XVIe s. *Caravelle.* Toulouse.

Calancha, Fray Antonio de la
1976/1638 *Crónica Moralizada.* Edited by Ignacio Prado Pastor. 6 vols. Lima.

Camino D. C., Alejandro
1980   Tiempo y Espacio en la estrategia de Subsistencia Andina: Un caso en las Vertientes Orientales Sud-Peruanas. In *El hombre y su ambiente en los Andes Centrales.* No. 10. Senri Ethnological Studies. National Museum of Ethnology. Osaka, Japan.

Castro, Fray Cristóbal, and Ortega Morejón, Diego
1974/1558 Relación y declaración del modo que este valle de Chincha y sus comarcanos se gobernaron antes que hobiese ingas y después que los hobo hasta que los cristianos entraron en esta tierra. *Historia y Cultura*, no. 8 pp. 91–104. Museo Nacional de Historia. Lima.

Cedulario del Peru Vol. 2:Sixteenth to eighteenth centuries
1534–38 Published by Raúl Porras Barrenechea. Colección de documentos inéditos para la historia del Perú. 1948.

Cerron-Palomino, Rodolfo
1985   Panorama de la lingüística andina. *Revista Andina*, 3, no. 2. December. Cusco.

Chapman, Anne
1957   Port of Trade Enclaves in Aztec and Maya Civilizations. In Karl Polanyi, *Trade and Market in the Early Empires.* The Free Press, Glencoe, Ill., pp. 114–53.

Cieza de León, Pedro
1943/1550 *Del Señorío de los Incas.* Ediciones Argentinas Solar. Buenos Aires.
1941/1553 *La Crónica del Perú.* Espasa Calpe. Madrid.

Cobo, Fray Bernabé
1956/1653 *Historia del Nuevo Mundo. Biblioteca de* Autores Españoles. Madrid.

Conrad, Geoffrey M., and Demarest, Arthur
1984   *Religion and Empire: The Dynamics of Aztec and Inca Expansionism.* Cambridge University Press. Cambridge.

Cook, Noble David
1975   *Tasa de la Visita General de Francisco de Toledo.* Universidad Nacional Mayor de San Marcos. Dirección Universitaria de Biblioteca y Publicaciones.

Diez de San Miguel, Garci
1964/1972   *Visita hecha a la provincia de Chucuito* . . . 1567. Casa de la Cultura. Lima.

Dollfus, Olivier
1981   *El reto del espacio andino.* Instituto de Estudios Peruanos. Lima.

Duviols, Pierre
1967   "Un inédit de Cristobal de Albornoz: La instrucción para descubrir las Guacas del Pirú y sus camayos y haziendas." *Journal de la Société des Américanistes,* vol. 56, no. 1. Paris.
1971   *La lutte contre les Religions autochtomes dans le Pérou Colonial.* L'extirpation de l'idolatrie entre 1532 et 1660. Institute Français d'Etudes Andine. Lima.
1974–76   Une petite chronique retrouvée: Errores, ritos, supersticiones y ceremonias de los yndios de la prouincia de Chinchaycocha y otras del Pirú. *Journal de la Société des Américanistes,* vol. 63. Paris.
1976a   Punchao Idolo Mayor del Coricancha. Historia y Tipología. *Antropología Andina,* nos. 1 and 2. Centro de Estudios Andinos. Cusco.
1976b   La Capacocha. *Allpanchis,* vol. 60. Cusco.
1979   La dinastía de los Incas ¿Monarquía o Diarquía? Argumentos heurísticos a favor de una tesis estructuralista. *Journal de la Société des Américanistes,* vol. 66. Paris.
1980   Algunas reflexiones acerca de la tesis de la estructura dual del poder incaico. *Histórica,* vol. 9, no. 2. Departamento de Humanidades. Pontificia Universidad Católica del Perú.

Edwards, Clinton R.
1965   *Aboriginal Watercraft on the Pacific Coast of South America.* University of California Press. Berkeley and Los Angeles.

Erickson, Clark L.
1987   The Dating of Raised-Field Agriculture in the Lake Titicaca Basin, Peru. In *Pre-Hispanic Agricultural Fields in the Andean Region,* edited by W. Denevan, K. Mathewson, and G. Knapp, pp. 373–84. BAR International Series 359, Oxford.

Espinoza Soriano, Waldemar
1963   La Guaranga y la reducción de Huancayo. *Revista del Museo Nacional.* Vol. 32. Lima.
1967   Los señoríos étnicos de Chachapoyas y la alianza hispano-chacha. *Revista Histórica.* Vol. 30. Publication of the Academia Nacional de Historia. Lima.
1970   Los mitmas yungas de Collique en Cajamarca. *Revista del Museo Nacional.* Vol. 36. Lima.
1971   *Los huancas aliados de la conquista.* Tres informaciones inéditas sobre la participación indígena en la conquista del Perú 1558, 1560, 1561. Universidad Nacional del Centro del Perú. Huancayo.
1972   Los Huancas aliados de la conquista. *Memoria* de don Jerónimo Guacrapaucar. *Revista de la Universidad Nacional del Centro del Perú.* Huancayo.
1974   El hábitat de la etnía Pinahua. Fifteenth and sixteenth centuries. *Revista del Museo Nacional.* Vol. 40. Lima.
1975   El valle de Jayanca y el reino de los Mochica. Fifteenth and sixteenth centuries. *Boletín del Instituto Francés de Estudios Andinos.* Vol. 4, no. 3–4. Lima.

Esquivel y Navia, Diego
1980   *Noticias cronológicas de la Gran Ciudad del Cuzco.* Biblioteca Peruana de Cultura. Fundación Augusto N. Wiese. Banco Wiese. Lima. 2 vols. (eighteenth century).

Estete, Miguel
      See Fernández de Oviedo Gonzalo.

Etnohistória y Antropología Andina
1981   Segunda Jornada del Museo Nacional de Historia. January 1979. Lima.

Evolución y Tecnología de la Agricultura Andina
1983   Proyecto de Investigación de los Sistemas Agrícolas Andinos. IICA/CIID. Instituto Indigenista Interamericano. Edición Ana María Fries. Cusco.

Falcón, Licenciado Francisco
1967 Ms.   Representación de los daños que se hacen a los indios. Biblioteca Nacional, Madrid. Manuscrito No. 3042 (previously numbered j.89). See Rostworowski, 1977. IEP.

Falk Moore, Sally
1958   *Power and Property in Inca Peru.* Columbia University Press. New York.

Farrington, Ian S.
1960   Un entendimiento de sistemas de riego prehistórico en Perú. *América Indígena,* vol. 40, no. 4. October–December.

1974   Irrigation and Settlement Pattern. Preliminary Research Results from the North Coast of Peru. In *Irrigation's Impact on Society*. Edited by Theodore E. Downing and McGuire Gibson. Anthropological Papers of the University of Arizona No. 25. Tucson, Arizona.

1978   Irrigación Prehispánica y establecimiento en la Costa Norte del Perú. In *Tecnología Andina*. Compiled by R. Ravines. Instituto de Estudios Peruanos.

1980   Un entendimiento de sistemas de riego prehistórico. *América Indígena*, vol. 40, No. 4. October–December.

Fernández, Diego, *el Palentino*
1963–65   *Crónica del Perú* Edition Pérez de Tudela Bueso, Juan. Biblioteca de Autores Españoles, vols. 164–68. Madrid.

Fernández de Oviedo, Gonzalo
1945/1549   *Historia General y Natural de las Indias*. Edition Guaraní. Asunción. Paraguay.

Flores Ochoa, Jorge
1981   Clasificación y nominación de camélidos sudamericanos. La tecnología en el mundo andino. Selected and prepared by Ana Maria Soldi. Vol. 1. Universidad Nacional Autónoma de México. Mexico.

Flores Ochoa, Jorge, and Paz Flores, Percy
1983   El cultivo en *Qocha* en la puna sur-andina. In *Evolución y Tecnología de la Agricultura Andina*. Edited by Ana María Fries. Proyecto de Investigaciones de Los Sistemas Agrícolas Andinos. Instituto Indigenista Interamericano. Cusco.

Gade, Daniel W.
1972   Bridge Types in the Central Andes. *Annals of the Association of American Geographers*, vol. 62, no. 1. March.

Galdos Rodríguez, Guillermo
1977   Visita a Atico y Caravelí (1549). *Revista del Archivo General de la Nación*, no. 4–5. Lima.

Gama, Sebastián de la
1974/1540   See Visita hecha en el valle de Jayanca (Trujillo). *Historia y Cultura*, no. 8.

Garanger, José
1976   Tradition orale et préhistoire en Océanie. Cahiers O.R.S.T.O.M. *Sciences humaines*, vol. 13, no. 2, pp. 147–61. Paris.

Garcilaso de la Vega, Inca
1943/1609   *Comentarios Reales de los Incas*. Emecé Edition. Buenos Aires.

Gasparini, Graziano, and Margolies, Luisa
1977   *Arquitectura Inka.* Centro de investigaciones históricas y estéticas. Facultad de Arquitectura y Urbanismo. Universidad Central de Venezuela. Caracas.

Geo-Ecologia de las Regiones Montañosas de las Americas Tropicales
1968   Proceedings of the UNESCO Mexico Symposium. August 1966. Edited by Carl Troll. Bonn.

Godelier, Maurice
1970   Un domaine contesté d'anthropologie économique. *Sur les société precapitalistes.* Editions sociales. Mouton.
1974   *Economía, fetichismo y religión en las sociedades primitivas.* Siglo Veintiuno de España. Editores S.A.
1978   L'appropriation de la nature. *La Pensée.* Ecologie et Sciences No. 198. April 1.

Gölte, Jürgen
1972   El trabajo y la distribución de tierras en el runa simi del siglo XVI. *Actas del XL Congreso Internacional de Americanistas.* Rome and Genova.
1980a   *La racionalidad de la organización andina.* Instituto de Estudios Peruanos. Lima.
1980b   Notas sobre la agricultura de riego en la costa peruana. *Allpanchis* 15. La agricultura andina II. Cusco.

González Carré, Enrique, Cosmopolis, E., and Levano, J.
1981   *La Ciudad Inca de Vilcashuaman.* Universidad Nacional de San Cristobal de Huamanga.

González Carré, Enrique, Pozzi-Escot, Denise, Pozzi-Escot, Muriel, and Vivanco Pomacanchari, Cirilo
1987   *Los Chankas: Cultura Material.* Laboratorio de Arqueología, Universidad de San Cristóbal de Huamanga.

Gonzáles García, M.
1978   Los acueductos incaicos de Nazca. *Technología Andina.* Edited by R. Ravines. Instituto de Estudios Peruanos.

González Holguín, Diego
1952/1608   *Vocabulario de la Lengua General de todo el Perú.* Llamada Quechua. Published by the Instituto de Historia. Universidad Nacional Mayor de San Marcos. Lima.

Guaman Poma de Ayala, Felipe
1936/1613   *Neuva coronica y buen gobierno.* Facsimile edition. Paris.
1980   *El primer nueva crónica y buen gobierno.* 3 vols. Edited by J. V. Murra and R. Adorno; translated by J. I. Urioste. Siglo Veintiuno. Mexico, D. F.

Guillén y Guillén, Edmundo
1963   Un documento para la historia social y económica de Ica (1594). *Revista del Archivo Nacional del Perú* Vol. 27. Lima.

Hardman, M. J.
1966   *JAQARU – Outline of phonological and Morphological Structure.* Mouton & Co. The Hague and Paris.

Hartmann, Roswith
1971   Mercados y ferias prehispánicas en el área andina. *Boletín de la Academia Nacional de Historia.* Vol. 54, no. 118. Quito.
1977   Otros datos sobre las llamadas "Batallas Rituales." *Actas y Memorias* del XXXIX Congreso Internacional de Americanistas. Lima.

Hernández, Max; Lemlij, Moisés; Millones, Luis; Péndola, Alberto; and Rostworowski, Maria
1987   Entre el mito y la historia. Imago Editores. Lima.

Herrera, Antonio de
1946/   *Historia General de los hechos de los Castellanos en las Islas y Tierra Firme*
1601–15   *de la Mar Océano.* Guarano, Buenos Aires.

Holm, Olaf
1966–67   Money Axes from Ecuador. *Folk.* Vols. 8–9. Copenhagen.
1975   La Pieza No. 3. *Casa de la Cultura Ecuatoriana.* Guayas.

Hyslop, John
1984   *The Inka Road System.* Academic Press. New York.
1985   *Inkawasi the New Cuzco.* Cañete, Lunahuaná Peru. BAR International Series 234. Oxford.

Imbelloni, J.
1946   *Pachakuti IX.* (El Inkario Crítico). Editorial Humanior. Buenos Aires.

Informaciones de Toledo
          See Levillier, Roberto. Vol. 2.

Jiménez Borja, Arturo y Alberto Bueno
1970   Breves notas acerca de Pachacamac. *Arqueología y Sociedad.* Museo de la Universidad Nacional Mayor de San Marcos. Lima.

Jiménez de la Espada, Marcos
1881–97   *Relaciones geográficas de indias.* 4 vols. Madrid.

Keatinge, Richard W.
1975   Urban Settlement System and Rural Sustaining Communities: An Example from Chanchan's Hinterland. *Journal of Field Archaeology,* vol. 2, no. 3.

Kendall, Ann

1976   Descripción e inventario de las formas arquitectónicas Inca. Patrones de
            distribución e influencias cronológicas. *Revista del Museo Nacional.* Vol.
            42. Lima.

Mss.   Report. Expedición 1. Departamento del Cusco 1980. Project Cusi-
            chaca, prepared by David Drew and Ann Kendall.

Kosok, Paul

1965   *Life, Land and Water in Ancient Peru.* Long Island University. New
            York.

Kubler, George

1948   Toward absolute time:Guano Archaeology. *Memoirs of the Society for
            American Archaeology.* No. 4. Salt Lake City.

Kus, J. S.

1974   Irrigation and Urbanization in Pre-Hispanic Peru: The Moche Valley.
            Yearbooks of the Association of Pacific Coast Geographers. Vol. 36, Cor-
            vallis.

La Gasca, Pedro de

1976/1549   Descripción del Perú. *Revista del Archivo Histórico del Guayas.* Junio
            No. 9. Guayaquil.

Larrabure y Unanue, C.

1941   *Manuscrito y publicaciones.* Vol. 2. Valle de Cañete. Historia y Arqueo-
            logía. Lima, (1893).

Las Casas, Bartolomé de

1923/1559   *Las Antiguas Gentes del Perú.* Colección de Libros y Documentos Refer-
            entes a la Historia del Perú, Lima.

Lecthman, Heather

1979   Issues in Andean Metallurgy. In *Pre-Columbian Metallurgy of South
            America.* A Conference at Dumbarton Oaks, October 18–19, 1975.
            Edited by Elizabeth Benson. Dumbarton Oaks, Washington D.C.

1981   Copper-Arsenic Bronzes from the North Coast of Peru. *Annals of the
            New York Academy of Sciences.* Vol. 376. December.

Léon Borja, Dora

1977   Los indios balseros como factor en el desarrollo del puerto de Guaya-
            quil. *Estudios sobre Política Indigenista Española en América.* Vol. 2.
            Universidad de Valladolid. Valladolid.

Levillier, Roberto

1940   Informaciones de Toledo. In *Don Francisco de Toledo.* Vol. 2. Espasa-
            Calpe. Buenos Aires.

Limlij, Moisés; Millones, Luis; Hernández, Max; Péndola, Alberto and
Rostworowski de Diez Canseco, María
1991   *El umbral de los dioses.* SIDEA, Biblioteca Peruana de Psicoanálisis. Lima.

Lisson y Chavez, Emilio
1943 and   *La iglesia de España en el Perú.* Colección de documentos para la His-
1944   toria de la Iglesia en el Perú. Sevilla. Vol. 1 – Nos. 2 and No. 3. Vol. 2 – No. 7.

Lizarraga, Fray Reginaldo de
1946   *Descripción de las Indias.* Los pequeños grandes libros de América. Edited by Loayza. Lima (1605).
1968/1605   *Descripción Breve del Perú.* Biblioteca de Autores Españoles. Vol. 216. Madrid.

Lopez de Gomara, Francisco
1941/1552   *Historia General de las Indias.* Edited by Espasa-Calpe. Madrid.

Lounsbury, F. G.
1978   La parenté inca. *Annales* 33 année No. 5–6. Septembre – December. Armand Colin.

Lumbreras, Luis G.
1969   *De los pueblos, las culturas y las artes del antiguo Perú.* Lima.
1972   *De los orígenes del Estado en el Perú.* Edited by Milla Batres. Lima.
1980   El Imperio Wari. Vol. 2. *Perú Antiguo en Historia del Perú.* Editorial Juan Mejía Baca.

Macera, Pablo
1979   *Pintores Populares Andinos.* Fondo del libro del Banco de los Andes. Lima.

Marco Dorta, Enrique
1975   Las pinturas que envió y trajo a España don Francisco de Toledo. *Historia y Cultura,* no. 9. Lima.

Marcos, Jorge G., and Norton, Presley
1981   Interpretación sobre la Arqueología de la Isla de La Plata. Miscelánea Antropológica Ecuatoriana. Boletín de los Museos del Banco del Ecuador. Year 1, no. 1.,

Marcus, Joyce, Matos Mendieta, Ramiro, and Rostworowski, María
1983–85   Arquitectura inca de Cerro Azul, Valle de Cañete.*Revista del Museo Nacional.* Vol. 47. Lima.

Mariscotti de Gorlitz, Ana María
1978   *Pachamama Santa Tierra.* Contribución al estudio de la religión autóc-
tona. Indiana-Suplemento 8. Ge-Mann Verlag. Berlín. Contribution to the Study of Indigenous Religion. Supplement 8

Martínez, Gabriel
1981   Espacio Lupaqa: algunas hipótesis de trabajo. *Etnohistoria y Antropología Andina.* Segunda Jornada del Museo Nacional de Historia. January 1979.

Martínez Cereceda, José Luis
1982 ms   *Una aproximación al concepto andino de autoridad, aplicado a los dirigentes étnicos durante el siglo XVI y principios del XVII.* Master's thesis in Anthropology. Pontificia Universidad Católica del Perú.

Masuda, Shozo
1981   Cochayuyo, macha, camarón e higos charqueados. *Estudios etnográficos del Perú meridional.* Masuda S. Editores. University of Tokyo.

Masuda, Shozo, Shimada, Izumi, and Morris, Craig, editors
1985   *Andean Ecology and Civilization. An Interdisciplinary Perspective on Andean Ecological Complementarity.* University of Tokyo. Japan.

Matos Mendieta, Ramiro
1980   La agricultura prehispánica en las punas de Junín. *Allpanchis* 15. La agricultura andina II. Cusco.

Mayer, Enrique, and Bolton, R., editors
1980   *Parentesco y matrimonio en los Andes.* Pontificia Universidad Católica del Perú.

Mellafe, Rolando
1965   La significación histórica de los puentes en el virreinato peruano del siglo XVI. *Historia y cultura.* Vol. 1. Lima.

Millones, Luis
1986   *Antología General de la Prosa en el Perú.* Vol. 1: Los orígenes de lo oral a lo escrito. Ediciones Edubanco. Lima.

Millones, Luis, editor
1990   *El Retorno de las Huacas.* Estudios y documentos sobre el Taki-Onquoy, Siglo XVI. Instituto de Estudios Peruanos, Sociedad Peruana de Psicoanálisis. Lima.

Millones, Luis, and Hiroyasu, Tomoeda, editors
1980   *El hombre y su ambiente en los Andes Centrales.* Papers presented in the 4th International Symposium. National Museum of Ethnology. Osaka, Japan.

Mitchell, William
1981   La agricultura de riego en la sierra central de los Andes: implicaciones para el desarrollo del Estado. In *La tecnología en el mundo andino.* Selected and prepared by Heather Lechtman and Ana María Soldi. Universidad Nacional Autónoma de México.

Mogrovejo, Toribio Alonso Arzobispo
1920   Diario de la Segunda Visita pastoral del Arzobispo de Los Reyes, Don Toribio de Mogrovejo. Publicado por Fray Domingo Angulo. Libro de visitas 1593. *Revista del Archivo Nacional del Perú.* Vol. 1, Parts 1 and 2.

Molina, Cristóbal (Parroco Cuzqueño)
1943/1575   *Fábulas y Ritos de los Incas.* Edition F. Loayza. Lima.

Molina, Cristóbal el Almagrista
1968/1552?   See Relación de muchas cosas acaecidas en el Perú. Biblioteca de Autores Españoles. Madrid.

Molinie-Fioravanti, Antoinette
1982   *La vallée Sacrée des Andes.* Travaux de l'Institut Français d'Etudes Andines. Vol. 18. Paris and Lima.
1985   Tiempo del espacio y espacio del tiempo en los Andes. *Journal de la Société des Américanistes.* Vol. 71. Paris.

Montesinos, Fernando de
1930   *Historiales y Políticas del Perú* Colección de Libros y Documentos referentes a la Historia del Perú Edition Horacio Urteaga. Vol. 6, second series. Lima.

Morlon, Pierre, Orlove, Benjamin, and Hibon, Alberic
1982   *Tecnologías agrícolas tradicionales en los Andes centrales.* Perspectivas para el desarrollo. Corporación Financiera de Desarrollo S. A. COFIDE. Proyecto Regional del Patrimonio Cultural. PNUD/UNESCO. Lima.

Morris, Craig
1981   Tecnología y organización Inca del almacenamiento de víveres en la sierra. *La tecnología en el mundo andino.* Selected and prepared by Heather Lechtman and Ana María Soldi. Universidad Nacional Autónoma. Mexico.

Morris, Craig, and Thompson, Donald E.
1985   *Huánuco Pampa. An Inca City and Its Hinterland.* Thames & Hudson. New York.

Moseley, Michael Edward
1974   Organizational Preadaptation to Irrigation: The Evolution of Early Water-Management Systems in Coastal Peru. In *Irrigation's Impact on Society,* edited by Theodore E. Downing and McGuire Gibson. Anthropological Papers of the University of Arizona, No. 25. Tucson.
1975   *The Maritime Foundation of Andean Civilization.* Cummings Publishing Company. Menlo Park, California.

Muelle, Jorge, and Wells, Robert
1939   Las pinturas del Templo de Pachacamac. *Revista del Museo Nacional.* Vol. 8, no. 3. Lima.

Murra, John V.
1964 Una apreciación etnológica de la Visita. In *Visita hecha a la Provincia de Chucuito por Garci Diez de San Miguel.* Casa de la Cultura. Lima.

1966 New Data on Retainer and Servile Populations in Tawantinsuyu. *Actas y Memorias.* XXXVI International Congress of Americanists. Vol 2. 1964. Sevilla.

1967 La Visita de los Chupachos como fuente etnológica. *Visita de la Provincia de León de Huánuco* en 1562. Iñigo Ortiz. Huánuco.

1970 La función del tejido en varios contextos sociales en el Estado inca (1960). *100 años de arqueología en el Perú.* Instituto de Estudios Peruanos. Lima.

1972 El "control vertical" de un máximo de pisos ecológicos en la economía de las sociedades andinas. Vol. 2. *Visita de la Provincia de León de Huánuco,* hecha por Iñigo Ortíz de Zúñiga. Huánuco.

1975 *Formaciones económicas y políticas del mundo andino.* Instituto de Estudios Peruanos. Lima.

1978 La organización económica del Estado Inca. Siglo XXI. México.

Murúa, Fray Martín de
1946/1600 *Los orígenes de los Inkas.* Edited by F. Loayza. Lima. serie 1, tomo XI.
and 1611

1962 Historia General del Perú. Origen y descendencia de Los Incas. Manuscrito del Duque de Wellington. Introduction and notes by Manuel Ballesteros Gaibrois. 2 vols. Madrid.

Navarro Del Aguila, Victor
1930 *Las tribus de Ankcu Wallokc.* Kosko-Peru.

Nuñez, Lautaro
1970 *La agricultura prehispánica en los Andes Meridionales.* Universidad del Norte. Antofagasta. Chile.

Oliva, Padre Anello
1895/1631 *Historia del Perú y varones insignes en Santidad de la Compañía de Jesús* por el padre . . . de la misma Compañia. Edited by J. F. Pazos Varela and Luis Varela Orbegoso. Lima.

ONERN
1974 Lineamiento de Política de Conservación de los recursos naturales renovables del Perú. Oficina Nacional de Evaluación de Recursos Naturales. Lima

Ordenanzas de los Tambos de Vaca de Castro
1908 Dictadas en el Cuzco el 31 de mayo 1543. *Revista Histórica.* Vol. 3. Lima.

Ortiz de Zuñiga, Iñigo
1967   *Visita de la Provincia de León de Huánuco en 1562*. Universidad Nacional Hermilio Valdizán. Huánuco. Vol. 1.
1972   Vol. 2.

Ortloff, C. R.
1981   La ingeniería hidráulica Chimú. *La tecnología en el mundo andino*. Selected and prepared by Heather Lechtman and Ana Maria Soldi. Universidad Nacional Autónoma de México.

Palacios Ríos, Félix
1981   Tecnología del pastoreo. *La tecnología en el mundo andino*. Selected and prepared by Heather Lechtman and Ana María Soldi. Universidad Nacional Autónoma de México.

Paulsen, Allison C.
1974   The Thorny Oyster and the Voice of God. Spondylus and Strombus in Andean Pre-History. *American Antiquity*, vol. 39, no. 4. Society for American Archaeology. Washington, D.C.

Pease, Franklin
1978   *Del Tawantinsuyu a la historia del Perú*. Instituto de Estudios Peruanos. Lima.
1980   Los Incas en Tomo II *Perú Antiguo*. *Historia del Perú*. Editorial Mejía Baca.
1981a   *Los últimos Incas del Cuzco*. Ediciones PLV. Lima.
1981b   Continuidad y resistencia de lo andino. *Allpanchis* 17/18. Cultura Andina: conflictos y permanencias. Cusco.

Pérez Palma, Recaredo
1938   *Evolución mítica en el Imperio Incaico del Tahuantinsuyu*. Lima.

Pizarro, Pedro
1944   *Relación del descubrimiento y conquista de los reinos del Perú y del gobierno y orden que los naturales tenían, y tesoros en ella se hallaron, y de las demás cosas que en él han subcedido hasta el día de la fecha, hecha por Pedro Pizarro . . .* Colección Eurindia, 1 Editorial Futuro. Buenos Aires.
1978/1571 Relación del descubrimiento y conquista de los Reinos del Perú. Edición de la Pontificia Universidad Católica del Perú.

Platt, Tristan
1978   Symetriées en miroir: le concepto de *yanantin* chez les Macha de Bolivie. In *Annales* 33, No. 5–6. September – December. Armand Colin. Paris.

Polanyi, Karl, Arenberg, C. A., and Pearson, H.
1957   *Trade and Market in the Early Empires*. The Free Press, Glencoe, Ill.

Polo de Ondegardo, Juan
1917/1571   *Relación de los fundamentos acerca del notable daño que resulta de no guardar a los indios sus fueros.* Colección libros y documentos referentes a la Historia del Perú, Urteaga. Serie 1, vol. 3. Lima.

Poole, Deborah
1982   Los santuarios religiosos en la economía regional andina (Cusco). *Allpanchis* 19. El cristianismo colonial. Cusco.

Porras Barrenechea, Raúl
1937   Las relaciones primitivas de la conquista del Perú. *Cuadernos de Historia del Perú.* No. 2. Series: Los cronistas de la conquista. Imprimeries Les Presses Modernes. Paris.
1948   See Cedulario del Perú.
1951   Crónicas perdidas, presuntas y olvidadas sobre la conquista del Perú. Biblioteca, series 1a, monographs. Sociedad Peruana de Historia. Lima.
1986   *Los cronistas del Perú* (1528–1530). Biblioteca Clásica del Perú/2. Ediciones del Centenario. Banco de Crédito del Perú.

Ramirez-Horton, Susan E.
1978   Chérrepe en 1572: Un análisis de la Visita General del Virrey Francisco de Toledo. *Historia y Cultura.* Vol. 11. Lima.

Ramos Gavilán, Fray Alonso
1976/1621   *Historia de Neustra Señora de Copacabana.* Publicaciones Culturales. La Paz, Bolivia.

Ravines, Rogger, editor
1970   *100 años de arqueoliogía en el Perú.* Instituto de Estudios Peruanos. Lima.
1978   *Tecnología andina.* Instituto de Estudios Peruanos. Lima.

Ravines, Rogger, and Solar la Cruz, Felix
1980   Hidráulica agrícola prehispánica. *Allpanchis* 15. La agricultura andina II. Cusco.
Recopilación de Leyes de los Reynos de la Indias Mandadas Imprimir y Publicar por la Magestad Católica del rey Don Carlos II, nuestro señor, 4 vols. In Madrid by Julian de Paredes, 1681; in Madrid by Ediciones Cultura Hispánica, 1973.

Regal, Alberto
1970   *Los trabajos hidráulicos del Inca en el antiguo Perú.* Lima.

Relación
1920   "Relación del origen e gouierno que los Ingas tuvieron, y del que había antes que lellos señoreasen a los indios deste Reyno, y de qué tiempo, y de otras cosas que el gouierno conuenia declaradas por Señores que sirvieron al Inga Yupanqui, y a Topa Inga Yupanqui y a Guaina Capac y a Guascar Inga." Colección de libros referentes a la Historia del Perú. 2a. serie. Lima (fines del siglo XVI).

Relacion del Sitio del Cusco
1934   Colección de libros y documentos referentes a la Historia del Perú.
            Tomo X, 2a. serie. Lima. 1535–1539.

Relaciones de Muchas Cosas Acaescidas en el Peru
1968/1552? Attributed to Cristóbal de Molina, "el Almagrista." Biblioteca de Autores Españoles. Madrid.

Relaciones Geográficas de Indias
1881–97   See Jiménez de la Espada. 4 vols. Madrid.

Rostworowski de Diez Canseco, María
1953   *Pachacutec Ynca Yupanqui.* Editorial Torres Aguirre. Lima.
1960   *Pesos y Medidas en el Perú Prehispánico.* Editorial Mariátegui. Lima.
1960a   Succession, Cooption to Kingship, and Royal Incest among the Inca.
            Southwestern Journal of Anthropology, vol. 16, no. 4. Winter. University
            of New Mexico, Albuquerque.
1961   *Curacas y Sucesiones.* Costa Norte. Lima.
1962   Nuevos datos sobre tenencia de tierras reales en el Incario. *Revista del
            Museo Nacional.* Vol. 31. Lima.
1963   Dos manuscritos inéditos con datos sobre Manco II, tierras personales
            de los Incas y mitimaes. *Nueva coronica* No. 1. Publication of the Departamento de Historia de San Marcos. Lima.
1964   Nuevos aportes para el estudio de la medición de tierras en el Virreinato
            e Incario. *Revista del Archivo Nacional.* Vol. 28, I and II.
1969–70   Los Ayarmacas. *Revista del Museo Nacional.* Vol. 36. Lima.
1970   El repartimiento de Doña Beatriz Coya, en el Valle de Yucay. *Historia
            y Cultura.* No. 4. Lima.
1970a   "Mercaderes del Valle de Chincha en la época prehispánica: Un documento y unos comentarios." *Revista Española de Antropología Americana.*
            Vol. 5, pp. 135–78. Madrid.
1976   El señorío de Changuco-Costa Norte. *Boletín del Instituto Francés de
            Estudios Andinos.* Vol. 5, no. 1–2. Lima.
1977   Algunos comentarios hechos a las Ordenanzas del Doctor Cuenca. *Historia y Cultura.* No. 9. Lima.
1977a   *Etnía y Sociedad Costa Peruana prehispánica.* Instituto de Estudios Peruanos.
1977b   La estratificación social y el Hatun Curaca en el mundo andino. *Histórica,* vol. 1, no. 2. Departamento de Humanidades. Universidad Católica del Perú. Lima.
1978a   *Señoríos indígenas de Lima y Canta.* Instituto de Estudios Peruanos.
            Lima.
1978b   Mediciones y Cómputos en el Antiguo Perú. *Cuadernos Prehispánicos*
            No 6. Seminario Americanista. Universidad de Valladolid. Valladolid.
1978c   Reflexiones sobre la reciprocidad andina. *Revista del Museo Nacional,*
            Vol. 62. Lima.

1978–80   Guarco y Lunahuaná dos señoríos prehispánicos, costa sur-central del Perú. *Revista del Museo Nacional.* Vol. 64. Lima.

1981a   La voz parcialidad en su contexto de los siglos XVI y XVII. *Etnohistoria y Antropología Andina.* Segunda Jornada del Museo Nacional de Historia. 9–12 January 1979.

1981b   Instituto de Estudios Peruanos, Lima. *Recursos naturales renovables y pesca. Siglos XVI y XVII.*

1981c   Mediciones y cómputos en el antiguo Perú. In *La tecnología en el mundo andino.* Vol. 1. Edited by Heather Lechman and Ana Maria Soldi. Universidad Nacional Autónoma de México.

1981–82   Dos probanzas de don Gonzalo, Curaca de Lima (1555–1559). *Revista Histórica.* Publication of the Academica Nacional de la Historia. Vol. 32. Lima.

1982   Comentarios a la Visita de Acarí de 1593. *Histórica,* vol. 6, No. 2. Pontificia Universidad Católica del Perú.

1983   *Estructuras andinas del poder.* Ideología religiosa y política. Instituto de Estudios Peruanos. Lima.

1983–84   La Tasa ordenada por el Licenciado Pedro de La Gasca (1549). *Revista Histórica.* Publication of the Academia Nacional de la Historia. Vol. 34. Lima.

1985   Patronyms with the Consonant F in the Guarangas of Cajamarca. In *Andean Ecology and Civilization. An Interdisciplinary Perspective on Andean Ecological Complementarity.* Edited by Shozo Masuda, Izumi Shimada and Craig Morris. University of Tokyo, Japan.

1985–86   La tasa de Capachica de 1575. *Revista Histórica.* Publication of the Academia Nacional de la Historia. Vol. 35. Lima.

1987   *Conflicts over Coca Fields in 16th Century Peru.* Joyce Marcus, General Editor. Vol. 4. Memoirs of the Museum of Anthropology. Studies in Latin American Ethnohistory and Archaeology. University of Michigan, Ann Arbor.

1988a   *Conflicts over Coca Fields in Sixteenth Century Peru.* Joyce Marcus, General Editor. Vol. 4. Memoirs of the Museum of Anthropology. Studies in Latin American Ethnohistory and Archaeology. University of Michigan, Ann Arbor.

1988b   La Antigua Región del Colesuyu. In *Sociedad Andina Pasado y Presente,* edited by Ramiro Matos Mendieta. FOMCIENCIA. Lima.

1989   *Costa peruana prehispánica. Etnía y Sociedad* (second edition). Instituto de Estudios Peruanos. Lima.

1990   Las macroetnías en el ámbito andino. *Allpanchis* 35/36.

Rostworowski de Diez Canseco, Maria, and Remy, Pilar

1992   *Las Visitas a Cajamarca 1571–72/1578.* 2 vols. Instituto de Estudios Peruanos. Lima.

Rowe, John H.

1945   Absolute Chronology in the Andean Area. *American Antiquity.* Vol. 10. January.

1946   Inca Culture at the Time of the Spanish Conquest. *Handbook of South American Indians.* Bureau of South American Ethnology. Bulletin 143, vol. 2. Washington, D.C.

1948   The Kingdom of Chimor. *Acta America,* vol. 6, no. 1–2.

1958   The Age-Grades of the Inca Census. *Miscellanea Paul Rivet.* Mexico.

1963   Urban settlement in ancient Peru. *Nawpa Pacha* I: 1–28. Institute of Andean Studies. Berkeley, California.

1967   What kind of a Settlement was Inca Cuzco? *Nawpa Pacha.* No. 5. Berkeley, California.

1978   La fecha de la muerte de Wayna Qhapaq. *História,* vol. 2, no. 1. July. Departamento de Humanidades, Pontificia Universidad Católica del Perú.

1979   An account of the shrines of the ancient Cuzco. *Nawpa Pacha.* No. 17. Institute of Andean Studies. Berkeley, California.

Rozas A., Jesús Washington

1986   El sistema de cultivo en Qocha. In *Andenes y Camellones en el Perú Andino.* Historia presente y futuro. Ministerio de la Presidencia. Consejo Nacional de Ciencia y Technología CONCYTEC. Edited by Carlos de la Torre y Manuel Burga.

Sabloff, Jeremy, and Lamberg-Karlovsky, C. C., editors

1975   *Ancient Civilization and Trade.* School of American Research. University of New Mexico Press. Albuquerque.

Sahlins, Marshall

1972   *Stone Age Economics.* Aldine Publishing Company. Chicago.

Saignes, Thierry

1986   En busca del poblamiento étnico de los Andes bolivianos (siglos XV y XVI). *Avances de Investigación.* No. 3. Museo Nacional de Etnografia y Folklore. La Paz, Bolivia.

Salas, Alberto Mario

1950   *Las armas de la Conquista.* Emecé-Buenos Aires.

Salinas Y Cordoba, Fray Buenaventura

1957/1631 *Memorial de las Historias del Nuevo Mundo-Pirú.* Universidad Nacional Mayor de San Marcos. Lima.

Sallnow, Michael J.

1974   La peregrinación andina. *Allpanchis 7.* La fiesta en los Andes. Cusco.

Salomon, Frank
1980   *Los señores étnicos de Quito en la época de los Incas. Colección pendones.* Instituto Otavaleño de Antropología. Ecuador.
1985   Ms. Frontera Aborigen y Dualismo Inca en el Ecuador Prehispánico: Pistas Onomásticas. Ponencia presentada en Simposio *"Fronteras del Estado Inca"* 450. Congreso Internacional de Americanistas. Bogotá, Colombia. July.

Salomon, Frank, and Urioste, George, translators and editors
1991   *The Huarochiri Manuscript. A Testament of Ancient and Colonial Andean Religion.* University of Texas Press, Austin.

Samano-Xerez
1937/1528 *Relación.* Cuadernos de Historia del Perú. Edited by Raúl Porras Barrenechea. Paris.

Santa Cruz Pachacuti Yamqui, Joan
1927/1613 *Relación de Antigüedades deste Reyno del Perú.* Colección de libros y documentos referentes a la Historia del Perú. Vol. 9, second series. Lima.
1968   *Relación de Antigüedades deste Reyno del Perú.* Biblioteca de Autores Españoles. Madrid.

Santillán, Hernando de
1927/1563 *Relación del origen, descendencia, política de los Incas. Colección de libros y documentos referentes a la Historia del Perú.* Tomo IX, second series. Lima.

Santo Tomas, Fray Domingo
1951a/   *Lexicón* Facsimile edition. Instituto de Historia. Universidad Nacional
1563   Mayor, San Marcos. Lima.
1951b   *Gramática o Arte de la Lengua General de los Indios de los Reynos del Perú.* Facsimile edition. Instituto de Historia. Universidad Nacional Mayor, San Marcos. Lima.

Santoro, Vargas Cologero
1983   Caminos del Inca en la Sierra de Arica. *Revista Chungara.* Instituto de Antropología, Universidad de Tarapacs. Arica, Chile

Sarmiento de Gamboa, Pedro
1943/1572 *Historia de los Incas.* Emecé Editores. Buenos Aires.

Sauer, Carl
1950   Cultivated Plants. *Handbook of South American Indians.* Vol. 6, pp. 487–543. Smithsonian Institution. Bureau of American Ethnology Bulletin 143. Washington, D.C.

Schaedel, Richard

  1966   Urban growth and ekistics on the Peruvian Coast. *Actas y Memorias,* XXXVI Congreso Internacional de Americanistas. 1964. Vol. 1. Seville, Spain.

  1972   The city and the origin of the State in America. *Actas y Memorias,* XXXIX Congreso Internacional de Americanistas. Vol. 2. Lima.

  1985a   Discussion: An Interdisciplinary Perspective on Andean Ecological Complementarity. In *Andean Ecology and Civilization,* edited by Shozo Masuda, Izumi Shimada and Craig Morris. University of Tokyo Press. Japan.

  1985b   Coast-Highland Interrelationships and Ethnic Group. In *Andean Ecology and Civilization.* Edited by Shozo Mazuda, Izumi Shimada, and Craig Morris. University of Tokyo Press. Japan.

Sherbondy, Jeanette E.

  1982a   *The Canal Systems of Hanan Cuzco.* Thesis. University Microfilms International of Illinois. Ann Arbor, Michigan.

  1982b   El regadío, los lagos, los mitos de origen. *Allpanchis* 17(20): 3–32. Cusco.

Shimada, Melody, and Shimada, Izumi

  1981   Explotación y manejo de los recursos naturales en Pampa Grande, sitio Moche V. significado del análisis orgánico. *Revista del Museo Nacional.* Vol. 45. Lima.

  1985   Perception, Procurement, and Management of Resources: Archaelogical Perspective. In *Andean Ecology and Civilization.* Edited by Shozo Masuda, Izumi Shimada, and Craig Morris. University of Tokyo Press. Japan.

Soldi, Ana María

  1982   *La agricultura tradicional en Hoyas.* Pontificia Universidad Católica del Perú. Fondo Editorial.

Squier, George E.

  1974/1877 *Un viaje por tierras incaicas.* Prologue by Raúl Porras B. Edition sponsored by the Universidad Nacional Mayor de San Marcos and the American Embassy in Lima.

Stiglich, Germán

  1922   *Diccionario Geográfico del Perú.* Torres Aguirre. Lima.

Taylor, Gerald

  1987   Rites et Tradiciones de Huarochiri: manuscrito quecha del siglo XVII, Instituto de Estudios Peruanos, Lima.

Thompson, Donald E., and Murra, John V.

  1966   Puentes incaicos en la región de Hupanuco Pampa. *Cuadernos de Investigación.* Universidad Nacional Hermilio Valdizán. Huánuco.

Topic, John, and Lange Topic, Theresa
1978   Prehistoric Fortification Systems of Northern Peru. *Current Anthropology*, vol. 19, no. 3. September.

Torero, Alfredo
1970   Lingüística e Historia de la Sociedad Andina. *Anales Científicos*, vol. 8, no. 3–4. Universidad Nacional Agraria. Lima
1974   *El quechua y la historia social andina.* Universidad Ricardo Palma. Dirección Universitaria Investigación.
1984   El comercio lejano y la difusión del quechua. El caso de Ecuador. Revista Andina 2, no. 2. December. Cusco.

Trujillo, Diego de
1920   *Relación del descubrimiento y conquista del Perú.* Escuela de Estudios Hispanoamericanos. Seville.

Vaca de Castro, Cristóbal
1908   "Ordenanzas de los Tambos dictadas en el Cuzco el 31 de mayo de 1543." *Revista Histórica.* Vol. 3. Lima.

Valensi, Lucette
1974   Anthropologie économique et Histoire: l'oveuvre de Karl Polanyi. *Annales* Economies, Sociétes, Civilizations. No. 6. November–December. Librairie Armand Colin. París.

Vargas Ugarte, Rubén
1942   Los mochicas y el cacicazgo de Lambayeque. *Actas y Trabajos Científicos del XXVII.* Congreso Internacional de Americanistas. Vol. 2, pp. 475–82. Lima.

Vasquez de Espinoza, Antonio
1942/1629   *Compendium and Description of the West Indies.* Smithsonian Miscellaneous Collection. Washington, D.C.

Visita a Atico y Caraveli (1549)
            See Galdos Rodríguez

Visita a la Provincia de Chucuito
            See Diez de San Miguel

Visita de Acari
1973/1593   *Historia y Cultura.* No. 7. Museo Nacional de Historia. Lima.

Wachtel, Nathan
1966   Structuralisme et Histoire: A propos de l'organisation sociale du Cuzco. *Annales* No. 1. January–February. Paris.
1971a   *La visión des vaincus.* Editions Gallimard. Paris.

1971b   Pensée sauvage et acculturation: l'espace et le temps chez Felipe Guaman Poma de Ayala et l'Inca Garcilaso de la Vega. *Annales*, nos. 3 et 4. May–August. Armand Colin. Paris.

1973   *Sociedad e ideología*. Ensayos de historia y antropología andina. Instituto de Estudios Peruanos. Lima.

1974   La réciprocité et l'Etat Inca: de Karl polanyi á John V. Murra *Annales*. Economies Société Civilizations. No. 6. November–December. Librairie Armand Colin. Paris.

1980–81   Les Mitmas de la Vallée de Cochabamba. La politique de colonisation de Huayna Capac. *Journal de la Société des Américanistes* Vol. 67. Paris.

Willey, Gordon R.

1953   *Prehistoric settlement in the Virú Valley, Peru*. Bureau of American Ethnology, Bulletin 155. Washington, D.C.

Williams, Carlos, and Merino, Manuel

1974   *Inventario, catastro y delimitación del patrimonio arqueológico del valle de Cañete*. 2 vol. Instituto Nacional de Cultura, Centro de Investigaciones y Restauración de Bienes Monumentales. Lima.

Zarate, Agustín

1944/1555   *Historia del Descubrimiento y Conquista del Perú*. Lima.

Ziolkowski, Mariusz

1984   La piedra del cielo: algunos aspectos de la educación e iniciación religiosa de los príncipes Incas. *Anthropologica*. Departamento de Ciencias Sociales No. 2, II. Pontificia Universidad Católica del Perú.

Zuidema, R. T.

1964   *The Ceque System of Cuzco*. The social organization of the capital of the Inca. Leiden.

1980   El sistema de parentesco incaico: una nueva visión teórica. En: *Parentesco y matrimonio en los Andes*. Edited by E. Mayer and R. Bolton. Pontificia Universidad Católica del Perú.

Index

DATE DUE

FEB − 5 1999	
APR 1 1999	
APR 2 8 1999	

UPI 261-2505 G   PRINTED IN U.S.A.